STEVEN H. SAWYERS
10103 BAKER STORMS
294-5626

INTRODUCTION TO
ANALOG COMPUTER PROGRAMMING

INTRODUCTION TO
ANALOG COMPUTER PROGRAMMING

DALE I. RUMMER, PH.D.
University of Kansas
Lawrence, Kansas

HOLT, RINEHART AND WINSTON, INC.
New York, Chicago, San Francisco, Atlanta, Dallas
Montreal, Toronto, London, Sydney

To My Wife
PAT

Copyright © 1969 by Holt, Rinehart and Winston, Inc.
All rights reserved
Library of Congress Catalog Card Number 69-17660
SBN: 03-080362-4
Printed in the United States of America
     1 2 3 4 5 6 7 8 9

PREFACE

Why should another book on analog computers be written? In particular, why should this book have been written? This book was produced in response to a need for an introductory text on analog computer programming written for second semester freshmen or first semester sophomores. Such a student would have previously taken a five credit course in calculus and analytic geometry. It is assumed that the student using this text has proficiency with the integration and differentiation of simple functions. Definitions and explanations are provided for the ideas needed from mechanics, thermodynamics, and electrical circuits.

Why teach analog computer programming at this level? Why not wait until the students have taken a course in differential equations? The experience that a student gets in learning about analog computer programming helps motivate his study both of mathematics and engineering. The student's concepts of integration and differentiation are strengthened by further application to real problems and by the graphic display of the solutions. Simple differential equations are introduced because such equations are needed to describe systems which involve rate processes. References to the analytical solutions to these equations are minimal because the student is not assumed to have previously seen these solutions. The background provided by a study of analog computer programming is most helpful to students when they later study the subject of differential equations.

The first chapter provides a perspective on computers in general and upon analog computers in particular. The second chapter introduces the arithmetic operations as implemented using potentiometers and operational amplifiers. Amplitude scaling of the problem variables to fit the limitations of the analog computer is described. These techniques are then applied to the solution of algebraic equations. The third chapter introduces the implementation of the operations of integration and differentiation using operational amplifiers. These techniques are applied to the generation of ramp, polynomial, and sinusoidal functions. Chapter 4 describes the various methods of recording the solutions generated by the analog computer. Chapter 5 shows how first-order differential equations naturally arise when one wishes to describe systems involving rate processes. The method of obtaining the analog computer block diagram from the mathematical equations describing the system is developed. The need for time scaling arises and a simple method of accomplishing time scaling is described. Time scaling and amplitude scaling are considered as separate operations which are to be done at distinctly different times in the process of preparing a problem for solution on an analog computer. Chapter 6 considers some systems which require second-order differential equations to adequately describe the physical phenomena. The physical processes are described fully to help the student understand how the equations for the mathematical model are produced. Time scaling is considered again to demonstrate the more general process of time scaling. Chapter 7 introduces some of the nonlinear operations which are possible on the analog computer. Again these new ideas are introduced in response to the need for new tools in solving certain classes of problems. If there is not time available to cover this material in an introductory course, the students can read the material later as it becomes appropriate to the problems which they are interested in solving.

Because there are many different analog computers in use in schools it is not practical to describe them all in detail. The details of the operation of some particular computers are placed in the appendix. The student can refer to the description of the computer which is available to him if it is described, or to the one which is most nearly like the one which he is using.

I am indebted to the many persons who have written papers and books on analog computing. This indebtedness is difficult to acknowledge specifically without a high probability of doing some persons an injustice. I do wish, however, to acknowledge that the approach which I have taken to scaling is due to the influence of a former colleague of mine, Dr. J. Robert Ashley.* This definition of scale factors in terms of problem units/volt seems to make both the creation of the analog model from the equations of the physical system, and the interpretation of the analog computer results in terms of the physical system being studied easier to understand. I urge that those teachers who may be accustomed to using the reciprocal scale factors try this other approach with their students.

I am most appreciative of the comments of students and teachers who have used these notes in mimeographed form over the past several years. My wife has been most helpful not only in typing the manuscript, but also in reading it critically. Her questions have eliminated many errors and have helped to clarify some obscure arguments.

D.I.R.

*J. Robert Ashley,
Introduction to Analog Computation (New York: John Wiley & Sons, 1963).

TABLE OF CONTENTS

PREFACE, vii

CHAPTER 1 PERSPECTIVE, 1
1.1 Digital vs. Analog, 2   1.2 Mathematical Modeling, 3   1.3 Active vs. Passive, 4   1.4 Past, Present, and Future, 5   1.5 Exercises, 6

CHAPTER 2 ANALOGS OF ARITHMETIC OPERATIONS, 7
2.1 Operational Amplifiers, 7   2.2 Amplitude Scaling, 9   2.3 Inversion, 11   2.4 Summation, 13   2.5 Multiplication by a Constant, 16   2.6 Solution of Algebraic Equations, 18   2.7 Solution of Simultaneous Linear Equations, 21   2.8 Exercises, 27

CHAPTER 3 ANALOGS OF CALCULUS OPERATIONS, 33
3.1 Differentiation, 34   3.2 Integration, 40   3.3 Generation of Ramp Functions, 47   3.4 Generation of Polynomial Functions, 49   3.5 Generation of Sinusoidal Functions, 53   3.6 Exercises, 54

CHAPTER 4 THE RECORDING AND DISPLAY OF SOLUTIONS, 61
4.1 Strip Chart Recorder, 62   4.2 X-Y Plotters, 62   4.3 Cathode Ray Oscilloscope, 64   4.4 Exercises, 65

CHAPTER 5 FIRST ORDER SYSTEMS, 70
5.1 Creation of Analog Models of Dynamic Systems, 71   5.2 Hydraulic System, 73   5.3 Time Scaling, 82   5.4 Freely Falling Body, 84   5.5 Falling Body with Viscous Drag, 88   5.6 Thermal Behavior of a Semiconductor Device, 92   5.7 Hydraulic System of Three Tanks, 98   5.8 Exercises, 104

CHAPTER 6 SECOND ORDER SYSTEMS, 109
6.1 Spring-Mass-Dashpot System, 110   6.2 Non-zero Forcing Function, 117   6.3 The Swinging Door System, 120   6.4 Simple Pendulum, 128   6.5 Exercises, 134

CHAPTER 7 NON LINEAR OPERATIONS, 137
   7.1 Diode Limiters, 137 7.2 Diode Function Generators, 144
   7.3 Multipliers, 145 7.4 Sine Cosine Generator, 148 7.5 Comparators, 152 7.6 Exercises, 154

BIBLIOGRAPHY, 156

APPENDICES

I-A BASIC OPERATION OF THE ELECTRONIC ASSOCIATES INC.
   TR-20 Analog Computer, 158 I-A-1 General Description, 158
   I-A-2 Multiplication by a Constant, 159 I-A-3 Inversion and Summation, 160 I-A-4 Integration, 162 I-A-5 Normal Operation of TR-20, 163 I-A-6 Repetitive Mode of Operation of TR-20, 163 I-A-7 References, 164

I-B BASIC OPERATION OF THE BURR-BROWN MODEL 600 ANALOG COMPUTER, 165
   I-B-1 General Description, 165 I-B-2 Multiplication by a Constant, 166 I-B-3 Inversion and Summation, 168 I-B-4 Integration, 169 I-B-5 Multiplier, 170 I-B-6 General Operation, 172 I-B-7 References, 172

I-C ELECTRONIC ASSOCIATES INC. TR-48 ANALOG COMPUTER, 173
   I-C-1 General Description, 173 I-C-2 Multiplication by a Constant, 174 I-C-3 Inversion and Summation, 175 I-C-4 Integration, 176 I-C-5 Non Linear Modules, 176 I-C-6 General Operation, 177

II DERIVATION OF ANALOG COMPUTER GAINS, 180
   II-A. Inversion, 180 II-B. Summation, 183 II-C Integration, 185

III ELECTRICAL CIRCUITS, 188
   III-A. Pot Set, 188 III-B. Initial Condition, 190

IV STABILITY OF SOLUTIONS FOR ALGEBRAIC EQUATIONS, 192

INDEX, 197

INTRODUCTION TO
ANALOG COMPUTER PROGRAMMING

CHAPTER 1 PERSPECTIVE

The purpose of this chapter is to place the contents of this book — an introduction to the programming of electronic differential analyzers, or EDA for short — into proper perspective in the larger realm of computers and the use of computers. A proper perspective is important in order to appreciate the advantages and the limitations of the EDA as compared to other kinds of computers. For many years there was a running battle between the proponents of analog computers and the advocates of digital computers. Much heat was generated, but very little light was shed on the subject because few people had adequate competence in both areas to make really valid comparisons. About 1960 some people realized that for some problems a combination of an analog computer and a digital computer would be advantageous. Such a combination is called a "hybrid computer," and much work is being done developing hybrid computation techniques.

1-1 Digital vs. Analog

Numbers are represented in a basically different way in these two types of computers. The digital computer represents a number by one of a set of discrete conditions. The analog computer, on the other hand, represents numbers in terms of a continuously variable condition. Consider a dial which has ten positions numbered 0 to 9. Mechanical detents prevent this dial being set at any position other than the numbered positions. This dial permits a digital representation of the numbers 0 through 9. Consider, on the other hand, a dial that has numbers in the same positions as before but that does not have the mechanical detents. This dial could be set half way between 7 and 8 to represent 7.5. Any device that represents numbers in terms of a continuous variable is analog in nature. Some examples of digital devices are as follows: the abacus, an adding machine, a desk calculator, a traffic counter. Some examples of analog devices are as follows: an ordinary ruler for measuring, a slide rule, a voltmeter, a micrometer, a mercury thermometer, a pressure gauge. The precision of the representation of numbers in analog computers seldom exceeds 0.05 per cent and is limited by the precision and stability of the components available. The critical components of analog computers are sometimes placed in temperature controlled ovens to improve the stability of the values of the components. The precision of the representation of numbers in digital computers is not determined by the accuracy or stability of the components, but rather depends on the quantity of components used to represent the number. The accuracy of representation of numbers in a digital computer is usually described in terms of the number of binary bits used to represent a number. Ten binary bits give an accuracy of one part in ($2^{10} - 1$) or one part in 1023. This is the order of 0.1 per cent which is the precision of good quality analog computers. Most digital computers use at least 16 binary bits to represent a number and many use as many as 32 bits or more. It is evident that the digital computer can represent numbers much more accurately than can the analog computer. Digital computers also may use what is called "floating point" representation of numbers to obtain an even greater range from very, very small numbers to very, very large numbers. For many problems the extreme accuracy of the digital computer is not needed, however, nor even appropriate, and the accuracy of the analog computer is adequate. By means of suitable scaling, the analog computer can represent numbers of any desired size. The digital computer solves a problem by performing a suitable number of computations one after another in serial fashion. The analog computer, on the other hand, performs many operations at the same time, that is, in parallel fashion. Typically the analog computer can solve systems of differential equations much more rapidly than can the digital computer. The complexity of the problem that can be handled by an analog computer is limited by how much computing equipment is available. The complexity of the problem that can be solved on the digital computer is limited by the rate at which the digital computer operates and by how much computer time is available. In both cases the ultimate limitation on the size of the problem is really one of money. If a problem can be solved by both the digital computer and the analog computer and if both kinds of computers are available, the decision should be made on the basis of which will do the job most economically and conveniently. This book is concerned with solving problems using the EDA, which is frequently called by the shorter name, analog computer.

1-2 Mathematical Modeling

Before a problem can be solved by any kind of computer, or indeed before it can be solved even by hand calculation, the problem must be described in quantitative terms. Frequently the actual relationships may be very complicated, or in some cases not precisely known. Simplifying assumptions are needed many times to permit solving the problem with or without the aid of computers. One of the advantages of using computers as an aid to solving problems is that fewer simplifying assumptions may be needed. The equations that define the relationships between the variables in a problem form the mathematical model for the problem. Another advantage of using computers is that several different models may be tried for one problem in order to find the one that is the best model. Before relying on a particular model for a given problem, the engineer must check the results in some way to find how good a model he has created. For example suppose that one is interested in how fast water will empty from a tank. As a first assumption one might consider that the rate at which the water runs out is proportional to the depth of the water in the tank, that is, the pressure at the bottom of the tank. A very simple experiment will show that this model may be grossly inaccurate. *See Exercise* 2. Once the accuracy of the assumed relationships has been verified, the engineer can proceed with confidence that the solutions which he produces based on the assumed models will be correct to the accuracy verified.

1-3 Active vs. Passive

If two devices have mathematical models of the same form, then one of these may be used as an analog of the other. The mathematical equation that relates angular velocity, ω, inertia, J, and mechanical damping, D, for a simple rotational mechanical system will later be shown to be

$$J\left[\frac{d\omega}{dt}\right] + D\omega = 0 \tag{1-1}$$

The mathematical equation that relates current, i, inductance, L, and resistance, R, for a simple series electrical circuit will be shown to be

$$L\left[\frac{di}{dt}\right] + Ri = 0 \tag{1-2}$$

Thus the electrical circuit could be considered to be an analog of the mechanical system by considering inductance, L, as analogous to inertia, J, current, i, as analogous to angular velocity, ω, and resistance, R, as analogous to mechanical damping, D. Results obtained by studying the electrical circuit can be interpreted in terms of performance expected from the mechanical system. This kind of use of analogies is very helpful in extending our understanding of, for example, electrical circuits to an understanding of the dynamics of mechanical systems, or conversely, if we are better acquainted with mechanical systems. We find as we study in different fields of engineering and science that the same mathematical equations occur repeatedly with only the names and/or the symbols changed.

If actual experiments were performed on an electrical circuit in order to predict the performance of a mechanical system as suggested above, then the electrical circuit could be called an analog computer. In order to provide a distinction between this kind of computer and the others which we will be studying, the former are called "passive analog computers." Passive analog computers have been built for modeling electric power distribution systems, water distribution systems, petroleum reservoir dynamics, ground water flow, and many other systems. Those models based on systems of simultaneous algebraic equations, such as models for electric power systems, can now be economically handled by large scale digital computers. Those models based on systems of simultaneous partial differential equations, such as models for ground water dynamics, can be solved on large digital computers, but a very large amount of time is required. Passive electrical analogs using networks of resistors and capacitors are still very useful for some studies in these areas. Passive electrical analogs using resistance paper are useful for solving problems in such diverse fields as electrostatics and the growth of cities. Although the passive analog computers have been very important and in some activities will continue to make useful contributions, the major applications of analog computing require the active type of analog computer, which is properly called the electronic differential analyzer, or EDA. Passive analog computers using resistance, inductance, and capacitance are limited in accuracy because physically realizable inductors may have appreciable power loss. The active analog computer using only resistors, capacitors, and operational amplifiers can model any linear physical system. For example, the EDA using resistance and capacitance elements can model an electrical circuit that has inductance present in addition to resistance and capacitance.

1-4 Past, Present, and Future

The electronic differential analyzer, EDA, as implied by the name, makes use of electronics. The theoretical groundwork was laid in the late 1920's by such men as Black at Bell Telephone Laboratories. The reduction of the theory to practical form did not occur until the late 1930's with improved vacuum tubes and with improved circuits for direct coupled amplifiers. One of the major problems with the first analog computers was adjusting the balance so that the output voltage would be zero when the input voltage was zero. Most present day computers have automatic balancing by a process called "chopper stabilization." Thus the user of such analog computers need not concern himself with the problem of balancing the amplifiers. A check on the balance is made periodically as part of preventive maintenance activity. The development of the transistor as a substitute for the vacuum tube has permitted the physical size and the electric power consumption of analog computers to be substantially reduced. A vacuum tube analog computer that had a volume of 75 cubic feet and consumed 3500 watts of electric power has been reduced to 15 cubic feet and consumes 500 watts. The accuracy of these two computers is comparable. The development of solid state multipliers and function generators as replacements for the electromechanical devices used on earlier analog computers permits the operation of the computer at higher frequencies. Thus 500 to 1000 solutions may be generated in the time previously required for the generation of one solution.

6　PERSPECTIVE

Digital computer programs exist today for taking the statement of a problem in equation form and producing the specifications for connecting up the analog computer model of the problem. The technology exists, though not at present in economical form, to have the digital computer connect up the analog computer components, to set all the coefficients, to operate the analog computer, and to record the results. Although such a system may not be appropriate for solving problems on analog computers, it is most probable that such a system will evolve in hybrid computing that makes use of both a digital computer and an analog computer to solve problems cooperatively more economically than would be possible using either computer separately. For example, launch windows, those time intervals during which it is possible to launch a rocket for a particular target in outer space, can be computed more economically on a hybrid system than on a purely digital system, and one would not consider doing it on a purely analog system. The development of transistor operational amplifiers makes it worthwhile to construct special purpose analog computers as part of a real-time data processing system, or as a part of a control system.

1-5 Exercises

1. Some devices and processes are basically analog and others are basically digital. For each device or process listed below, state whether it is digital or analog in nature and state your reasons. Some of these devices or processes may be either depending on certain variations of the device or the process.
    a. a stop watch
    b. an automobile speedometer
    c. the odometer on an automobile
    d. the tuning of a radio receiver
    e. the computation of the cost of gasoline delivered by a gasoline pump
    f. the playing of a piano
    g. the playing of a violin
2. You are to create a mathematical model that describes the relationship between the rate at which water flows from a hole in the side of a tank and the height of the water above the hole. Devise and describe a procedure using only materials normally found in a kitchen to obtain data on this process.
3. If it is convenient to do so, carry out the experiment devised in Exercise 2 and determine an appropriate mathematical model from the data obtained. Hint: semilog graph paper may be useful. If it is not convenient to carry out the experiment, determine an appropriate mathematical model based on the data provided below.

Height-in.	2	3	5	7	9
Flow rate-oz/sec	.284	.347	.448	.529	.600

CHAPTER 2 ANALOGS OF ARITHMETIC OPERATIONS

The purpose of this chapter is to show how the basic arithmetic operations of addition, subtraction, and multiplication can be performed on an analog computer. These methods will then be applied to solve some algebraic equations. Since most of the operations performed on an analog computer make use of operational amplifiers, the properties of operational amplifiers will be considered first. The problems must be amplitude scaled because the operational amplifiers are capable of operating only over a limited range.

2-1 Operational Amplifiers

An operational amplifier is an electronic device that amplifies or multiplies electrical voltages. Amplifiers are used in many familiar situations such as radios, phonographs, tape recorders, and hi-fi music systems. The strength of an electrical voltage is measured in volts by an instrument called a voltmeter. Voltage is always measured between two points and so may be referred to as potential difference. One of these points, particularly in the case of analog computers, is frequently a reference point called ground. Thus when we speak of the output voltage of Amplifier 1 on an analog computer, we mean the potential difference between the output terminal of Amplifier 1 and computer ground. The potential difference between the terminals of an ordinary flashlight cell (a zinc-carbon cell) is 1.5 volts. Most automobiles today have a battery consisting of six lead-acid cells connected in series. The potential difference for each cell is about 2.2 volts and thus the battery has a terminal voltage of 13 volts. Since the voltage under operating conditions drops to about 12 volts, the system is described as a 12-volt system. The voltage between the terminals of a phonograph pickup is a few millivolts. A millivolt is 0.001 volt. A phonograph amplifier amplifies or increases this potential difference to a few volts applied to the loudspeaker. Thus the phonograph amplifier multiplies the input voltage by a factor of approximately 1000. The ratio of the output voltage to the input voltage for an amplifier is called voltage gain. The phonograph amplifier described has a voltage gain of approximately 1000. The operational amplifiers used in analog computers typically have voltage gains of 50,000 to 50 million. This very high voltage gain is maintained as long as the output voltage is within prescribed limits. These limits for transistorized amplifiers are usually ± 10 volts, and the limits for vacuum tube type amplifiers are usually ± 100 volts. Some transistorized amplifiers have a ± 100-volt range. These limits impose the need for amplitude scaling that is discussed in the next section. Another property of operational amplifiers is that the input resistance is very high. This means that the input current is very small, since by Ohm's law the input current is the ratio of the input voltage to the input resistance. Consider the following example:

EXAMPLE 2-1

An operational amplifier has a voltage gain of 100,000 and an input resistance of 5 megohms. Compute the input current when the output voltage is 75 volts.

$$V_{in} = \frac{V_{out}}{gain} = \frac{75}{100,000} = 75 \times 10^{-5} \text{ volt}$$

$$I_{in} = \frac{V_{in}}{R_{in}} = \frac{75 \times 10^{-5}}{5 \times 10^{6}} = 15 \times 10^{-11} \text{ amp}$$

2-2 Amplitude Scaling

Amplitude scaling is required in order to place the range of the problem variables within the range of voltage possible on the analog computer. This is similar to the process used in making a scale model of a ship. Assume that the real ship is 200 ft long and the block of wood available for the model is 10 in. long. The scaling used must be such that the maximum dimension of the ship when reduced by a scaling factor will produce a length which is not greater than the length of the block, that is, 10 in. If a larger scale factor is used, one end of the model ship will be beyond the end of the block of wood, and hence the model will not be complete and accurate. The scale factor needed to convert from distance on the real ship to distance on the model ship can be computed as follows:

$$k_d = \frac{(\max |L| \text{ of model})}{(\max |l| \text{ of ship})} = \frac{10 \text{ in.}}{200 \text{ ft}} = 0.05 \text{ in./ft}$$

To convert any distance (length, width, or height) on the real ship to the corresponding distance on the model ship the distance in feet is multiplied by the scale factor, k_d. Assume that a cabin on the real ship has the following dimensions:

length, l = 40 ft; width, w = 20 ft; height, h = 10 ft

The dimensions of the cabin on the model ship are computed as

length, $L = k_d * l$ = (0.05 in./ft) * (40 feet) = 2.0 in.
width, $W = k_d * w$ = (0.05 in./ft) * (20 feet) = 1.0 in.
height, $H = k_d * h$ = (0.05 in./ft) * (10 feet) = 0.5 in.

Notice how the units of distance, feet and foot, cancel when the product is taken to yield the unit of distance, the inch, for the model ship dimensions. A conversion factor to convert from distance on the model ship to distance on the real ship is sometimes desired. This factor can be computed as:

$$K_d = \frac{(\max |l| \text{ of ship})}{(\max |L| \text{ of model})} = \frac{(200 \text{ ft})}{(10 \text{ in.})} = 20 \text{ ft/in.}$$

A distance, L, on the model ship is multiplied by the scale factor, K_d, to give the corresponding distance, l, on the real ship. Assume that the mast on the model is 3.0 in. high. The height of the mast on the real ship is as follows:

$$h = K_d * H = (20 \text{ ft/in.}) * (3.0 \text{ in.}) = 60.0 \text{ ft}$$

The maximum voltage that an operational amplifier is rated to deliver corresponds to the length of the block of wood used to make a model of a real ship. If the scaling is incorrect such that the model is required to produce a larger voltage than the rated maximum value, the model will be distorted and inaccurate. A convenient symbol for this maximum voltage is Cm, which stands for "computer maximum." Assume as before that the maximum distance on the real device to be modeled is 200 ft and the rated maximum output voltage from the operational amplifiers is 10 volts. The scale factors, referred to as amplitude scale factors to distinguish them from time scale factors to be discussed in Chapter 5, are computed as follows:

$$k_d = \frac{(Cm \text{ of computer})}{(\text{mas } |d| \text{ of device})} = \frac{(10 \text{ volts})}{(200 \text{ ft})} = 0.05 \text{ volt/ft}$$

$$K_d = \frac{(\max |d| \text{ of device})}{(Cm \text{ of computer})} = \frac{(200 \text{ ft})}{(10 \text{ volts})} = 20 \text{ ft/volt}$$

A distance of 50 ft would be represented on the computer by

$$D = k_d * d = (0.05 \text{ volt/ft}) * (50 \text{ ft}) = 2.5 \text{ volts}$$

A voltage of 5 volts on the computer would represent an actual distance of

$$d = K_d * D = (20 \text{ ft/volt}) * (5.0 \text{ volts}) = 100 \text{ ft}$$

Throughout this book lower-case symbols will be used for variables in the real device or system, and the corresponding upper-case letters will be used for the related variables in the analog computer model. Note also that the lower-case letter is used for k_d, which multiplies actual system variables (lower-case) to obtain the computer model variables. Likewise the upper-case letter is used for K_d, which multiplies computer model variables (upper-case) to obtain system variables. The word system has been introduced as a means of referring to the thing being modeled. When a specific case is considered, there may be appropriate adjectives to further identify the system of interest, that is, hydraulic system, vertical position control system, speed regulating system, suspension system. After the amplitude scaling has been established, the next step in creating a model on an analog computer is to model the mathematical operations required by the problem. These will be considered next.

2-3 Inversion

Inversion is the name used in analog computing to identify the process of multiplying a variable by -1.0. Thus if a voltage of 5.0 volts is inverted, the result is -5.0 volts. If a voltage of -8.0 volts is inverted, the result is $+8.0$ volts. If a variable, X, is inverted, the result is $-X$. The interconnection of analog computing equipment to create the model of the real system is described by block diagrams. The analog computer block diagram serves a function very similar to that of the flow chart for a digital computer program. The block diagram symbol for the process of inversion, an inverter, is shown in Fig. 2-1. The triangle indicates that an operational

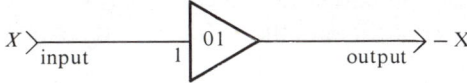

FIG. 2-1

Block Diagram Symbol for an Inverter.

amplifier has been connected as an inverter. The line from the vertex on the right side is the output of the operational amplifier. The line connecting to the left side of the triangle is the input to the inverter. The number "1" shown beside this line means that the input is to be multiplied by -1.0. If the number "1" is omitted, the implication is that the factor is still -1.0. In some cases a different multiplying factor such as 0.1, 2.0, 5.0, or 10.0 may be desired. The presence of such a number instructs the person connecting up the analog computer to connect the operational amplifier to give the indicated multiplying factor, or gain, as it may be called. The connection of an operational amplifier as an inverter is shown in Fig. 2-2. The pie-shaped symbol represents the operational amplifier. The right vertex is the output terminal and G and B are the input terminals. The number 01 identifies which operational amplifier is used. For a detailed explanation of how this circuit functions see Appendix 2-A. The following is a simplified explanation. The potential difference between the input terminals of the operational amplifier, B and G, is very small because the voltage gain of the operational amplifier is very high, for example 100,000. When the output voltage of the amplifier is 100 volts, the input voltage would be 0.001 volt. For output voltages less than 100 volts

ANALOGS OF ARITHMETIC OPERATIONS

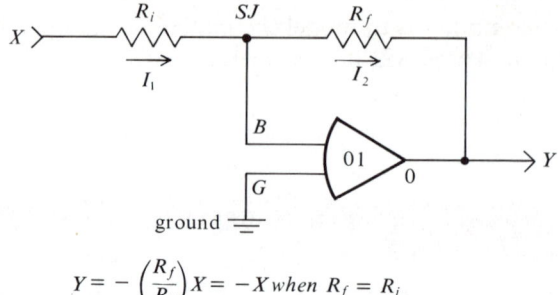

$$Y = -\left(\frac{R_f}{R_i}\right)X = -X \text{ when } R_f = R_i$$

FIG. 2-2
Connection of an Operational Amplifier as an Inverter.

the input voltage would be even smaller. Since the input resistance of the operational amplifier is very high, the current into the B terminal of the amplifier is very small. The potential difference, V, across a resistor, the current, I, through the resistor, and the value of the resistor, R, are related by Ohm's law as follows:

$$R = \frac{V}{I} \qquad (2\text{-}3a)$$

The potential difference is measured in volts, the current is measured in amperes, and the resistance is measured in ohms. Ohm's law can be solved for current, I, to show that the electrical current flowing in a resistor is equal to the ratio of the potential difference across that resistor and the value of that resistor. The potential difference across the input resistor, R_i, in Fig. 2-2 is essentially the voltage, X, because the potential of the point SJ with respect to ground, G, is very nearly zero. Therefore the current, I_1, is as follows:

$$I_1 = \frac{X}{R_i} \qquad (2\text{-}3b)$$

By Ohm's law, the potential difference across a resistor is equal to the product of the current flowing through that resistor and the value of resistance of that resistor. Thus the potential difference across the feedback resistor, R_f, is $I_2 * R_f$ with the right end of R_f being at a lower potential than the point SJ. Since the potential of SJ is nearly zero, the potential of the output terminal with respect to ground is as follows:

$$Y = -I_2 * R_f \qquad (2\text{-}3c)$$

Since the current into the summing junction is very, very small, the currents I_1 and I_2 are essentially equal, and the substitution of Eq. (2-3b) into Eq. (2-3c) yields the general relationship:

$$Y = -\frac{X}{R_i} R_f = -\frac{R_f}{R_i} X \qquad (2\text{-}3d)$$

2-4 Summation

The name summation describes the analog computer process of adding up a set of variables. Subtraction is not considered separately, but rather is accomplished by summing the negative of the quantity to be subtracted. This need for the negative of a quantity points to an application of the inverter of the previous section. The block diagram symbol for the process of summation, called a summer, is shown in Fig. 2-3. The triangle indicates that the operational Amplifier 1 has been connected as a summer.

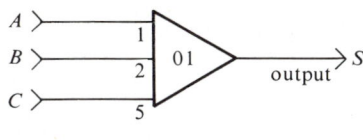

$$S = -(A + 2.0\,B + 5.0\,C)$$

FIG. 2-3
Block Diagram of a Summer.

The line from the vertex on the right side is the output of the operational amplifier and is identified by the symbol, S. The three inputs to the summer are identified as A, B, and C. The number by each of the inputs shows the factor by which that input is multiplied before being summed. The output from the summer is therefore as follows:

$$S = -(A + 2.0 * B + 5.0 * C) \qquad (2\text{-}4a)$$

The negative sign on the process arises for the same reason that the sign change takes place in the inverter. In fact, if the variables B and C are made equal to zero, the summer shown in Fig. 2-3 reduces to the inverter shown in Fig. 2-1. Fig. 2-4 shows the connection of an operational amplifier as a summer. The gain for each input is computed as:

$$G = -\left[\frac{R_f}{R_i}\right] \tag{2-4b}$$

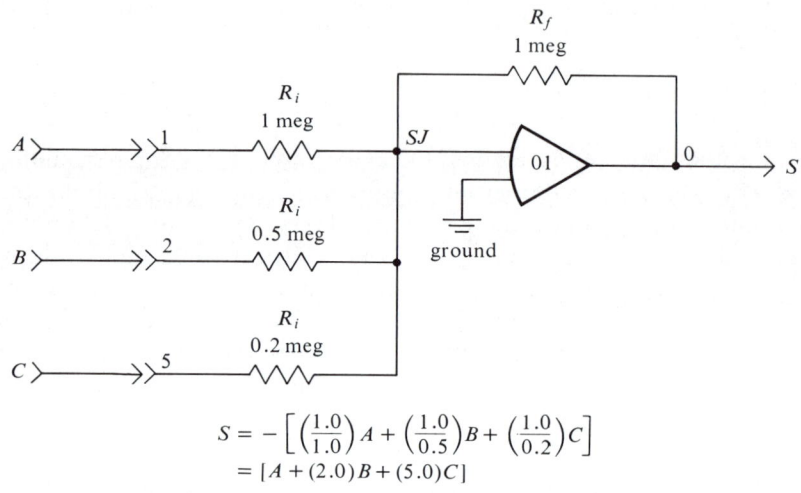

$$S = -\left[\left(\frac{1.0}{1.0}\right)A + \left(\frac{1.0}{0.5}\right)B + \left(\frac{1.0}{0.2}\right)C\right]$$
$$= [A + (2.0)B + (5.0)C]$$

FIG. 2-4

Connections of an Operational Amplifier as a Summer.

The possible gains are determined by the available values of resistance for the feedback and input resistors. On some computers the operator must plug in these resistors and therefore has a wide choice of ratios and hence a wide choice of gains. On other computers these resistors are permanently connected, the gains are marked for each input terminal, and the operator selects from those which are available. If the positive sum of a set of variables is needed, the result can be obtained as shown in

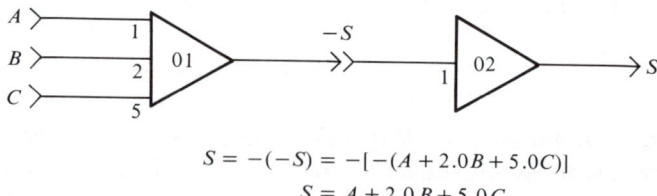

$$S = -(-S) = -[-(A + 2.0B + 5.0C)]$$
$$S = A + 2.0B + 5.0C$$

FIG. 2-5

Connection of Summer and Inverter to Obtain a Positive Sum.

Fig. 2-5 by combining an inverter with the circuit used previously. The same result could have been obtained by inverting A, B, and C before summing, but this procedure would have required the use of four operational amplifiers (three inverters, and one summer) rather than the use of one inverter and one summer. Such a reduction in the amount of computing equipment required to perform a particular job can frequently be made by proper choice of the sequence of operations. If Eq. (2-4c) was to be modeled:

$$S = A + 2.0 * B - 5.0 * C \qquad (2\text{-}4c)$$

the desired result could be obtained by inverting C as shown in the upper portion of Fig. 2-6. The block diagram in the lower portion of Fig. 2-6 accomplishes the same result with two summers rather than one summer and two inverters.

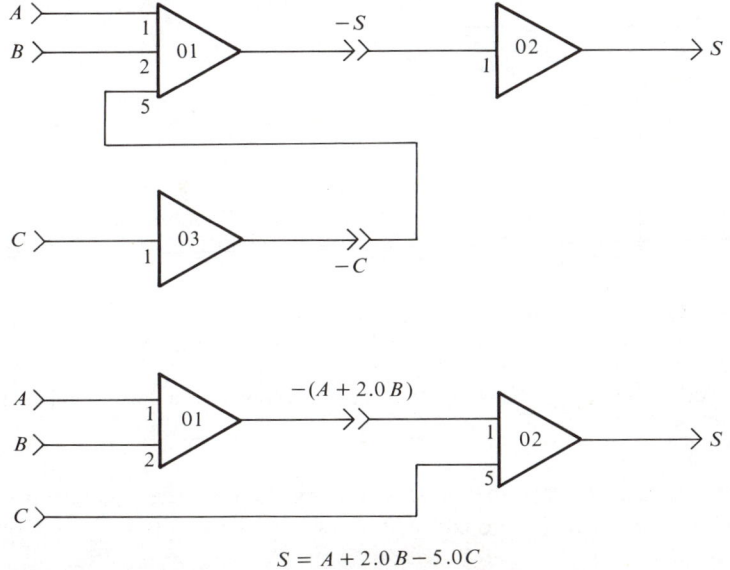

FIG. 2-6

Connections of a Summer and Inverters to Implement Subtraction.

In the process of summing and inverting the variables can be multiplied by constants such as 0.1, 1.0, 2.0, 5.0, and 10.0. For some purposes multiplication by a more general constant is required. Such multiplication is considered in the next section.

2-5 Multiplication by a Constant

The volume control on a radio or phonograph provides an adjustment in the intensity of the sound that is produced. A device that is identical in electrical function is used on analog computers to provide a continuously adjustable multiplying factor. These devices are properly called coefficient setting potentiometers but are frequently referred to as potentiometers, or pots. The name potentiometer is derived from the words "potential meter" which describes the use of such a device to measure voltage or potentials. The use considered here is more adequately described as a voltage divider. The block diagram symbol and the actual electrical circuit for a potentiometer are shown in Fig. 2-7. The circle represents the

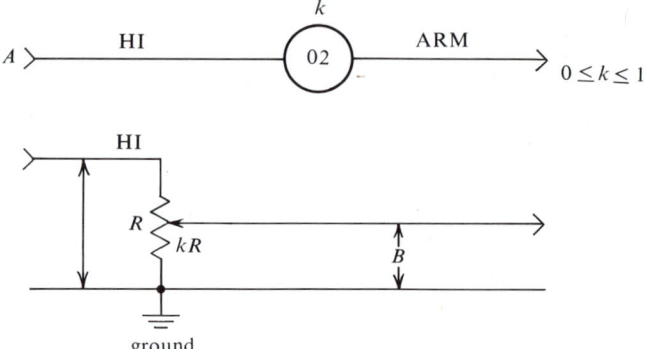

FIG. 2-7

Block Diagram Symbol and Electrical Connections for a Two-Terminal Potentiometer.

potentiometer, the number inside the circle identifies which potentiometer is used, and the constant k shows what ratio is to be set on the potentiometer. The symbol A identifies the potential difference with respect to ground G, the voltage which is applied to the upper or HI terminal of the potentiometer. The symbol B identifies the voltage at the output or ARM terminal of the potentiometer with respect to ground. As the adjustable tap on the potentiometer is moved from the bottom to the top, the ratio k changes from zero to 1.0. This ratio is shown on a calibrated dial if the potentiometer has such a dial. In actual operation the ratio may be less than indicated on the dial because some electrical current flows from the ARM of the potentiometer to the input resistor on the

MULTIPLICATION BY A CONSTANT 17

operational amplifier. Most analog computers are equipped with a POT BAL or POT SET mode of operation. After actuating a switch associated with the potentiometer, the ratio on the potentiometer can be set with reference to the ratio set on a master potentiometer or can be set by reading the ratio directly on a digital voltmeter. See Appendix 3-A for details. These procedures automatically compensate for any current flowing from the ARM of the potentiometer and hence give greater accuracy than if the potentiometers are set according to the indication of a calibrated dial on the potentiometer. This procedure also permits the use of less expensive potentiometers because a linear relationship between the resistance and mechanical rotation is no longer essential.

The potentiometers discussed thus far have two terminals, HI and ARM, available for making connections. The ARM terminal should never be connected to the output of an operational amplifier or to any other source of voltage. If the ARM terminal is connected to a voltage source and the potentiometer set for a low ratio, the potentiometer may be overheated or damaged. Some potentiometers have the lower terminal, marked LO, available for patching. For normal operation this terminal is connected to ground potential. The block diagram symbol and the electrical circuit for a three-terminal potentiometer is shown in Fig. 2-8. The

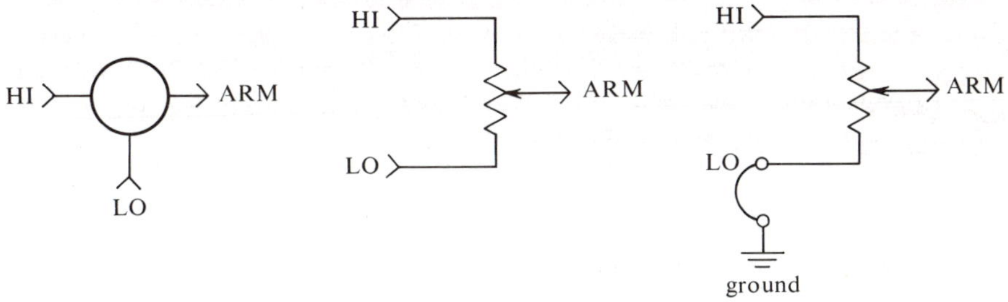

FIG. 2-8

Block Diagram Symbol and Electrical Connections for a Three-Terminal Potentiometer.

electrical circuit on the right shows the LO terminal grounded. This connection is electrically equivalent to the two-terminal potentiometer shown in Fig. 2.7.

The use of potentiometers permits the realization of more general coefficients in analog computer modeling. Fig. 2-9 shows how the potentiometers are used to obtain ratios that are not available on the basic summer. The resulting gain is the product of the ratio set on the potentiometer and the gain of the input channel to which the pot is connected.

18 ANALOGS OF ARITHMETIC OPERATIONS

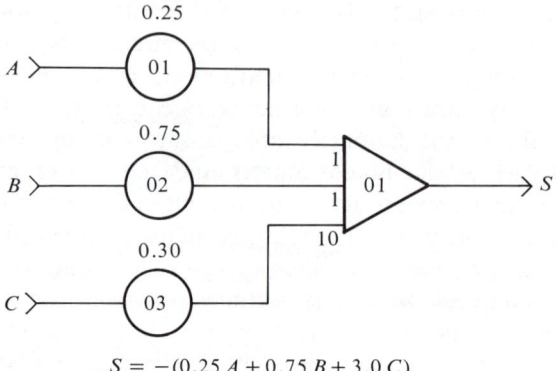

$$S = -(0.25\,A + 0.75\,B + 3.0\,C)$$

FIG. 2-9

Block Diagram Showing Potentiometers and a Summer Used for More General Summation.

The variables A and B are connected to inputs with a gain of 1.0 on the summer and hence appear at the output multiplied by the negative of the ratio set on potentiometers 01 and 02. Since the variable C feeds through an input on the summer with a gain of 10.0, the variable C appears at the output multiplied by $-(0.3 * 10.0)$ or -3.0. Potentiometers, summers, and inverters can be used to create analog computer models for some problems involving algebraic equations.

2-6 Solution of Algebraic Equations

The simplest kind of algebraic equation is a variable equal to the sum of several constants. This equation is so simple to evaluate analytically that the analog computer is not an appropriate tool for solving it. However, the solution of this equation provides a simple example with an obvious answer to demonstrate how the analog computer can be used to model algebraic processes.

EXAMPLE 2-2

Consider Eq. (2-6a):

$$Y = 5.0 - 3.0 \qquad (2\text{-}6a)$$

SOLUTION OF ALGEBRAIC EQUATIONS 19

Assume that the operational amplifiers to be used have an output voltage rating of ± 10 volts. Then an amplitude scaling of one unit per volt would be appropriate. A voltage of 5.0 volts is needed to represent the number 5.0 and a voltage of -3.0 volts is needed to represent the number -3.0. These voltages can be obtained by multiplying the reference voltages available on the computer by a suitable ratio using a potentiometer. These reference voltages are available at terminals on the computer marked $+\text{REF}$ and $-\text{REF}$. Sometimes these terminals are marked with the value of the voltage. If the operational amplifiers are rated for ± 10 volts, the reference voltages might be marked $+10$ and -10. Since the summer introduces an inversion, the equation should be rewritten as Eq. (2-6b).

$$Y = -(-5.0 + 3.0) \tag{2-6b}$$

This equation shows that a -5.0 volts should be summed with a $+3.0$ volts to obtain the variable Y. The block diagram for implementing this equation is shown in Fig. 2-10.

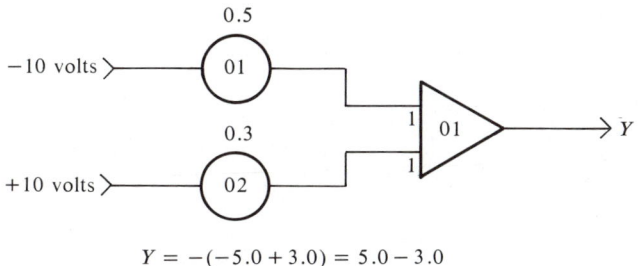

$$Y = -(-5.0 + 3.0) = 5.0 - 3.0$$

FIG. 2-10
Block Diagram for a Variable Equal to the Difference of Two Constants.

EXAMPLE 2-3

Consider now Eq. (2-6c) with the independent variable X.

$$Y = 5.0 - 3.0 * X \tag{2-6c}$$

The assumption now is that a voltage analogous to the variable X is available. The equation is modeled by the block diagram shown in Fig. 2-11. Note the change in the gain to which the ARM of POT 02 is connected. This change was made on the assumption that the amplitude scaling of the variable X is one unit per volt, that is, the same amplitude

ANALOGS OF ARITHMETIC OPERATIONS

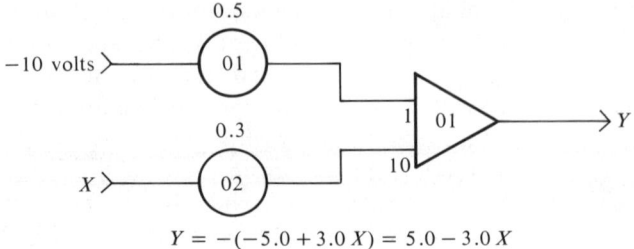

$$Y = -(-5.0 + 3.0\,X) = 5.0 - 3.0\,X$$

FIG. 2-11

Block Diagram for a Variable Equal to the Difference of a Constant and Another Variable.

scaling as on the variable Y. For purposes of experimenting with this circuit, a voltage is needed to represent the variable X. The first thought might be to obtain it by means of a potentiometer from the $+10$ volt reference as shown in Fig. 2-12. The ratio set on POT 03 is equal to $0.1X$.

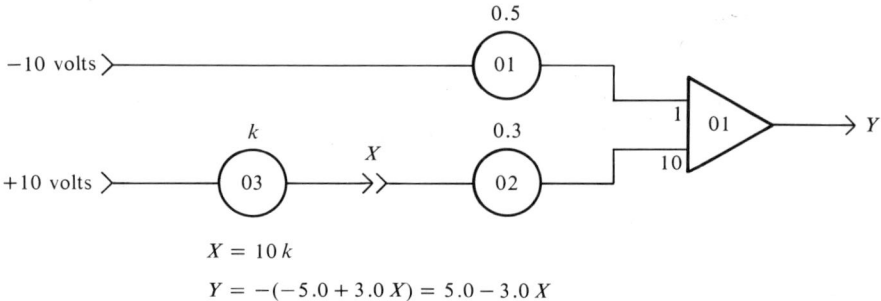

$$X = 10\,k$$
$$Y = -(-5.0 + 3.0\,X) = 5.0 - 3.0\,X$$

FIG. 2-12

Unsatisfactory Connection to Supply Variable X For Equation 2-6c.

If this circuit is tried, the voltage, X, will be found to be too small because the current flowing in the ARM of POT 03 is much too large. This difficulty can be overcome by using an inverter between the two potentiometers as shown in Fig. 2-13. Note the change from $+10$ to -10 on the HI terminal of POT 03. This change was needed to compensate for the sign change introduced by the inverter 02. These ideas can be applied to more complicated circumstances. The only difficulty that may arise is a limitation on the number of inputs to a summer. These ideas are more useful as applied to solving a set of simultaneous linear algebraic equa-

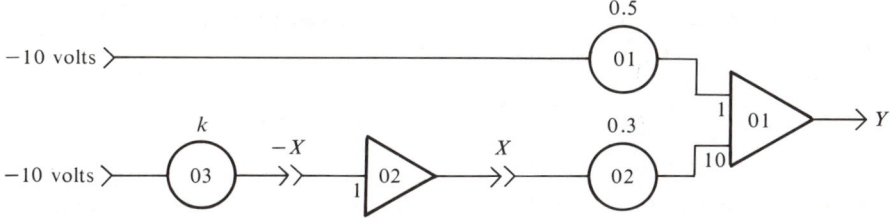

FIG. 2-13
Satisfactory Connection to Supply the Variable X For Equation 2-6c.

tions than for solving single equations. The method of creating an analog model of simultaneous equations will be considered next.

2-7 Solution of Simultaneous Linear Equations

In the period from 1940 to 1950 there was considerable interest in using analog computers for solving sets of simultaneous equations because the only alternative method of solution was hand computation. Today the interest has declined because it is possible to obtain solutions more easily and economically by means of the digital computer. This discussion of the analog solution of simultaneous algebraic equations is included because the basic method is the same as that to be considered later for solving sets of simultaneous differential equations. The process also provides an opportunity to practice on the analog computer the techniques learned thus far.

EXAMPLE 2-4

Consider the set of Eqs. (2-7a) and (2-7b).

$$5.0 * X - Y = 3.0 \qquad (2\text{-}7a)$$
$$-X + 3.0 * Y = 5.0 \qquad (2\text{-}7b)$$

The first step is much like that learned in algebra class, that is, solve Eq. (2-7a) for the variable X.

$$X = \frac{3.0 + Y}{5.0} = 0.6 + 0.2 * Y \qquad (2\text{-}7c)$$

The next step is different because rather than substitute into Eq. (2-7b), we solve Eq. (2-7b) for the variable Y.

$$Y = \frac{5.0 + X}{3.0} = 1.66 + 0.333 * X \qquad (2\text{-}7\text{d})$$

The next step is to model each of these equations on the analog computer as shown in the block diagram of Fig. 2-14. The circuit shown in the

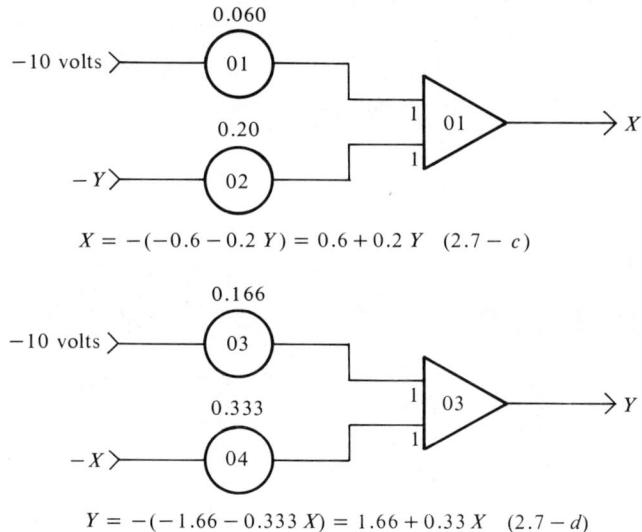

FIG. 2-14

Block Diagram of Analog Model for Equation 2-7c and 2-7d.

upper part of the figure would produce the variable X provided that the negative of the variable Y was available. The circuit shown in the lower part of the figure would produce the variable Y if the negative of the variable X was available. Although it may seem like "black magic," the model can be completed by connecting these two circuits together as shown in Fig. 2-15 with the output of AMP 01 providing the variable X to the input of the circuit which computes the variable Y, and conversely the output of AMP 03 providing the variable Y needed by the circuit which computes the variable X. An amplitude scaling of one unit per volt has been assumed. After this circuit is connected on the analog computer and the potentiometers adjusted to the values indicated on the block diagram, the output of AMP 01 will be found to be 1.0 volt and the output of

SOLUTION OF SIMULTANEOUS LINEAR EQUATIONS   23

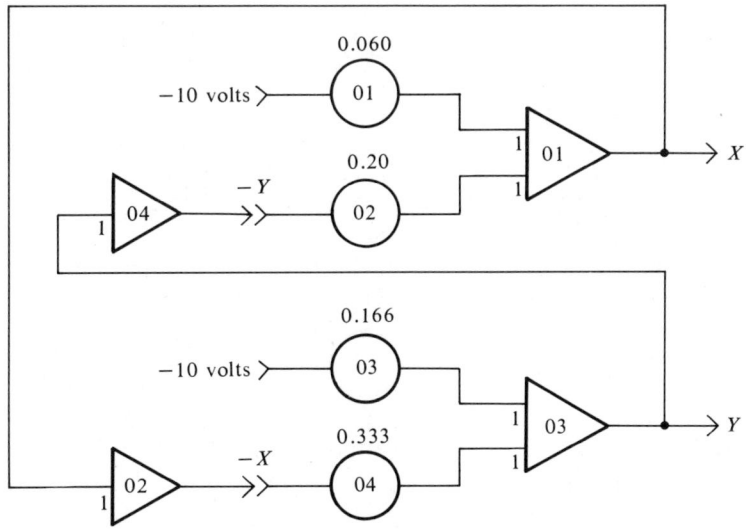

FIG. 2-15

Completed Block Diagram for Analog Model for Equation 2-7c and 2-7d.

AMP 03 will be 2.0 volts. These values will check if substituted in the original equations. Although these results also check if substituted into the derived Eqs. (2-4c) and (2-4d), a check here is a necessary but sufficient check on the correctness of the solution. If a mistake had been made in obtaining the second set of equations, the analog computer results would check the second set of equations but not the original set. The process takes on even more the aura of "black magic" if the equations are interchanged and the solution repeated. The block diagram for this case is shown in Fig. 2-16. When this circuit is connected on the analog computer, the output voltages of the amplifiers take on one of the two possible extreme values and the overload signal is actuated. For operational amplifiers rated for ±10-volt outputs, the limiting values will have a magnitude of 12 to 14 volts. The form of the block diagram is the same for the two cases, and both cases represent the same set of algebraic equations.

The reason for this seemingly strange behavior is not immediately obvious, but some insight into this problem can be gained by considering an analytical solution by successive approximations. Assume that X is zero and then solve Eq. (2-7d) for Y. Substitute this value of Y, 1.667, into Eq. (2-7c) and solve for X. Substitute this value of X, 0.9334, into Eq. (2-7d) and solve again for Y. This result, $Y = 1.9711$, when substituted into Eq. (2-7c), yields an improved value for X of 0.99422. Thus

24   ANALOGS OF ARITHMETIC OPERATIONS

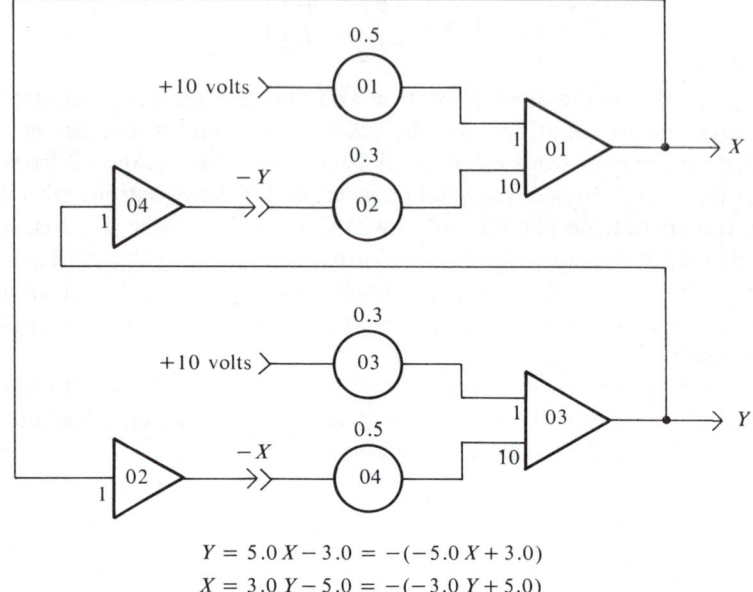

$$Y = 5.0\,X - 3.0 = -(-5.0\,X + 3.0)$$
$$X = 3.0\,Y - 5.0 = -(-3.0\,Y + 5.0)$$

FIG. 2-16

Block Diagram for an Unstable Analog Model for Equation 2-7c and 2-7d.

the successive values of X and Y are seen to converge to the values of (1.0, 2.0), which can be shown to be the correct solution. If a value of X greater than 1.0 is chosen as the starting point, the series of approximations converges from above to the same limit. If on the other hand Eq. (2-7a) were solved for Y and Eq. (2-7b) were solved for X, and the process repeated as outlined above, the series of approximations will diverge from the correct solution regardless of where the process is started unless of course one assumes the correct answer. The demonstration of this divergence is left for the student to explore. A sketch of a graphical solution for these simultaneous linear equations may be helpful in seeing the process of convergence and divergence.

The analog computer model can be thought of as solving the equations by successive approximations. If the process is convergent, a correct solution is obtained, but if the process is divergent, no solution is possible, and the operational amplifiers will overload. Once again it is demonstrated that "black magic" is only a phenomenon that is imperfectly understood by the person in whose eyes it appears to be magic.

Consider the matrix A for the coefficients of the unknowns for the set of Eqs. (2-7a) and (2-7b):

SOLUTION OF SIMULTANEOUS LINEAR EQUATIONS

$$A = \begin{bmatrix} +5 & -1 \\ -1 & +3 \end{bmatrix}$$

As a general rule the analog solution and also the analytical solution by successive approximations will be stable if the larger coefficients are located on (or near for a larger than 2 by 2 array) the diagonal from the upper left corner to the lower right corner, and if the equations are solved from top to bottom for the unknowns from left to right. That is, solve equation 1 for X_1, equation 2 for unknown $X_2, \ldots,$ and the nth equation for X_n. A discussion of the question of the convergence of the solution for systems of simultaneous equations from yet another point of view is given in Appendix IV.

Another reason for the amplifiers to overload is that the solution requires numbers that with the assumed amplitude scaling cannot be represented within the ratings of the amplifiers.

EXAMPLE 2-5

Consider the following set of linear algebraic equations:

$$4.0x - 3.0y = 3.0 \qquad (2\text{-}7e)$$

$$-x + y = 4.0 \qquad (2\text{-}7f)$$

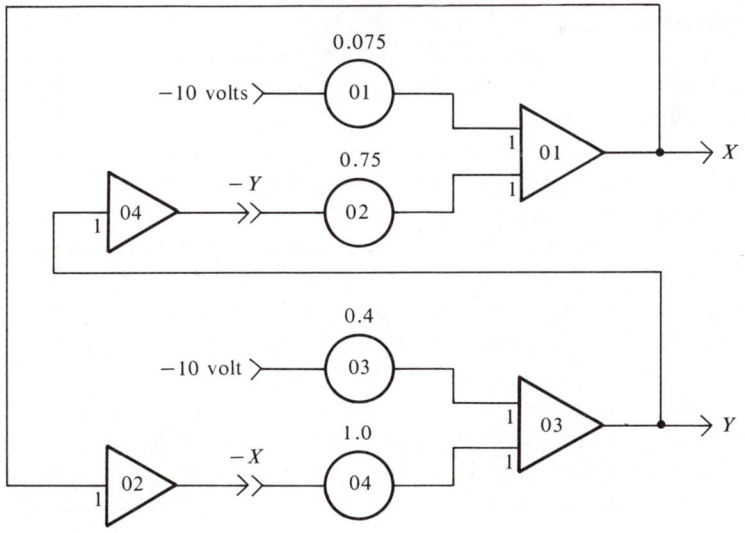

FIG. 2-17

Block Diagram for Analog Computer Model for Equations 2-7e and 2-7f.

26 ANALOGS OF ARITHMETIC OPERATIONS

These equations are solved by the same process as in the previous example, and the resulting block diagram is shown in Fig. 2-17. The amplifiers will overload under these conditions because the solution to the problem is $x = 15$ and $y = 19$ and hence the problem is not properly scaled. The same problem would arise if this problem were solved graphically on a graph 10 in. by 10 in. if the scale were assumed to be one unit of x or y equal to 1 in. The lines would intersect somewhere above and to the right of the upper righthand corner of the page. We can solve this problem either by taking a sheet of graph paper 20 in. by 20 in., or by rescaling the problem to make 10 in. on the graph equal to 20 units of x or y.

$$K_d = \frac{\max |x|}{Cm} = \frac{20 \text{ units}}{10 \text{ volts}} = 2.0 \text{ units/volt}$$

Therefore, x and y are related to the computer variables X and Y by Eqs. (2-7g) and (2-7h).

$$x = K_d * X = 2.0 * X \qquad (2\text{-}7g)$$
$$y = K_d * Y = 2.0 * Y \qquad (2\text{-}7k)$$

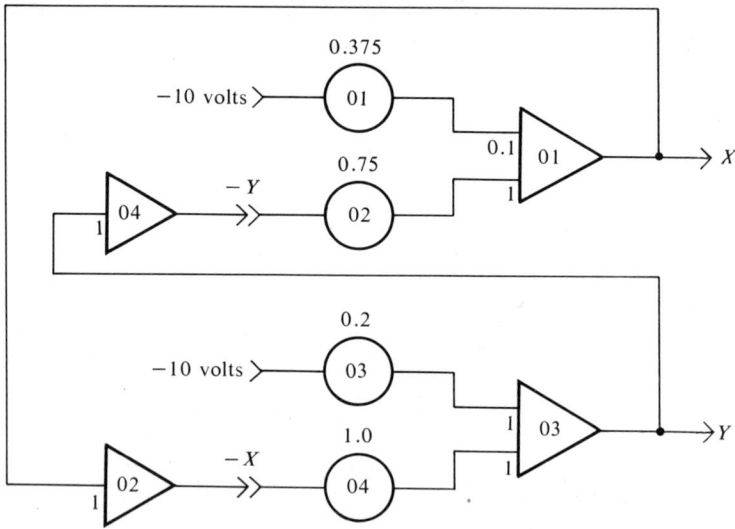

FIG. 2-18
Block Diagram for Analog Computer Model of Equations 2-7i and 2-7j.

These last two equations are substituted into the original set of simultaneous equations, Eqs. (2-7e) and Eq. (2-7f), to yield the amplitude scaled set of equations that can be modeled on the analog computer.

$$4.0(2.0 * X) - 3.0(2.0 * Y) = 3.0 \qquad (2\text{-}7\text{i})$$

$$-(2.0 * X) + (2.0 * Y) = 4.0 \qquad (2\text{-}7\text{j})$$

After these equations are processed, as in the previous examples, the block diagram shown in Fig. 2-18 is obtained. The ARM of POT 01 has been connected to an input on summer 01 with a gain of 0.1. If the lowest gain available is 1.0, then the ratio set on POT 01 must be 0.0375. The accuracy of low ratios is not as great as for larger ratios, and, therefore, low ratios should be avoided when possible. The analog model obtained with the analog computer connected as shown by Fig. 2-18 yields a value of 7.5 for X and 9.5 for Y. These values are converted by use of the amplitude scale factor Eqs. (2-7g) and (2-7h), to a value of 15.0 for x and 19.0 for y. These values satisfy the original set of Eqs. (2-7e) and (2-7f).

2-8 Exercises

1. An operational amplifier has a voltage gain of $-200,000$ and an input impedance of 2 megohms. What is the input voltage and input current when the output voltage is $+8$ volts?
2. The hull of a ship is 500 ft long, has a beam of 60 feet, and a height from keel to the main deck of 80 ft. A model is to be carved from a block of wood which is 20 in. long, 2 in. wide, and 4 in. high.
   a. Compute appropriate amplitude scale factors K_d and k_d. Show complete units.
   b. Compute the dimensions of the model that correspond to the 500 ft, 60 ft, and 80 ft.
3. The variable x for a problem ranges from -20 to $+30$ ft. The variable y ranges from -50 to $+40$. Compute appropriate amplitude scale factors k_x, K_x, k_y, and K_y.
4. The scale factor K_x has been determined as 4 ft/volt.
   a. Compute the values of the problem variable, x, which is represented by a voltage of 6 volts.
   b. Compute the value of the voltage, X, which corresponds to a value of 20 ft for x.
5. An operational amplifier is connected as shown in Fig. 2-19. What is the output voltage when the input voltage is 2 volts?

28   ANALOGS OF ARITHMETIC OPERATIONS

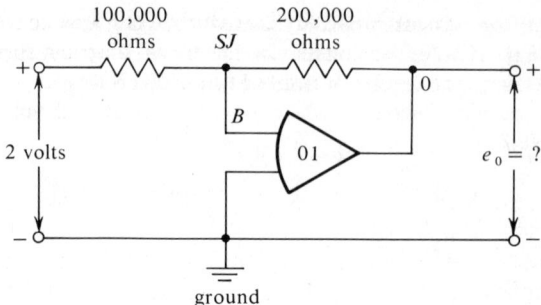

FIG. 2-19

6. Sketch a block diagram representation of the analog computer circuit in Exercise 5.
7. An operational amplifier is connected as shown in Fig. 2-20. What is the output voltage when the input voltages are as shown.

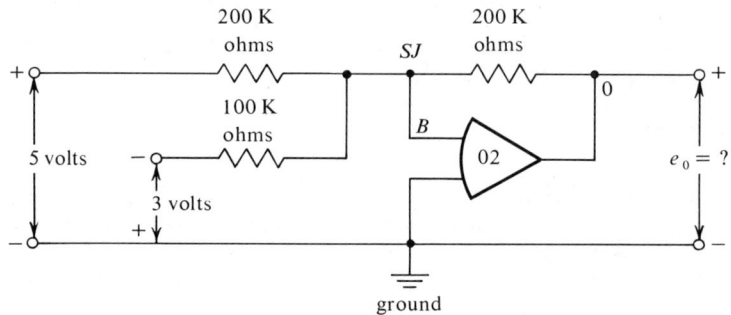

FIG. 2-20

8. Sketch a block diagram representation of the analog computer circuit in Exercise 7.
9. a. Sketch an analog computer circuit diagram showing how to connect an operational amplifier to implement the block diagram shown in Fig. 2-21. Assume that the feedback resistor is 1 megohm.
   b. What is the output voltage for an input voltage of $+20$ volts?

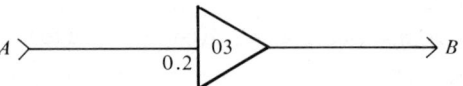

FIG. 2-21

10. a. Sketch an analog computer circuit diagram showing how to connect an operational amplifier to implement the block diagram shown in Fig. 2-22. Assume the feedback resistor to be 100 Kohms.
    b. What is the output voltage D when $A = 5$ volts, $B = 2$ volts, and $C = -8$ volts?

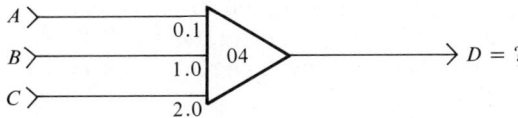

FIG. 2-22

11. Sketch an analog computer block diagram to implement the mathematical relations given. Assume that gains of 1, 2, and 5 are available. Use the minimum number of operational amplifiers. No potentiometers are to be used for this problem.
    a. $SA = A - 2B + 5C - D$
    b. $SB = 4A + 2B - 5C$
12. Determine the mathematical relation between the output and the inputs for each of the block diagrams in Fig. 2-23.

(a)

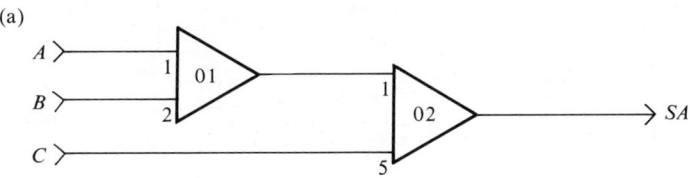

(b)

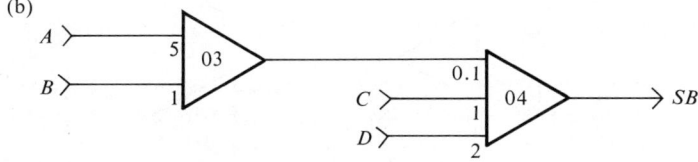

FIG. 2-23

13. The block diagram representation of a potentiometer is shown in Fig. 2-24. What is the output voltage when the input voltage is as follows:
    a. 10 volts
    b. Y volts

30 ANALOGS OF ARITHMETIC OPERATIONS

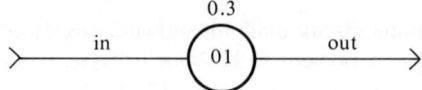

FIG. 2-24

14. Sketch the analog computer block diagram to implement the mathematical relation given. Assume that gains of 0.1, 1.0, and 10.0 are available on the inverter-summers. Use a minimum number of operational amplifiers and potentiometers.
   a. $SA = -0.8A + 0.5B + 2.0C - 0.05D$
   b. $SB = 3.0A + B - 0.15C - D$
15. Determine the mathematical relation between the output and the inputs for each of the block diagrams in Fig. 2-25.

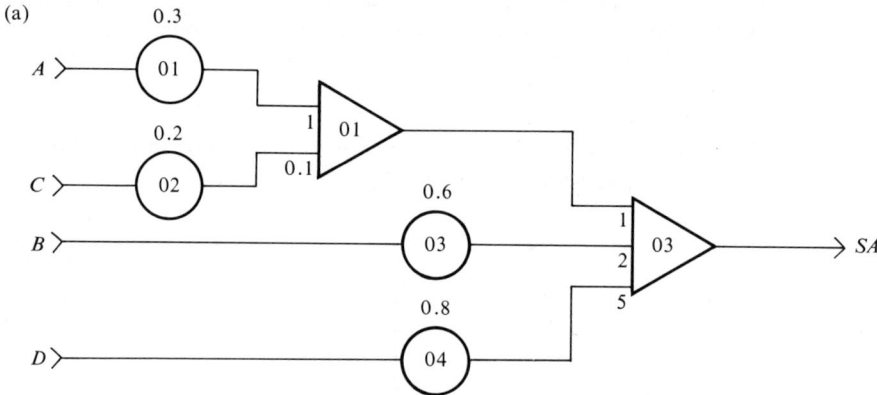

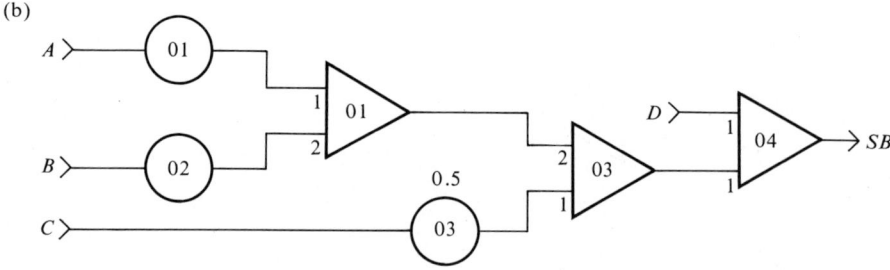

FIG. 2-25

16. Can the block diagram for part b of Exercise 15 be simplified to use fewer amplifiers? Assume the gains of 1, 2, and 5 are available on the summer-

inverters. Sketch the simplified block diagram and verify that the relation between the output voltage and the input voltage is the same as for the original system.

17. Show all of the connections required to implement the block diagram shown in Fig. 2-26 on one or more of the analog computers described in Appendix I. Sketches of the panels will be found in these appendices. Assume that the voltages X and Y are available.

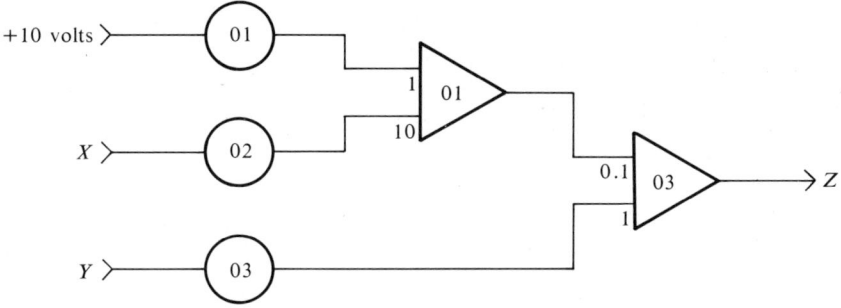

FIG. 2-26

18. Sketch the analog computer block diagrams to implement the equations listed below. Assume that voltages to represent all variables on the right are available.
   a. $P = 8.0 - 4.0Q$
   b. $P = 6.0 + 5.0Q$
19. Set up on the analog computer available to you the block diagram shown in Fig. 2-13. If your computer has a reference voltage other than 10 volts, use that voltage rather than 10 volts. Measure Y for the following values of k:

$$k = 0.1, 0.2, 0.3, 0.4, 0.5$$

Compare the measured values of Y with the expected values.

20. Set up on the analog computer available to you the model described by the block diagram of Fig. 2-15. Verify the solution given.
21. Set up on the analog computer available to you the model described by the block diagram of Fig. 2-16 and confirm that the model is unstable.
22. Sketch the analog computer block diagram to solve the system of equations given below.

$$4.0X + 0.8Y = 7.0$$
$$0.5X + 3.0Y = 9.0$$

ANALOGS OF ARITHMETIC OPERATIONS

23. Solve algebraically the system of equations for Exercise 22. Would a computer with a Cm of 10 volts be able to model this system adequately?

24. Set up on an analog computer a model of the system of equations given in Exercise 22. Rescale if necessary to fit the model to your computer. Compare the answers obtained with those computed in Exercise 23.

25. Determine the general relationship between Y and X for the system shown in Fig. 2-27. For what purpose might this circuit be useful?

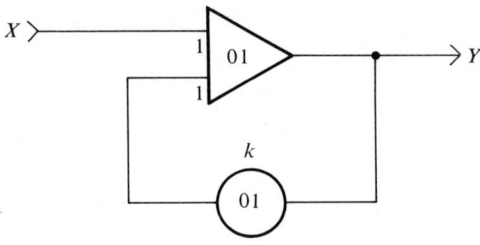

FIG. 2-27

CHAPTER 3 ANALOGS OF CALCULUS OPERATIONS

Many problems and systems of interest to engineers involve rates of change with respect to time or some other independent variable. Thus models for such systems require models for integration and differentiation. For example, consider velocity, v, and displacement, x:

$$v = \frac{dx}{dt} \quad \text{and} \quad x = \int v\,dt$$

Velocity, v, is the derivative with respect to time of the related displacement, x. Displacement, x, is the integral with respect to time of the velocity, v. This chapter considers analog computer models for the processes of differentiation and integration. These processes are then applied to show how various functions can be generated on the analog computer.

3-1 Differentiation

Consider a tank for storing water such as is shown in Fig. 3-1. Assume that this tank is a right-circular cylinder with circular cross section located in the horizontal plane. The amount of water, Q, stored in the tank is

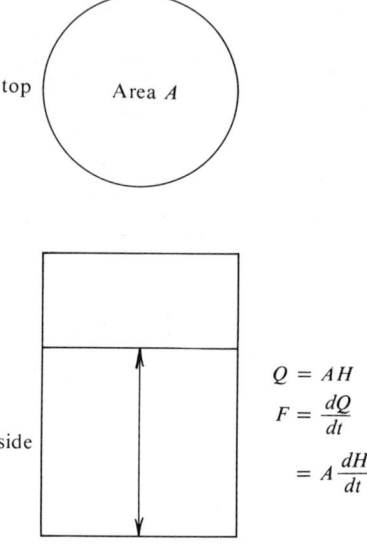

FIG. 3-1
Water Storage Tank Analogy to Capacitor.

proportional to the depth of the water, H. The factor of proportionality is the cross-sectional area, A, of the tank. Thus the relation between the quantities Q, A, and H is as follows:

$$Q = A * H \tag{3-1a}$$

If the area of the tank is expressed in square feet and the depth of the water is expressed in feet, then the volume of water in the tank is expressed in cubic feet. The rate at which water is flowing into the tank, F, is the derivative of Q with respect to time, that is,

$$F = \frac{dQ}{dt} = A * \frac{dH}{dt} \tag{3-1b}$$

A capacitor consists of two electrically conducting plates separated by an insulator. For example, two pieces of aluminum foil separated by a sheet of paper form a capacitor. Frequently strips of foil separated by strips of insulating material are rolled up to form capacitors. A capacitor stores electrical charge in a manner analogous to the way in which a tank stores water. The amount of electrical charge, Q, stored in a capacitor is proportional to the potential difference, V, across the capacitor, that is,

$$Q = C * V \qquad (3\text{-}1c)$$

The factor of proportionality is the electrical capacitance, C. A capacitance of one farad charged to a potential difference of one volt contains a charge of one coulomb. Since typical values of capacitance are usually very, very much smaller than one farad, capacitance is usually measured in units of one millionth of a farad, that is, one microfarad.

The time rate at which charge flows past a point is called electric current and is represented by the symbol I. Thus the rate of flow of charge into a capacitor is the current flowing into the capacitor. Electric current is defined by the relation

$$I = \frac{dQ}{dt} \qquad (3\text{-}1d)$$

If the charge is measured in coulombs and if time is measured in seconds, the current is measured in amperes. On the assumption that the capacitance is constant, the current flowing into a capacitor is the time rate of change of charge in the capacitor, that is,

$$I = \frac{dQ}{dt} = C * \frac{dV}{dt} \qquad (3\text{-}1e)$$

If the voltage across a capacitor is constant, the current flowing is equal to zero, because the derivative with respect to time of the voltage is zero. See Fig. 3-2 for a summary of the relations for a capacitor as a model of

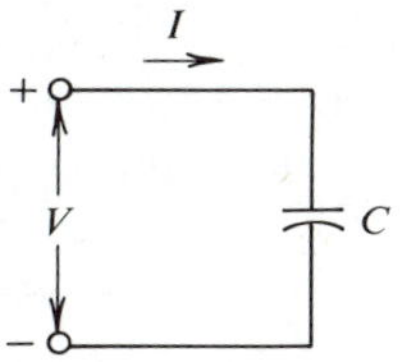

FIG. 3-2

Electrical Capacitor as a Model for Differentiation.

differentiation. Before considering how the capacitor can be useful as an analog for the process of differentiation, let us consider the analogy between the capacitor and the water tank described previously.

The amount of charge stored in the capacitor is analogous to the volume of water stored in the water tank. The potential difference across the capacitor is analogous to the depth of water in the tank. Thus a pressure gauge connected to the bottom of the tank could be calibrated to read the depth of water in the tank. This pressure gauge would function in a manner analogous to a voltmeter connected across the capacitor to read its electrical pressure, or potential difference. The capacitance of the capacitor is a measure of the number of coulombs of charge stored in the capacitor per volt of potential difference. Capacitance is analogous to the area of the tank that is a measure of the volume of water stored per foot depth of water in the tank. The rate of flow of charge into the capacitor, coulombs per second, is analogous to the rate of flow of water into the tank, cubic feet per second. These ideas of analogy are summarized in Table 3-1.

TABLE 3-1. ANALOGY BETWEEN ELECTRICAL CAPACITOR AND WATER TANK

	CAPACITOR			WATER TANK	
Symbol	Name	Unit	Symbol	Name	Unit
Q	charge	coulomb	Q	volume of water	cubic ft
V	potential difference	volt	H	depth of water	ft
C	capacitance	coulomb/volt or farad	A	area of tank	cubic ft/ft or square ft
I	current	coulomb/sec or amp	F	flow of water	cubic ft/sec

$$Q = C * V$$
$$I = C * \frac{dV}{dt}$$

$$Q = A * H$$
$$F = A * \frac{dH}{dt}$$

The capacitor could be used as an analog of the process of differentiation if a current proportional to the change of voltage was satisfactory.

The most desirable kind of analog, however, would be one which produced a voltage proportional to the derivative of the input voltage. By Ohm's law the potential difference across a resistor is proportional to the product of the resistance and the current that flows through the resistance. The combination of a capacitor, a resistor, and an operational amplifier as shown in Fig. 3-3 produces the desired analog model. The relationship

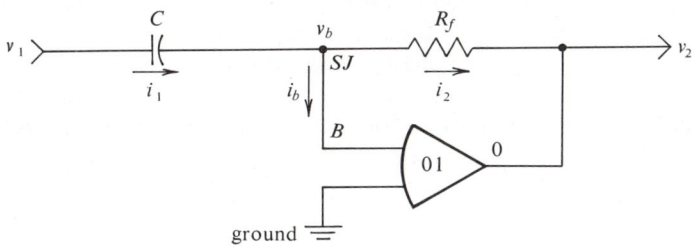

FIG. 3-3

Analog Computer Model for Differentiation.

between the input voltage, v_1, and the output voltage, v_2, can be derived as follows assuming that the operational amplifier is ideal, that is, $v_b = 0$, $i_b = 0$.

$$v_c = v_1 - v_b = v_1, \text{ since } v_b = 0 \tag{3-1f}$$

The current through the capacitor, i_1, is computed by Eq. (3-1e) as

$$i_1 = C\frac{dv_c}{dt} = C\frac{dv_1}{dt} \tag{3-1g}$$

The current i_2 is equal to the current, i_1, since the current into the input of the operational amplifier, i_b, is zero for an ideal operational amplifier. Therefore

$$i_2 = i_1 - i_b = i_1 = C\frac{dv_1}{dt} \tag{3-1h}$$

The potential difference across the resistor, R_f, is by Ohm's law

$$v_b - v_2 = i_2 * R_f \tag{3-1i}$$

Since the input voltage, v_b, for an ideal operational amplifier is zero, the output voltage, v_2, is as follows:

ANALOGS OF CALCULUS OPERATIONS

or
$$-v_2 = +i_2 * R_f$$
$$v_2 = -i_2 * R_f \tag{3-1j}$$

Substituting from Eq. (3-1h) the desired result is as follows:

$$v_2 = -C\frac{dv_1}{dt} * R_f$$
$$= -R_f * C\frac{dv_1}{dt} \tag{3-1k}$$

Appendix II-C derives the relationships in greater detail to show the effect of a nonideal operational amplifier.

EXAMPLE 3-1

Consider the analog computer circuit for differentiation shown in Fig. 3-4. For the numbers given for the capacitor, C, and the resistor, R_f, the $R_f * C$ product has a numerical value of 2.0. Thus the relationship between the output voltage, v_2, and the input voltage, v_1, is as follows:

$$v_2 = -R_f * C\frac{dv_1}{dt} = -2.0\frac{dv_1}{dt} \tag{3-1l}$$

The input voltage, v_1, is defined as a function of time by the upper graph shown in Fig. 3-4. This is called a trapezoidal waveform. The derivative with respect to time of the voltage, v_1, is plotted in the middle graph of Fig. 3-4. During the time interval from 0 to 4 seconds, the derivative of v_1, that is, the slope of the graph, is as follows:

$$\frac{dv_1}{dt} = \frac{(20 - 0)}{(4 - 0)} = \frac{20}{4} = 5 \text{ volts/sec} \tag{3-1m}$$

The slope of the graph for v_1 in the interval from 4 to 8 seconds is equal to zero since the function is constant. For the interval from 8 to 16 seconds the derivative is as follows:

$$\frac{dv_1}{dt} = \frac{(-20 - 20)}{(16 - 8)} = \frac{(-40)}{(8)} = -5 \text{ volts/sec} \tag{3-1n}$$

The remainder of the graph for dv_1/dt is computed in the same way. Eq. (3-1l) relates the output voltage, v_2, and the derivative of v_1 with respect to time, and thus relates the lower and middle graph of Fig. 3-4.

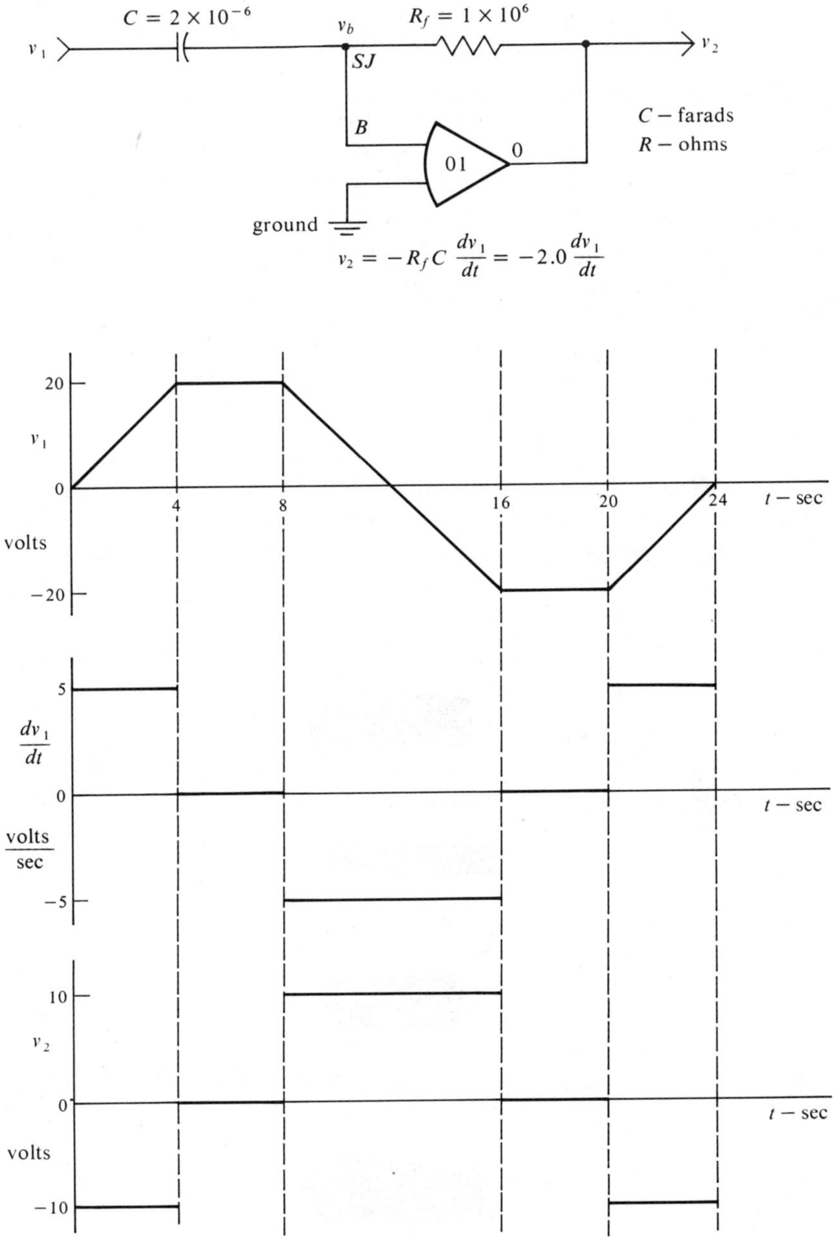

DIFFERENTIATION   39

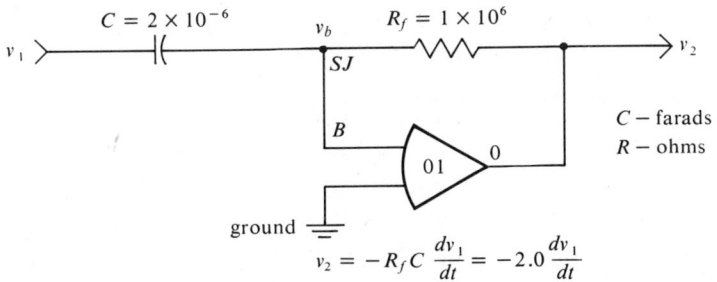

$$v_2 = -R_f C \frac{dv_1}{dt} = -2.0 \frac{dv_1}{dt}$$

FIG. 3-4

Example of Differentiation of a Voltage.

The reversal of sign in the process of differentiation occurs for the same reason as in the case of the process of summation and in fact occurs with all operations involving operational amplifiers.

Although the analog model of the process of differentiation can be created easily as shown above, this analog is not used very frequently in analog computation because differentiation accentuates noise. In most cases the model can be created using only the process of integration. This process is preferred because the averaging inherent in integration tends to reduce noise that may be present. The creation of the electrical analog to the process of integration also uses a capacitor-resistor network and will be considered next.

3-2 Integration

The processes of integration and differentiation are inverses of each other. That is, if A is the derivative of B, then B is the integral of A. Since the current, i, through a capacitor is proportional to the derivative of the voltage across the capacitor, then the voltage across the capacitor would be proportional to the integral of the current through the capacitor. Since current is the derivative of charge with respect to time,

$$i = \frac{dq}{dt} \tag{3-2a}$$

then charge, q, is related to current, i, by:

$$q = \int i\,dt \tag{3-2b}$$

Since $q = Cv$ by definition, then

$$v = \frac{q}{C} \tag{3-2c}$$

The substitution of the integral relation for q into the last equation yields the following:

$$v = \frac{1}{C}\int i\,dt \tag{3-2c}$$

These relations are summarized in Fig. 3-5. This analog model for integration has a disadvantage similar to that of the simple capacitor circuit for

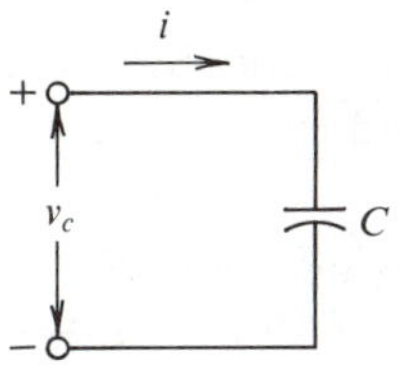

INTEGRATION 41

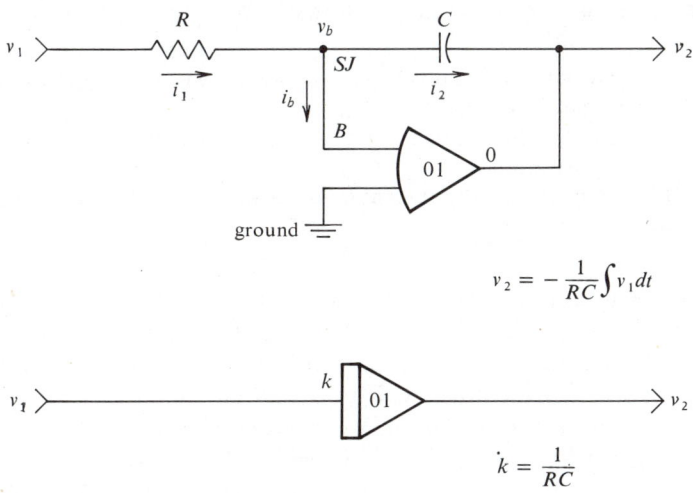

FIG. 3-5

Electrical Capacitor as an Integrator.

differentiation, that is, a voltage is proportional to the integral of a current. The most desirable process would produce an output voltage that was proportional to the integral of the input voltage. The combination of a capacitor, a resistor, and an operational amplifier as shown in Fig. 3-6 produces the desired result. The validity of this circuit will now be demonstrated by the following derivation.

FIG. 3-6

Analog Computer Model of Integration.

This derivation assumes that the operational amplifier is ideal, that is, the input voltage, v_b, and the input current, i_b, are small enough to be considered to be zero. Refer to Fig. 3-6 for the circuit diagram. The input current, i_1, and the output current, i_2, are as follows:

$$i_1 = \left[\frac{(v_1 - v_b)}{R}\right] = \frac{v_1}{R} \qquad (3\text{-}2\text{e})$$

ANALOGS OF CALCULUS OPERATIONS

$$i_2 = i_1 - i_b = i_1 = \frac{v_1}{R} \tag{3-2f}$$

The potential difference across the capacitor, v_c, is as follows:

$$v_c = v_b - v_2 \tag{3-2g}$$

Since the voltage, v_b, is negligible compared to the voltage, v_2, the output voltage, v_2, is as follows:

$$v_2 = -v_c = -\frac{1}{C}\int i_2 dt = -\frac{1}{C}\int \frac{v_1}{R} dt \tag{3-2h}$$

$$v_2 = -\frac{1}{RC}\int v_1 dt$$

This result can be remembered as follows:

1. the input voltage, v_1, divided by the input resistor, R, determines the current that is flowing,
2. this current is integrated with respect to time to determine the charge on the capacitor,
3. this charge divided by the value of capacitance, C, gives the value of output voltage.

The block diagram symbol for the analog model of integration is also shown in Fig. 3-6. The difference between this symbol and that for the inverter is the addition of the rectangular box on the left side of the symbol. The number 01 identifies which operational amplifier is to be connected as an integrator. The number represented by the symbol k is the reciprocal of the RC product of the integrator. This constant is called the gain of the integrator. When the capacitance is measured in microfarads (10^{-6} farad) and the resistance is measured in megohms (10^6 ohms), the RC product has units of farad-ohms or seconds. The analog model for integration has associated with it the sign inversion seen previously for the analog models of the process of summation and differentiation. Although the sign inversion for these processes could be eliminated by including an inverter with each of the analogs, this addition would needlessly increase the cost of the equipment. As will be seen later, the sign inversion is taken into account in setting up the problem and an inverter is added only if needed.

EXAMPLE 3-2

Consider the analog integrator set up as shown in Fig. 3-7, which is integrating the voltage, v_1, which has the waveform shown in the upper graph. The second graph from the top shows the result of integrating the voltage, v_1. The integral of a function can be considered to be the area under the graph of that function. Thus the area between the graph for v_1 and the t-axis is -10 volts per sec, and the slope of the graph for the integral is -10 volt-sec per sec over the interval from 0 to 4 sec. The value of the integral at 4 sec is the area between the graph for v_1 and the t-axis over the interval from 0 to 4 sec. This area is -40 volt-sec. Since the voltage, v_1, is zero over the interval from 4 to 8 sec, the value of the integral is constant at -40 volt-sec during this interval. In the interval between 8 and 16 sec, the area under the v_1 curve is $+10$ volts per sec, and the slope of the graph for the integral of v_1 is $+10$ volt-sec per sec. The area under the v_1 curve over the interval from 8 to 12 sec is $+10$ volts * 4 sec or 40 volt-sec. Thus the value of the integral at time equal to 12 sec is zero. After 4 more sec the value of the integral is $+40$ volt-sec, and the process continues in similar fashion to complete the curve. The output voltage from the integrator is related to the integral of the input voltage by the reciprocal of the *RC* product for the integrator and the sign inversion common to all analog operations with operational amplifiers. The output voltage v_2 is shown on the lower graph of Fig. 3-7. Compare the voltages v_1 and v_2 shown in Fig. 3-4 and Fig. 3-7. The voltage v_1 to be integrated in Fig. 3-7 is the same as the voltage v_2 obtained by differentiating the voltage v_1 in Fig. 3-4. Furthermore, the output voltage v_2 of Fig. 3-7 is the same as the input voltage v_1 of Fig. 3-4. These relations between the input and output voltages demonstrate the inverse nature of the operations of integration and differentiation.

Frequently it is desirable to integrate the sum of two or more variables. This could be accomplished by first summing the variables with a summer and then integrating the result with an integrator. The two processes can, however, be combined and performed by one operational amplifier. Since problems may be frequently large enough to use all of the computing equipment that is available, it is appropriate to economize wherever possible. Such a combination is shown in Fig. 3-8. The result can be inferred by considering each input separately and then adding up the result. The process suggested is an example of the principle of superposition. The principle of superposition states that the net effect of several independent causes is the same as the sum of the effects of each cause

44 ANALOGS OF CALCULUS OPERATIONS

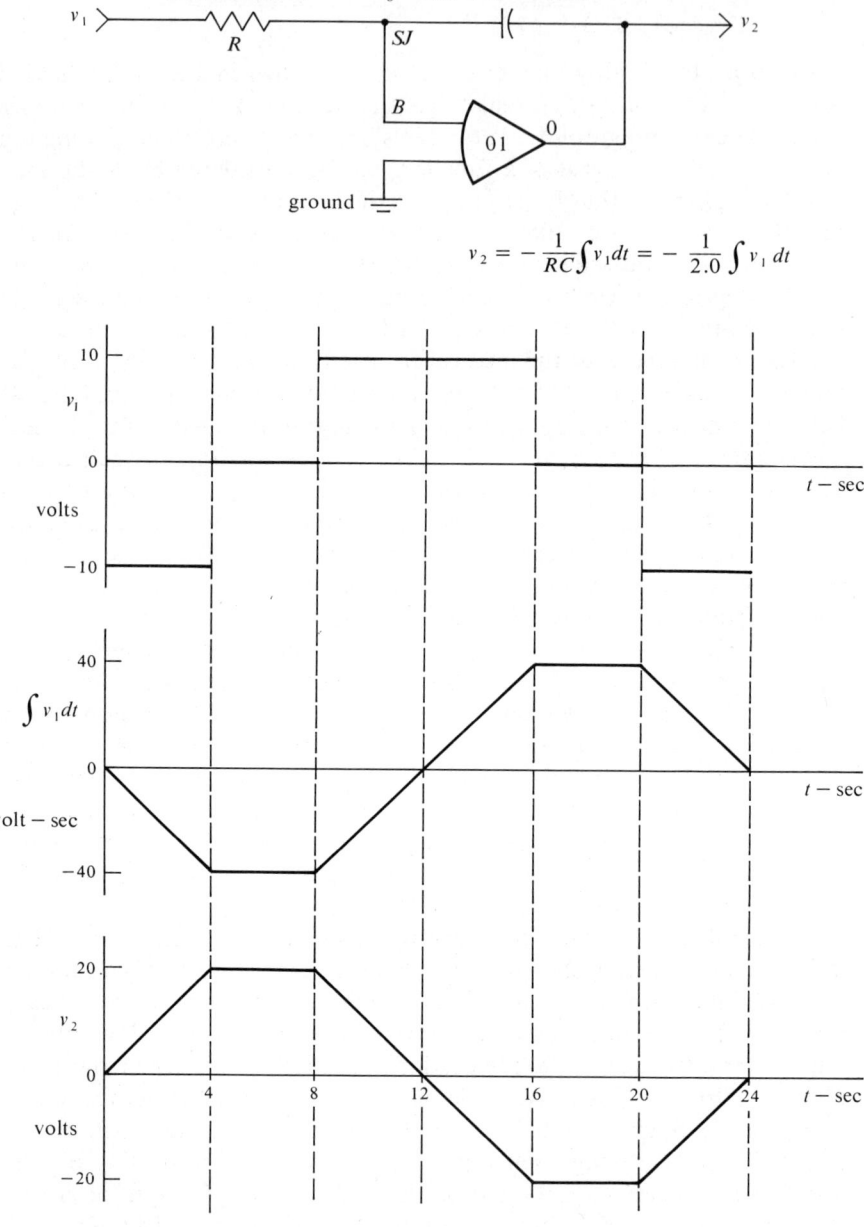

FIG. 3-7
Example of Integration of a Voltage.

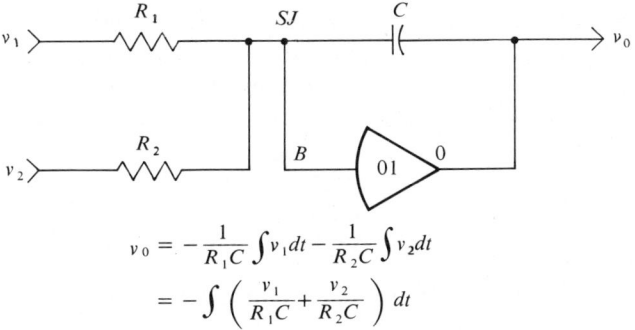

FIG. 3-8

Combined Summation and Integration.

acting separately. For example, consider a scale for measuring the weight of people. If one person weighs 125 pounds and a second person weighs 150 pounds, the scale registers 275 pounds if both are on the scale at the same time. The block diagram for the combined operation of summation and integration is shown in Fig. 3-9.

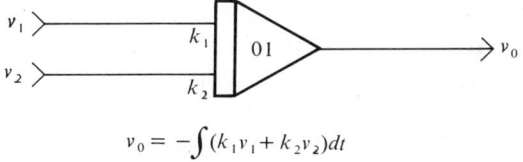

$$v_0 = -\int (k_1 v_1 + k_2 v_2) dt$$

FIG. 3-9

Block Diagram for Combined Summation and Integration.

The integrals that we have been considering are not complete. In calculus you learned that the integral of $6x^2$ is as follows:

$$\int 6x^2 dx = 2x^3 + IC \qquad (3\text{-}2\text{i})$$

The symbol IC stands for the initial value of the integral. This initial value will be a constant and its derivative will be zero. Thus the integral of $6x^2$ could be $2x^3$, $2x^3 + 3$, or $2x^3 +$ any constant. The derivative of all these functions is $6x^2$. Thus the analog model may also require provision for an initial condition. An initial value for the output of an analog integrator requires that the capacitor be charged initially to a suitable voltage. This is accomplished by connecting a suitable voltage to the terminal on the integrator marked IC. The nature of the process of obtaining the initial condition involves the sign change common to all operations using operational amplifiers. Thus the initial condition obtained by connecting a voltage $+A$ to the *IC* terminal is $-A$. The block diagram for an integrator with an initial condition connected is shown in Fig. 3-10. If no initial con-

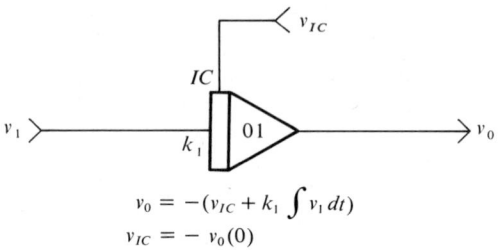

FIG. 3-10

Block Diagram for Integration with Initial Condition.

dition is desired, the connection is omitted on both the block diagram and in the connections made on the analog computer. The initial condition is then zero. The value of voltage needed for an initial condition may not be directly available on the computer. In this case a potentiometer can be used to attenuate or reduce the reference voltage to provide the desired value. The coefficient required on the integration process may be a value other than the standard gains available on the patch panel. In this circumstance the potentiometer is used to obtain the desired value. The general case of integration with an arbitrary gain and initial condition is shown in Fig. 3-11. A specific example of this general case will be used in the next section to generate a ramp function.

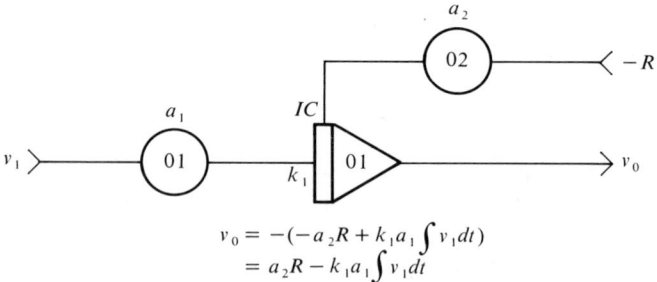

FIG. 3-11

Block Diagram for Integration with General Constants.

3-3 Generation of Ramp Functions

The simplest function after constants are linear functions. The graph of a linear function is shown in Fig. 3-12 in the familiar "slope-intercept" form. The slope m is the ratio of Δy to Δx, and the intercept is the value of b. Because the graph of such functions looks similar to ramps used to move from one level to another, these functions are called ramp functions.

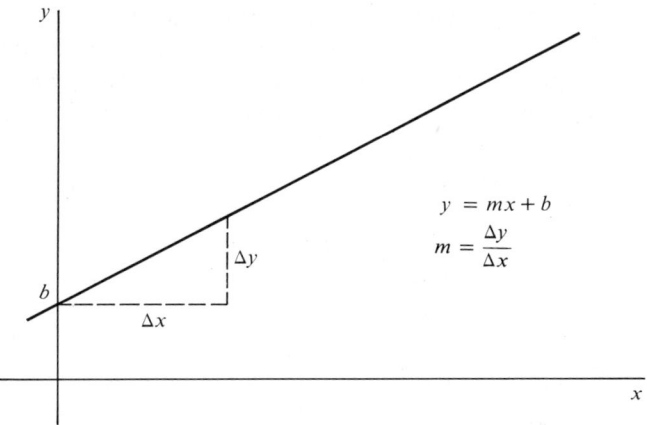

FIG. 3-12
Graph of Linear Function or Ramp.

Consider the block diagram shown in Fig. 3-13. Potentiometer 01 attenuates the -10 volt reference to -0.5 volt. Since the input to an integrator is the derivative of the output of the integrator, the output will

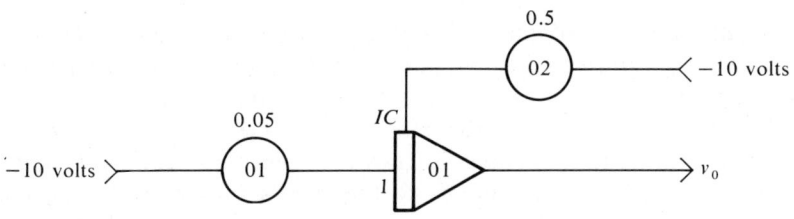

FIG. 3-13
Ramp Function Generator.

48 ANALOGS OF CALCULUS OPERATIONS

change at the rate of 0.5 volt per second. Thus the ramp generated will have a slope of -0.5 volt/second. Potentiometer 02 attenuates the -10 volts to -5.0 volts, and the inversion makes the initial value of the output voltage equal to $+5.0$ volts. The output voltage can be calculated as follows:

$$v_0 = -[(-10.0 * 0.5) + (1.0 * 0.05 \int -10.0 dt)]$$
$$v_0 = 5.0 + 0.5 \int dt = 5.0 + 0.5t \qquad (3\text{-}3)$$

The result is plotted in Fig. 3-14. Since the analog computer is assumed to start calculating at time equal to zero, there is no curve to the left of the origin. The limited range of the output voltage of the operational amplifier provides a limit on the magnitude of the function that can be generated. This limit was assumed to be 10 volts for the present example.

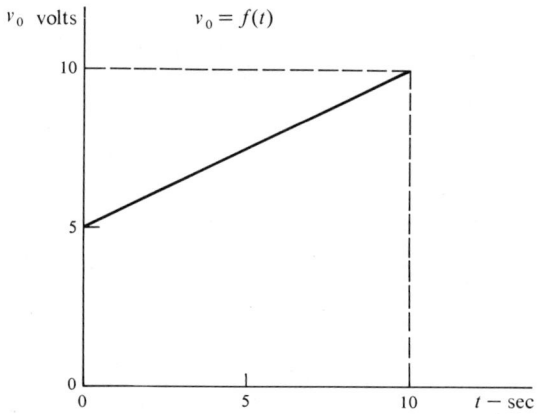

FIG. 3-14

Ramp Function Generated by Model Shown in Fig. 3-13.

The usual process of interest is not to compute the function that will be generated by a given analog computer configuration, but rather, given the function that one wishes to generate, to create the analog computer configuration that will do the job. The former process is known as analysis, and the latter process is known as synthesis. The usual activity of engineers is that of creating or synthesizing a system or device to perform a specified job. The analog computer is a useful tool for synthesis because models can be easily created on the analog computer and tested to see whether the performance is satisfactory. Consider the problem of generating the function shown in Fig. 3-15. The slope is positive and has a

GENERATION OF POLYNOMIAL FUNCTIONS

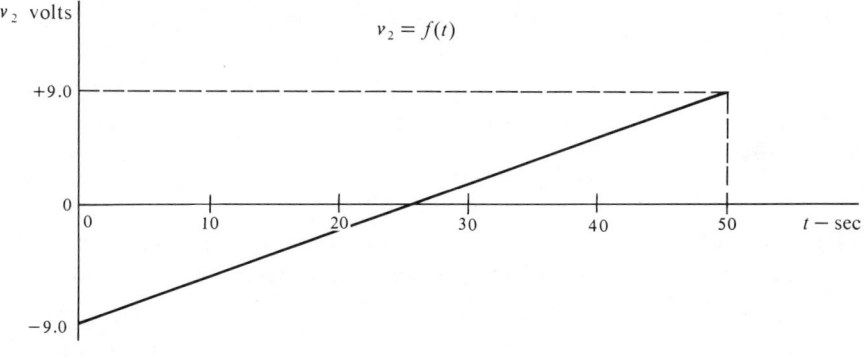

FIG. 3-15
Ramp Function Desired.

value of (18/50) or 0.36 volt per second. Therefore, the input voltage should be -0.36 volt, which can be obtained by potentiometer 01 set for 0.036 and connected to -10 volts. The initial condition is -9.0 volts, which can be obtained by connecting $+9.0$ volts to the *IC* terminal. This is obtained from potentiometer 02 set for a ratio of 0.90 and connected to $+10$ volts. See Fig. 3-16 for the block diagram of the analog model to generate the desired ramp function. Ramp functions are frequently needed in analog computer models to provide a voltage that is a linear function of time to drive one axis of an *X-Y* plotter or other display device. This application will be discussed in the next chapter.

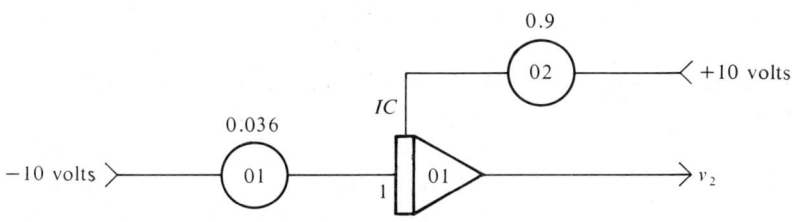

FIG. 3-16
Block Diagram of Analog Model for Generating Ramp Function of Fig. 3-15.

3-4 Generation of Polynomial Functions

Consider the integration of a linear function *y* such as generated in the last section:

ANALOGS OF CALCULUS OPERATIONS

$$z = \int y\,dx + C = \int [mx + b]\,dx + C$$

$$z = \frac{mx^2}{2} + bx + C$$

$$z = ax^2 + bx + C \tag{3-4a}$$

Thus the integration of a linear function is a quadratic function. This process can be repeated as many times as desired to obtain any desired

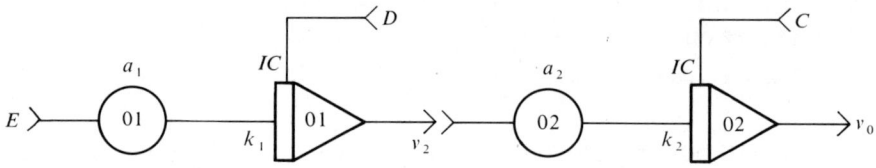

FIG. 3-17
Block Diagram for Generation of a Quadratic Function.

polynomial function. Consider the block diagram shown in Fig. 3-17. The output v_2 of amplifier 01 is by application of the principles of Section 3-2.

$$v_2 = -(D + k_1 a_1 \int E\,dt)$$

$$v_2 = -D - [Ek_1 a_1]t \tag{3-4b}$$

The output voltage v_0 of amplifier 02 is the integral of the voltage v_2 as follows:

$$v_0 = -[+C + k_2 a_2 \int v_2\,dt]$$

$$= -C - k_2 a_2 \int [-D - Ek_1 a_1 t]\,dt$$

$$= -C + k_2 a_2 Dt + \frac{Ek_1 k_2 a_1 a_2 t^2}{2}$$

$$v_0 = -C + [k_2 a_2 D]t + [0.5\ Ek_1 k_2 a_1 a_2]t^2$$

$$v_0 = -C + Bt + At^2 \tag{3-4c}$$

GENERATION OF POLYNOMIAL FUNCTIONS

Suppose that it is desired to generate the polynomial below:

$$v_0 = -10 + 2.0t - 0.05t^2 \quad (3\text{-}4d)$$

A comparison of Eqs. (3-4c) and (3-4d) shows that:

$$C = +10.0$$

The product of the constants k_2, a_2, and D must be 2.0. If D is chosen to be $+10$ and k_2 chosen to be 1.0, then a_2 is 0.20, which is an appropriate value to set on potentiometer 02. The value of 10 for D is appropriate if the reference voltage is 10 volts. The value of 1.0 is generally an appropriate gain for an integrator. From Eq. (3-4c) it can be found that:

$$-0.05 = A = (0.5[E\ k_1\ a_1]\ k_2\ a_2) \quad (3\text{-}4e)$$

Since $k_2 a_2 = 0.2$,

Therefore: $k_1 a_1 E = -0.5$.

Assume: $E = -10$

Therefore: $k_1 a_1 = +0.05$

Assume: $k_1 = 1.0$

Therefore: $a_1 = 0.05$

The block diagram for the analog computer model to generate the polynomial of Eq. (3-4d) is shown in Fig. 3-18. A graph of the voltages v_0 and v_2 plotted as a function of time is shown in Fig. 3-19.

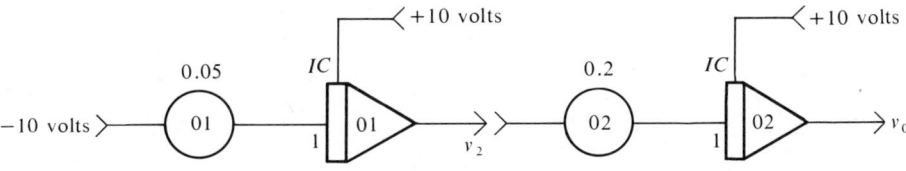

FIG. 3-18
Block Diagram for Generation of $v_0 = -10 + 2.0t - 0.05t^2$.

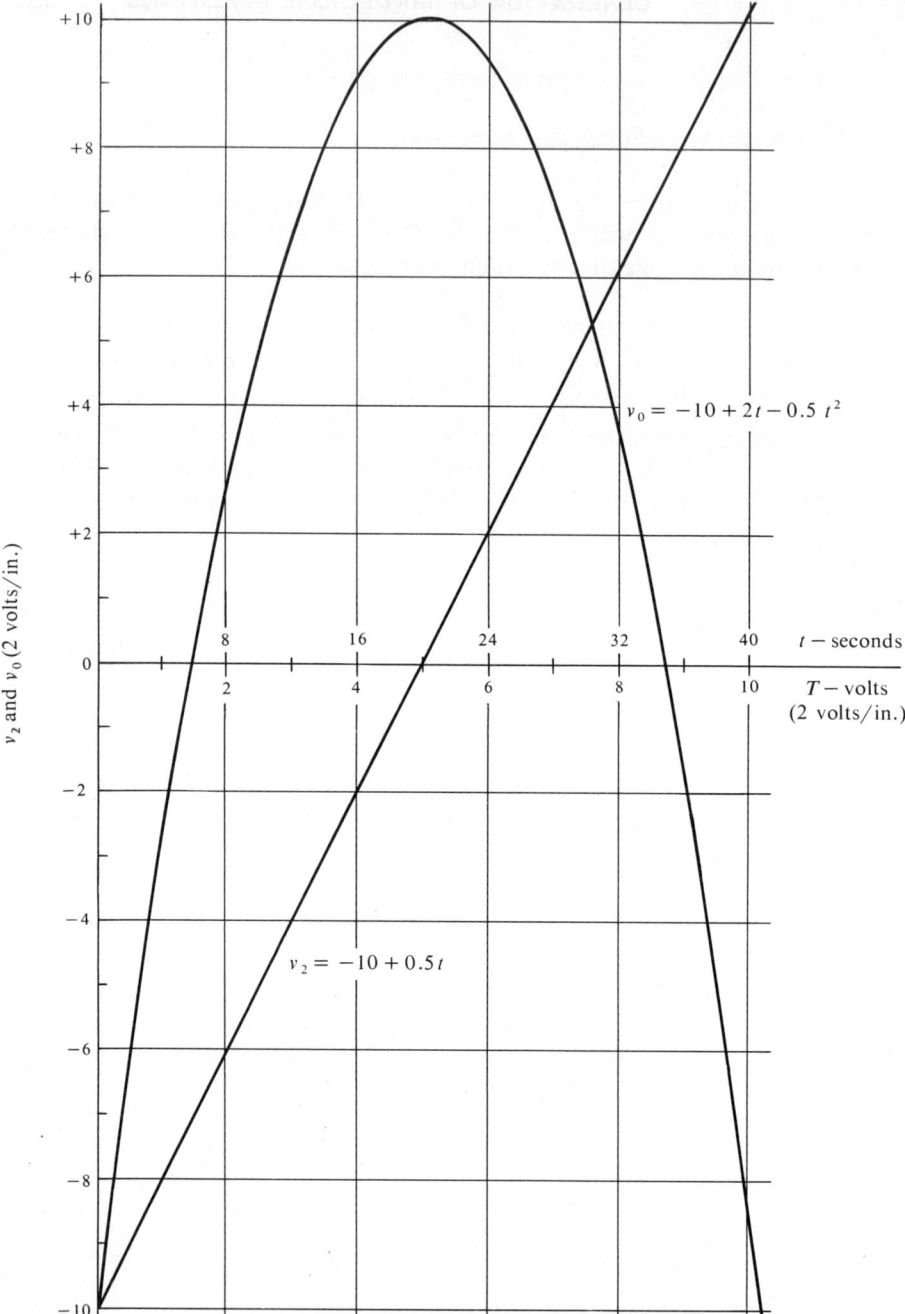

FIG. 3-19

Graphs Produced by Analog Computer Model of Fig. 3-18.

3-5 Generation of Sinusoidal Functions

The sine and cosine functions have an interesting property in that repeated integrations will produce the function with which one started except for a multiplicative constant. For example:

$$\int \omega \sin(\omega t) dt = \int \sin(\omega t) d(\omega t) = -\cos(\omega t)$$

$$\int \omega \cos(\omega t) dt = \int \cos(\omega t) d(\omega t) = \sin(\omega t)$$

The constants, ω, were added to facilitate the integrations. The implementation of the integration of the cosine function on an analog computer is shown in Fig. 3-20. Because of the inherent inversion (sign change) the resulting voltage v_2 is a negative sine function.

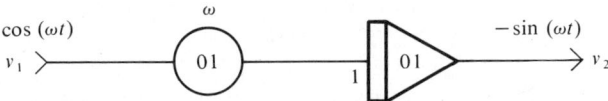

FIG. 3-20
Integration of a Cosine Function.

Next we will consider the integration of the negative sine function, since we wish to make an iterative type operation. See Fig. 3-21. Again the input voltage, v_2, has been multiplied by the constant ω to facilitate the integration. The result, v_3, is a negative cosine function. The inverter 03 has been added to produce a positive cosine function.

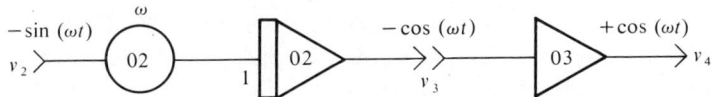

FIG. 3-21
Integration of a Sine Function.

The analog models shown in Figs. 3-20 and 3-21 can be combined to form a sinusoidal function generator. Before reading on, the student should try to put the two parts together to form this generator.

The terminals marked v_2 are connected together and the terminals marked v_4 and v_1 are connected together. The complete system is shown

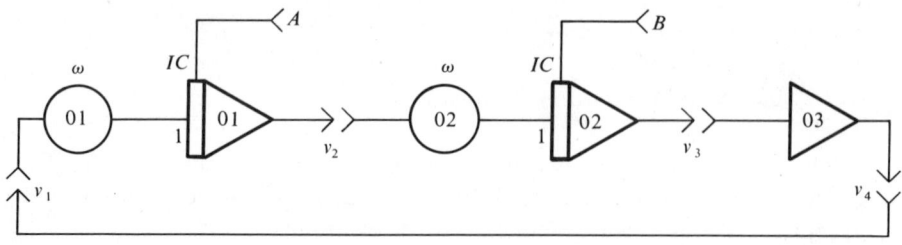

FIG. 3-22

Sinusoidal Function Generator.

in Fig. 3-22. The feature added here that was not in the preceding two figures are the initial conditions A and B. If the initial conditions are both zero, nothing is generated. If A is zero and B is -10 volts, the voltage, v_3, and the voltage, v_2, will be as follows:

$$v_3 = 10.0 * \cos(\omega t)$$

$$v_2 = 10.0 * \sin(\omega t)$$

Although the reason for these results is not obvious, the correctness of the statements can be easily verified by successive integrations and consideration of the sign inversion of the analog integrators. In similar fashion the result for initial conditions of $A = -10.0$ volts and $B =$ zero are as follows:

$$v_2 = +10.0 * \cos(\omega t)$$

$$v_3 = -10.0 * \sin(\omega t)$$

Sinusoidal generators such as described are very useful for analog computer modeling because the value of the function at the start of the computation can be adjusted and can be depended upon to be repeatable for a fixed value of adjustment. Most signal generators, such as those used in electronics laboratories, cannot be started in this fashion. The conditions at the start would vary in a random fashion.

3-6 Exercises

Note: The real problems that an engineer or other person solves in practice are not usually like the typical textbook problems that have just the right amount of information and one unique answer. One of the first steps in solving such real problems is to sort out the relevant material from that which is irrelevant. On occasion the information provided is not sufficient and certain assumptions must be made. If it is necessary to make assumptions, they should be clearly labeled as such. Some of the problems in this book will have too much or too little information. The student should therefore be alert.

1. A water tank is a rectangular parallelopiped 100 feet high with a base which is 20 ft by 30 ft. Compute the rate at which water is flowing into the tank when the rate of change of height is 2 ft/min.
2. Water is 20 ft deep in the tank of Exercise 1 at time equal to zero. Water flows into the tank at a constant rate of 1000 cu ft/min. Compute the rate at which the height is changing at:
   a. time equals 30 minutes
   b. time equals 90 minutes
3. Compute the depth of the water for the conditions of Exercise 2 at
   a. time equals 20 minutes
   b. time equals 80 minutes.
4. Does an answer to Exercise 3 suggest a possible error in an answer to Exercise 2? If so, what is the error? If this problem were modeled on an analog computer, what would occur at the problem time equal to 80 minutes?
5. a. What is the relationship between the output voltage and the input voltage for the analog computer circuit shown in Fig. 3-23?
   b. Sketch the block diagram representation of this analog computer circuit.

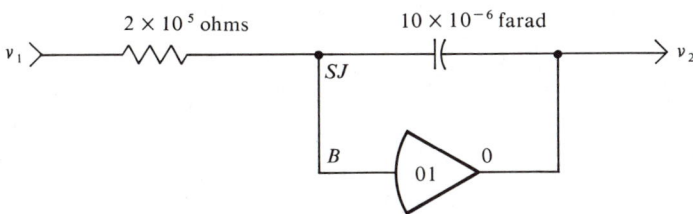

FIG. 3-23

6. a. What is the relationship between the output voltage, v_2, and the input voltage, v_1, for the analog computer circuit represented by the block diagram shown in Fig. 3-24?
   b. Sketch the analog computer circuit represented by this block diagram. Assume that the feedback capacitor has a value of 1×10^{-6} farad.

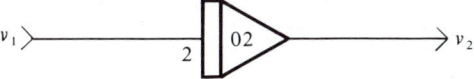

FIG. 3-24

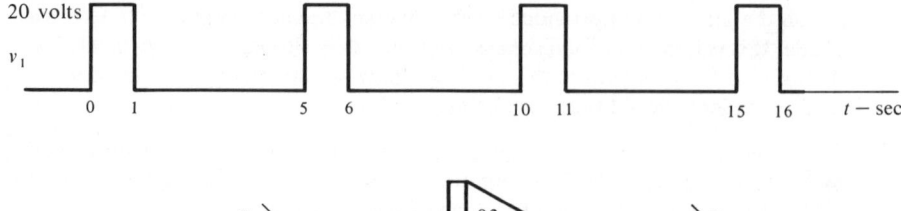

FIG. 3-25

7. a. The voltage v_1 has the waveform shown in Fig. 3-25. This voltage is operated on by an analog computer circuit represented by the block diagram shown below. Sketch the output voltage v_2 over the time interval 0 to 10 seconds.
   b. Assume that the operational amplifier used is rated for operation over a range of output voltage from -10 to $+10$. Does the 20 volt input signal create any problems? Why or why not? How long can this system operate before problems will arise? What is the problem?
8. a. What is the relationship between the input voltage and the output voltage for the analog computer circuit represented by the block diagram shown in Fig. 3-26?
   b. Sketch the analog computer circuit represented by this block diagram. Assume that the feedback capacitor has a value of 10×10^{-6} farad.

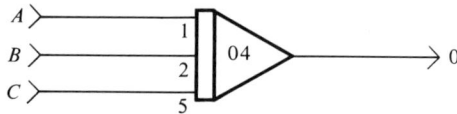

FIG. 3-26

9. What is the relationship between the output voltage and the input voltage for the analog computer circuit represented by the block diagram shown in Fig. 3-27?

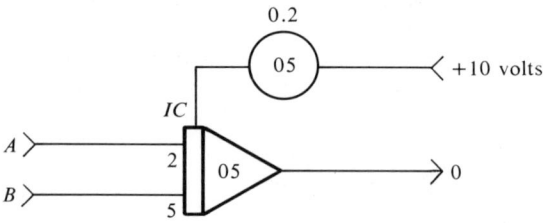

FIG. 3-27

10. What is the mathematical expression for the voltage v_2 in the analog computer circuit represented by the block diagram shown in Fig. 3-28?

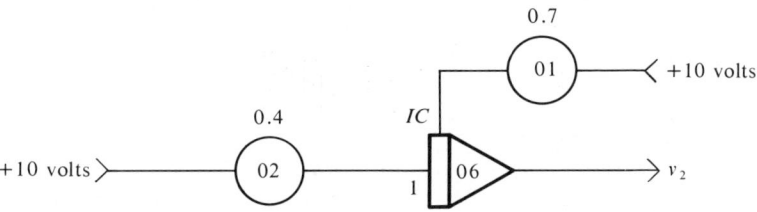

FIG. 3-28

11. A voltage waveform as shown in Fig. 3-29 is desired. Sketch the block diagram representation of the analog computer circuit that will generate this waveform. Assume that the reference voltage on the computer to be used is 100 volts. Assume that the integrators to be used have gains of 1, 2, and 5.

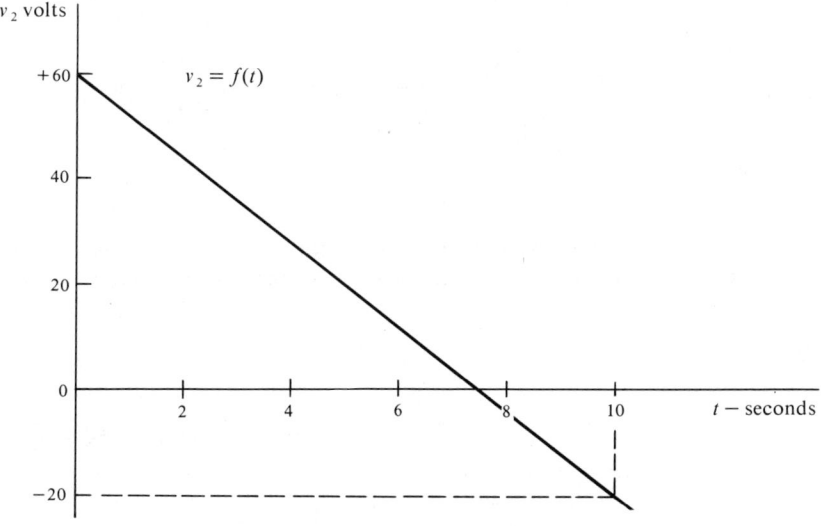

FIG. 3-29

12. What is the mathematical expression for the output voltage, v_2, in the analog computer circuit represented by the block diagram shown in Fig. 3-30?

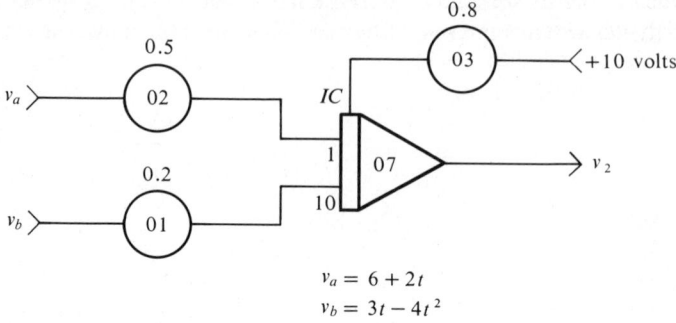

FIG. 3-30

13. What is the mathematical expression for the output voltage, v_2, in the analog computer circuit represented by the block diagram shown in Fig. 3-31?

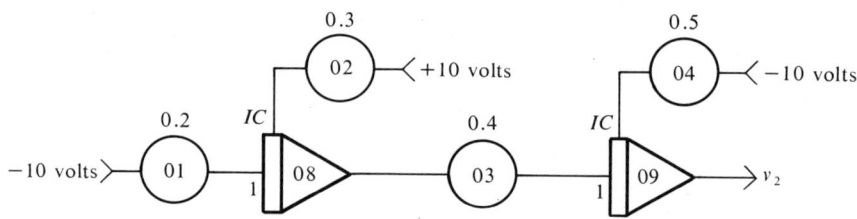

FIG. 3-31

14. What is the mathematical expression for the output voltage, v_2, in the analog computer circuit represented by the block diagram shown in Fig. 3-32?

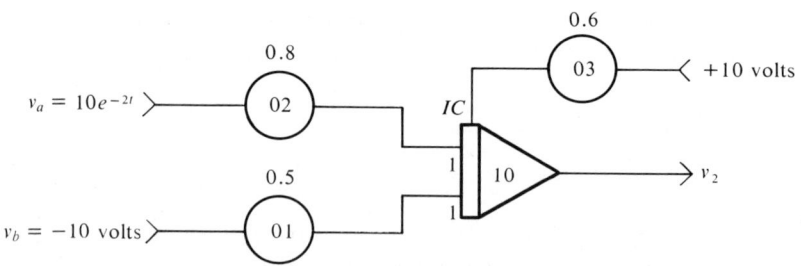

FIG. 3-32

15. Sketch the block diagram representation of the analog computer circuit which will generate the given function. Assume that the analog computer used has a reference voltage of 100 volts, and that the integrators used have gains of 1, 2, and 5.

$$v_2 = 30 - 4t + 2t^2$$

16. a. What is the *general* mathematical expression for the voltage v_2 generated by the analog computer circuit represented by the block diagram shown in Fig. 3-33?

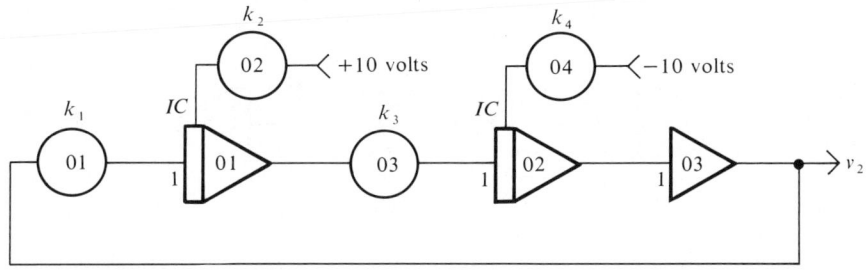

FIG. 3-33

b. What is the *specific* mathematical expression for the voltage v_2 generated for each set of potentiometer ratio listed below?

POTENTIOMETER	01	02	03	04
CASE 1	0.20	0.80	0.20	0.00
CASE 2	0.20	0.00	0.20	0.60
CASE 3	0.20	0.80	0.20	0.60
CASE 4	0.40	0.80	0.40	0.60

17. Sketch the block diagram representation for the analog computer circuit that will generate each of the voltages listed below. Assume that the reference voltage on the computer being used is 10 volts and that the integrator gains are 1 and 10.
    a. 5 cos (2t)
    b. 8 sin (0.5t)
18. Show by means of detailed sketches how one or more of the analog computers described in Appendix 1 would be connected to implement the block diagrams shown in Fig. 3-34.

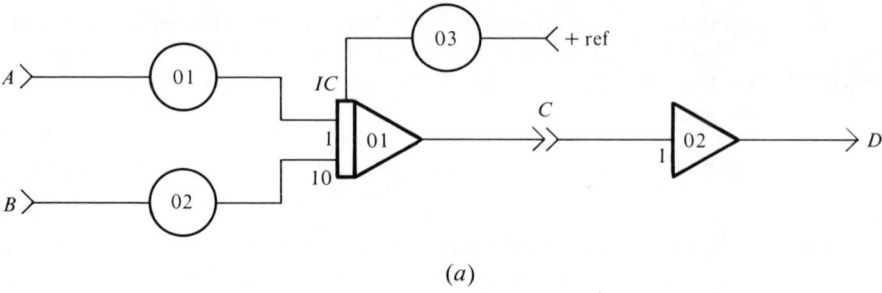

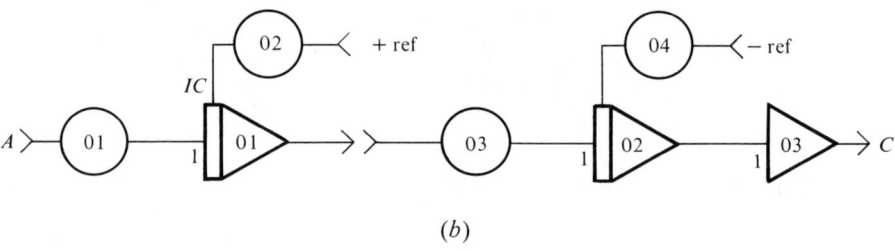

FIG. 3-34

19. a. Create an appropriate mathematical model for the system shown in Fig. 3-35, and show by means of a block diagram how this can be implemented on an analog computer. Assume that the analog computer to be used has a reference voltage of 100 volts and amplifier gains of 1, 2, and 5. The variable of interest is the height, $h(t)$, of the water in the tank.
   b. Since the rates at which the water flows into the tank, q_{in}, and out of the tank, q_{out}, are constant and not equal, the tank will either run dry, or overflow. Which of these happens and at what time does it happen?

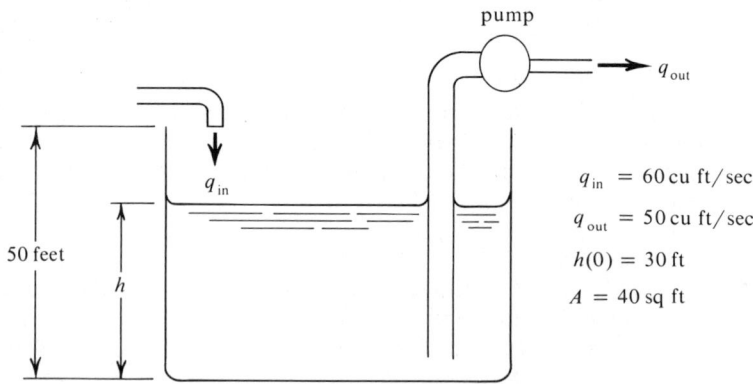

$q_{in} = 60$ cu ft/sec
$q_{out} = 50$ cu ft/sec
$h(0) = 30$ ft
$A = 40$ sq ft

FIG. 3-35

CHAPTER 4 RECORDING AND DISPLAY OF SOLUTIONS

The answer produced by an analog computer is usually a nonconstant function of the independent variable of the problem. Such an answer is most easily interpreted when plotted as a graph showing the functional relationship between the variables. Three of the most commonly used methods of presenting the answer are cathode ray oscilloscopes, strip chart recorders, and electromechanical X-Y plotters. The human ear is less sensitive to sounds as the frequency increases, and ultimately the ear has no response for sufficiently high frequencies. In the same way, these recorders and display devices are limited with regard to the highest frequency of electrical signal that they can handle without excessive error. The cathode ray oscilloscope can reproduce signals of much higher frequency (0.5 megacycle and higher) than are produced by analog computers. This is true even when the analog computer is operating in the REP-OP mode, which increases the frequencies by a factor of 500 to 1000. The usual strip chart recorders can record signals with fre-

62 RECORDING AND DISPLAY OF SOLUTIONS

quencies up to 100 cycles per second. The electromechanical *X-Y* plotter can record signals up to a few tenths of a cycle per second. For signals with frequencies less than a few tenths of a cycle per second the *X-Y* plotter is capable of the greatest accuracy. Such plotters may have an accuracy of 0.05 to 0.1 per cent. The strip chart recorder and the oscilloscope are useful where the signals have higher frequencies and accuracy of the order of 1.0 per cent is adequate.

4-1 Strip Chart Recorder

These recorders have provision for moving a strip of chart paper under one or more pens at one of several fixed speeds. The motion of the pen is perpendicular to the direction of motion of the paper. In some cases the tip of the pen moves in a circular arc, rather than a straight line. Since in this case the ordinate lines on the chart paper are also arcs of the same radius, the coordinates on the graphs can be read in spite of this distortion. See Fig. 4-2 associated with Exercise 1. The deflection of the pen is proportional to the voltage applied to the terminals of the recorder. Therefore, the trace on the paper is a graph of the voltage applied to the terminals as a function of time. If a recorder has more than one pen, then several different variables can be recorded simultaneously, and the values of these variables can be conveniently compared. These recording systems usually have amplifiers with an attenuator calibrated in volts/cm. The setting of this control should always be written on the chart to permit the graph to be interpreted in terms of computer voltage levels. For example, if the control were set for 2 volts/cm, then a distance on the chart of 3 cm corresponds to a voltage of 6 volts. There is usually a mechanical centering control on each pen, and the pen should be centered with zero volts applied to the recorder. There is also an electrical positioning control that can be used to set the pen off center with zero volts applied to the terminals of the recording system. After the pen has been properly positioned, the reference voltage of the computer should be applied to check on the correctness of the calibration. For example, if the attenuator is set for 2 volts/cm, then a computer reference voltage of 10 volts would cause a deflection of 5 cm. The setting of the speed control on the strip chart recorder should also be written on the chart to permit interpreting the time axis properly in seconds per cm.

4-2 X-Y Plotters

One of the disadvantages of the strip chart recorders is the limited chart width available, usually 4 cm. *X-Y* plotters are designed for standard graph paper such as 8½ by 11 in. or 10 by 15 in. Larger sizes such as 30 by 30 in. are also sometimes used. The position of the pen is controlled by two electric motors that cause the pen to move parallel to each axis. The position of the pen along an axis is proportional to the voltage applied at the input terminals for that axis. The factor of proportionality is determined by the attenuator control for that axis. Suppose that the controls for both the X and the Y axes are set for one volt per inch. A voltage of 5 volts applied to the X-axis and 8 volts applied simultaneously to the Y-axis would cause the pen to move to the position (5, 8) if the zero position were at the origin of the plot. The position of the pen with zero volts applied to the input terminals can be adjusted to any position desired by means of centering controls. These controls can also be used to draw the axes of the graph directly on the graph paper. This method of drawing the axes checks the correctness of the alignment of the paper on the plotting table. The procedure is as follows:

a. With the pen lifted off the paper, center the pen at the position desired for the origin.
b. Lower the pen and cause it to move along the X-axis by changing the X-axis centering control.
c. Return the pen to the origin and repeat with the Y-axis control to draw the Y-axis. Return the pen to the origin and proceed with recording the solutions.

The setting for the attenuator controls for each axis should be written on the graph paper to permit proper labeling of the axes with voltages and problem units. Suppose that the Y-axis attenuator was set for 2 volts per in. and the scale factor for the y variable was 5 ft per volt. Then 1 in. on the Y-axis equals a distance of 10 ft in terms of the problem variable plotted on the Y-axis. The scale factor on the Y-axis is 10 ft/in.

The independent variable in many problems solved on the analog computer is time. Thus a voltage proportional to time is needed to drive one axis of the plotter. This voltage can be obtained by integrating a constant voltage as discussed in Section 3-3. Suppose that the reference voltage on the computer being used is 10 volts and that the solution is to be plotted over a time interval of 20 seconds. The voltage on the time axis of the recorder should change at the rate of 10 volts in 20 sec or 0.5 volt per sec. The attenuator on the X-axis of the recorder should be set for 1.0 volt/in. assuming that the X-axis is 10 in. long. The circuit shown in Fig. 4-1 will provide the proper operation of the pen on the X-axis of the recorder. It has been assumed that the pen is located at the lefthand side of the paper when zero volts is applied to the recorder. When the computer is switched to OPERATE, the time-base integrator 01 begins

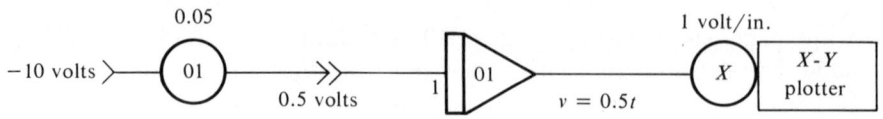

FIG. 4-1

Generation of Time Base for *X-Y* Plotter.

integrating and the pen moves to the right at the rate of 0.5 in. per sec. The *X*-axis would be marked to a scale of 2.0 sec per in.

Some plotters have an automatic pen lift connected to the analog computer, and others have a manually operated pen lift. In the latter case, the pen must be lowered before the computer is placed in OPERATE. When the solution has been completed, the computer should be placed in HOLD. After the pen has been lifted, the computer can be switched to RESET, and the pen will return to the origin. If the computer is switched directly to RESET, the pen will trace an unwanted line across the graph paper. If the automatic pen lift feature is available, one should pause briefly in the HOLD mode to give the pen lift time to function.

Some *X-Y* plotters have a built in time-base generator. The rate at which the pen moves on the *T*-axis is controlled by a knob calibrated in in. per sec. The desired rate is selected by positioning the knob. This time-base generator must be placed in operation automatically by the computer MODE control so that the plotter will start when the problem starts. This synchronization is accomplished by connecting a special cable between the plotter and the computer.

On the patch panel of some computers is a special set of terminals that connect the plotting equipment. The voltages to be recorded are patched into these terminals. A special cable between the plotter and the analog computer completes the connection. On other computers the connections are made directly from the appropriate amplifier outputs on the patch panel to the recorder input terminals. It is appropriate also with the *X-Y* plotters to check the calibration of the plotter by connecting the reference voltages to the plotter input terminals and observing that the proper deflection is obtained.

4-3 Cathode Ray Oscilloscope

The cathode ray oscilloscope is usually referred to by the shorter name, oscilloscope. The general procedure for using the oscilloscope to display computer results is similar to that for the *X-Y* plotter. The deflection of the spot on the screen is proportional to the voltage applied to the input terminals. The voltage applied to the X-input moves the spot horizontally, and the voltage applied to the Y-input moves the beam vertically. Assume that the attenuators are set for 2 volts per cm. If a voltage of 5 volts is applied to the X-input and a voltage of 10 volts is applied to the Y-input, the spot will move 2.5 cm to the right and 5 cm up from the initial position. The same comments made above for the X-Y plotter apply to establishing the proper scales on the display in terms of problem variables.

The oscilloscope may have a built in time-base generator to provide the voltage to deflect the spot linearly with time on the horizontal axis. This sweep must be started, or triggered, by a proper voltage from the analog computer to the trigger input on the oscilloscope. Frequently the oscilloscope will be used to check out the setup of the problem with the computer operating in the REP-OP mode, and then the computer will be run in the regular mode while the solution is being recorded by the X-Y plotter. In this case it is desirable to generate the time base for the oscilloscope presentation on the analog computer because the same time-base generator can then be used to provide the time voltage for the X-Y plotter.

The oscilloscope also has controls for centering the spot at the desired location when zero voltage is applied to the input terminals. There also will be controls for brightness (intensity) of the spot and for focus of the spot. Some oscilloscopes have two or more input channels on the vertical axis. The spot may make one trace for the first signal, and a second trace for the next signal, and then repeat the sequence. This switching is performed automatically in an ALTERNATE sweep mode of operation. There may also be a CHOPPED mode in which the two inputs are switched alternately onto the spot. This switching is done at a high enough rate so that the two traces appear to be continuous.

4-4 Exercises

1. The computer variables X and Y were recorded on a strip-chart recorder. The calibration on the X, Y, and T axes is shown. The amplitude scale factors on X and Y are given below. Determine the values of the problem variables x and y for times $t = 2$, 6, and 12 sec. The strip-chart record is shown in Fig. 4-2.

$$K_x = 20 \text{ ft/volt}$$

$$K_y = 5 \text{ ft/volt}$$

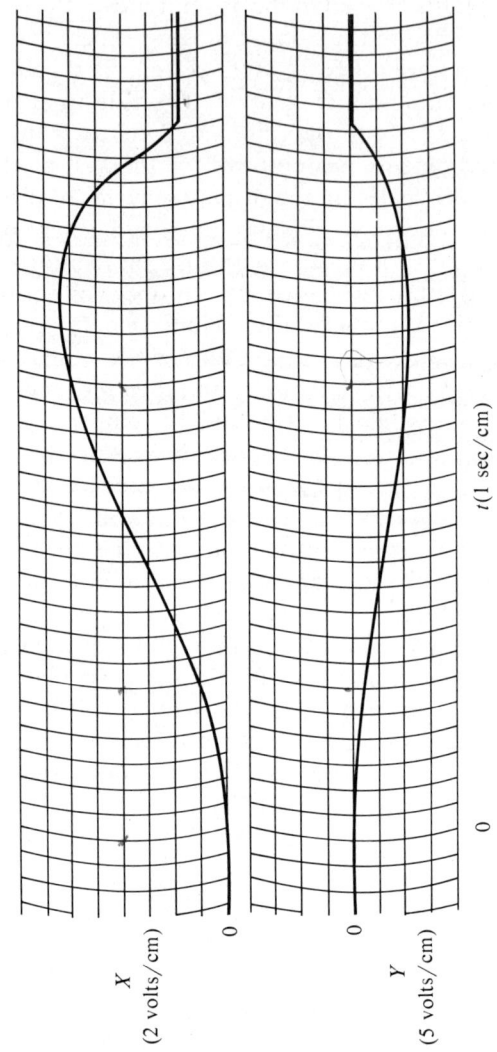

FIG. 4-2 Strip Chart Recording for Exercise 1.

2. The computer variables P and Q were recorded on an X-Y plotter as a function of time as shown in Fig. 4-4. The calibration is shown on the axes. The ramp function to drive the time axes is shown in Fig. 4-3. The amplitude scale factors are also listed below. Determine values of the problem variables p and q for times $t = 5$, 8, and 10 sec.

$$K_p = 25 \text{ gal/volt}$$

$$K_q = 2 \text{ gal/sec-volt}$$

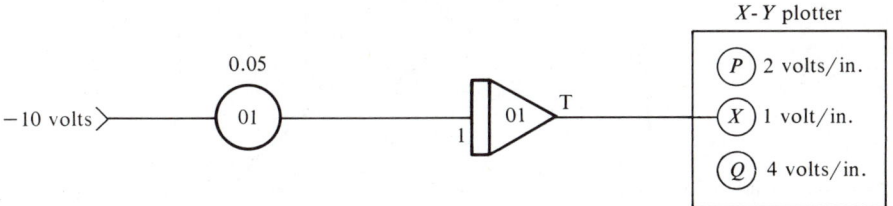

FIG. 4-3

3. Select appropriate gains and attenuator settings for generating a 0 to 30-sec time base for the 15-inch axis of a 10 by 15 inch X-Y plotter. Assume that the computer being used has reference voltages of ± 100 volts; that the amplifiers have gains of 1, 2, 5; and that the X-Y plotter has attenuator settings of 1, 2, 5, 10, 20, 50 volts/in. A positive voltage moves the pen to the right. See Fig. 4-5.

4. Specify appropriate settings for the Y-axis attenuator on the X-Y plotter of Exercise 3 above to record the following signals. Where would the pen be positioned for $Y = 0$? All limits are given in volts.
   a. $0 \leq Y \leq 50$
   b. $0 \leq Y \leq 100$
   c. $-30 \leq Y \leq +75$
   d. $-50 \leq Y \leq +25$

5. A cathode ray oscilloscope was used to make the record shown in Fig. 4-6. The block diagram and attenuator settings are as shown. The amplitude scale factors are as shown below. Determine the values of the problem variable y at $t = 2$, 6, and 15 sec.

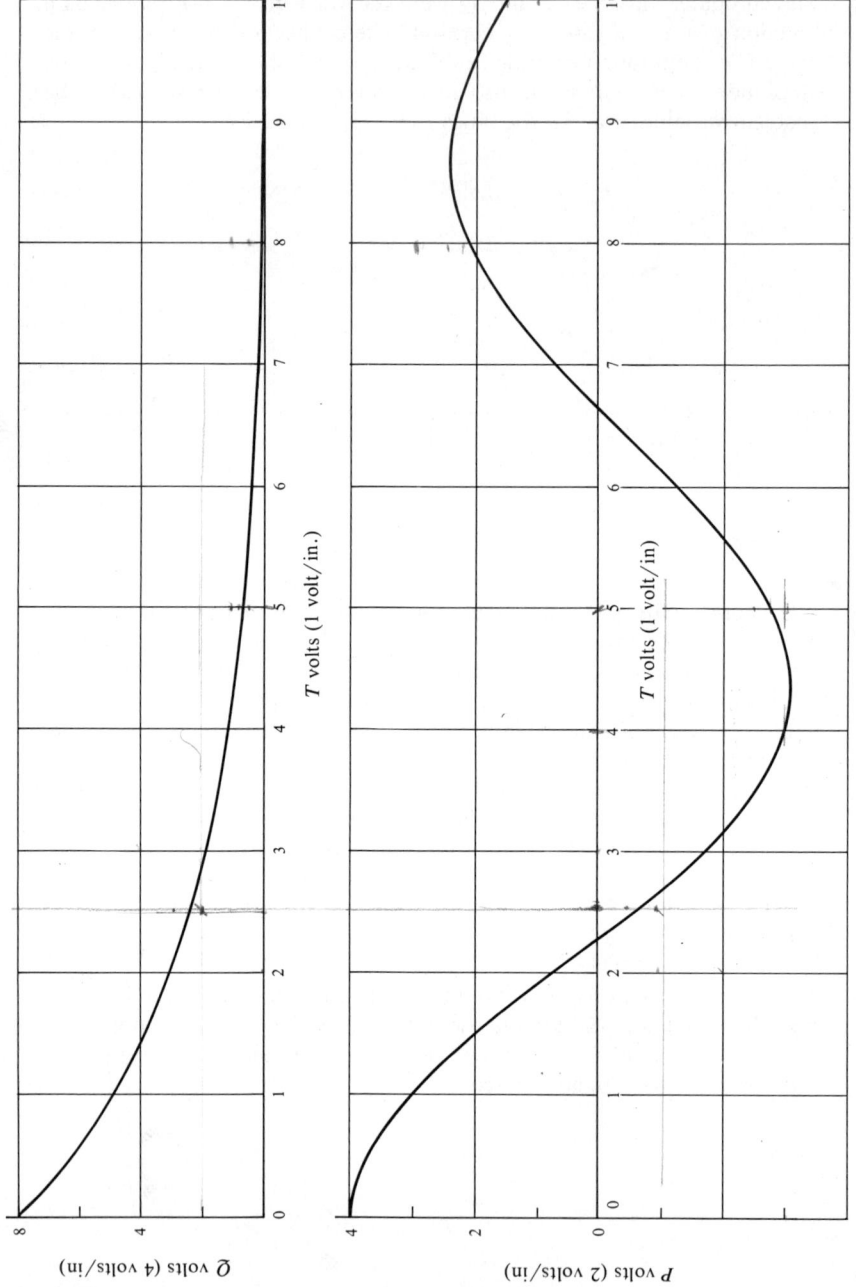

FIG. 4-4 X-Y Plotter Recording for Exercise 2.

EXERCISES 69

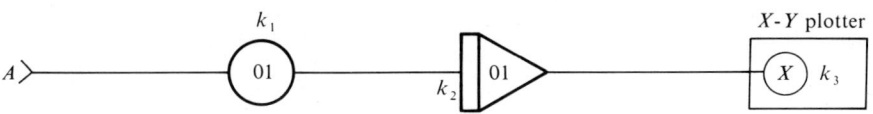

FIG. 4-5

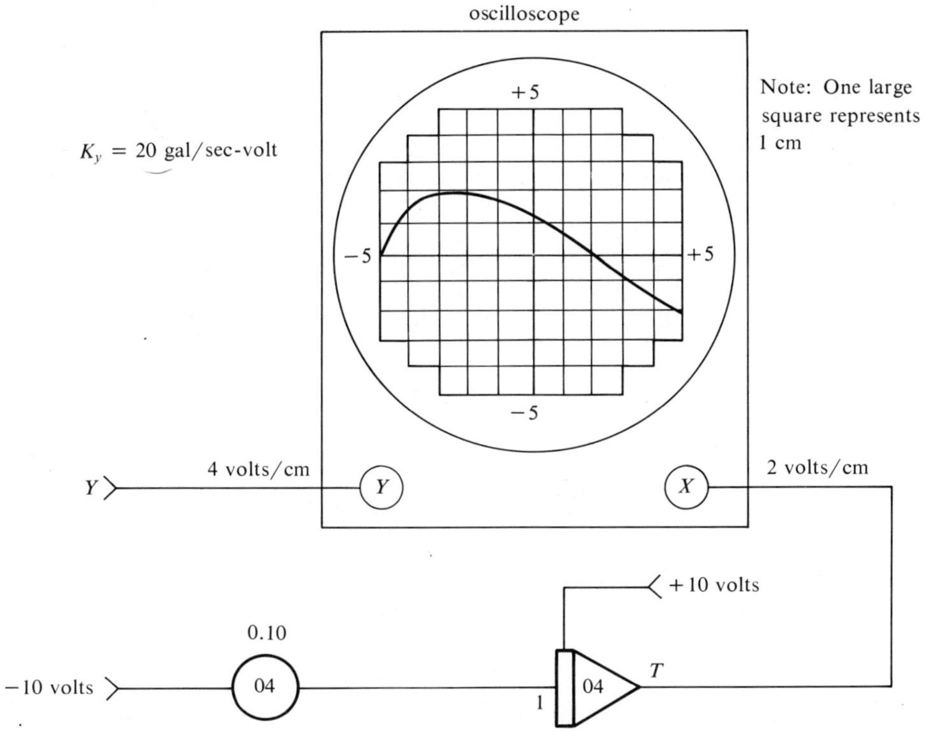

FIG. 4-6
Cathode Ray Oscilloscope Recording for Exercise 5.

CHAPTER 5 FIRST-ORDER SYSTEMS

The word SYSTEM was used in the title of this chapter to indicate generality. Suitable adjectives will be used as appropriate to limit the scope in particular applications. A system is as simple or as complex as needed. For example, the life support system for a manned spacecraft is very complex. Complex systems may usually be broken down into smaller, simpler subsystems. For example, the life support system for the spacecraft may have a temperature regulating system, a CO_2 regulating system, a humidity regulating system, and probably many others. By way of contrast, the brakes of an automobile are a relatively simple system. The words "first-order" in the title limit the scope of this chapter to systems in which no derivatives of higher order than the first appear in the mathematical relations. Second-order and higher-order systems are the subject of Chapter 6. A very strong thread of similarity runs through all of analog simulation regardless of the subject matter of the problem. The analog computer model for a hydraulics problem may have the same form as the analog computer model for cooling of a hot body. This of course results from the similarity of the mathematical models. Examples will be chosen from thermodynamics, dynamics, hydraulics, transient electrical circuits, and chemical rate dynamics.

The analog computer cannot make up for any lack of understanding of the problem on the part of the user. If the user creates a good mathematical model and implements it correctly on the analog computer, the resulting analog model will be a good model. A poor mathematical model, even if correctly implemented on the analog computer, will still result in a poor analog model. Needless to say, a correct mathematical model incorrectly implemented will result in an erroneous analog model. Careful checking at all stages of the process of analog simulation is necessary to insure the validity of the results that will be obtained.

5-1 Creation of Analog Models of Dynamic Systems

Chapter 2 was concerned with the creation of analog models of static systems. The procedures for amplitude scaling and for arithmetic operations developed in Chapter 2 together with the procedures for integration from Chapter 3 form the basis for creating models of dynamic systems. A dynamic system is one in which the rates of change of quantities, that is, their derivative or derivatives, are important in addition to the values of these quantities. For example, the question of determining the maximum speed of an automobile is a static problem. It is a static problem because the force developed by the engine to cause the car to move can be related to the speed of the automobile by an algebraic equation. Likewise an algebraic expression relates the drag force which opposes the motion of the car to the speed at which it moves. The maximum speed of the automobile will be that speed for which the force developed by the engine to propel the car is equal to the drag force opposing the motion of the automobile. The determination of the intersection of curves of drag force and engine force is an algebraic problem, and hence a static model is adequate for this problem. If the question was to determine how long a time is required for the automobile to accelerate from 10 to 50 miles per hour, the problem requires a dynamic model because in addition to the speed of the car, the rate of change of speed, or acceleration is important. Generally the analog computer is more useful as a tool for modeling dynamic systems than for modeling static systems.

72   FIRST-ORDER SYSTEMS

The first step in creating an analog model is to create the mathematical model for the system. The mathematical model is the collection of mathematical relations between the variables which result from physical laws and the relationships which result from the structure of the system. The relation between the rate at which heat is transferred across a boundary and the temperature difference across the boundary results from a physical law. The fact that in a particular problem the temperature on one side of the boundary is constant results from the structure of the system.

The second step in creating an analog model is to suitably scale the mathematical model so that the scaled model will fit within the limitations of the analog computer being used. This scaling will depend upon the specifications of the particular analog computer being used. A problem may require either amplitude scaling or time scaling, or may require both amplitude and time scaling. Some procedures for scaling operate in a way such that these two scalings if required are interdependent. The procedures used in this book treat the two processes of scaling as independent processes. Therefore, changes can be made in either the amplitude scaling or in the time scaling without changing the other. The subject of scaling involves making estimates about the amplitudes of problem variables. The student should not spend too much time making these estimates because the trial solution obtained on the analog computer will tell how satisfactory the estimate was. On the basis of the trial solution, the estimate can be improved if necessary. There is a relatively wide range of suitable scalings for any problem.

The third step in creating the analog model is to implement the scaled mathematical model on the analog computer. For simple systems the user may work directly from the scaled equations to the connection of the analog computer modules. Generally, however, the creation of a block diagram of the analog computer setup is helpful and may even save time in the long run. The block diagram shows how the analog computer modules are to be connected, the assignment of the modules, and the settings of all the potentiometers. Such a block diagram contains all the information needed to connect and adjust the analog computer. In complex systems it is very easy to miss one or more of the connections when connecting the analog computer from the block diagram. Each connection should be marked with a check on the block diagram as it is made on the analog computer to insure that no connections are missed.

The fourth step in creating the analog computer model is to run a trial solution. The resulting solutions are compared with what is expected, and the range of amplitudes of all of the computer variables are observed to see that the scaling selected was appropriate. If a variable has a range from -2 volts to $+5$ volts, then the scaling on that variable could be adjusted to give a range from -4 volts to $+10$ volts, and thus give greater accuracy, assuming a range of computer voltage of -10 volts to $+10$ volts. If the range of a variable was -0.5 volt to $+1.0$ volts, then a change in scaling would certainly be needed to improve the accuracy of the results, although the analog model would function. On the other hand, if the scaling is in error such that the voltage representing a variable exceeds the limit of the voltage possible for the particular computer being used, then the computer may be stopped because of the overload. Even if the computer is not stopped automatically, the results will be in error. The presence of an overload is indicated by a light, an audible alarm, or perhaps both. An overload indicates that the problem must be rescaled to reduce the offending variable. The initial values of all variables should be checked to see that they are in agreement with the problem specifications. The final values of some or all of the variables may be known and should be checked. The only easy check on intermediate values of the variables is in cases where the sum of several variables is a constant. The repetitive mode of operation is very useful in running trial solutions.

The fifth step is to operate the analog computer model for the various values of the parameters which are of interest and record the solutions. The attenuator settings and scale factors used should be carefully recorded so that the results can be interpreted quantitatively. The graphs should be completely labeled with variable names, problem units, and titles.

The application of these five steps to the creation and testing of analog models for several physical systems will be demonstrated by means of some completely worked out examples. The student should look for the thread of similarity in these examples because the same thread will be found in all models of first-order systems regardless of the context of the problem.

5-2 Hydraulic System

STEP 1. Formulation of Mathematical Model

Consider a hydraulic system consisting of two tanks, A and B, which are connected at the bottom by a pipe and valve as shown in Fig 5-1. The water level in Tank A is maintained constant at a level of 20.0 ft by an automatic system which is not shown. The valve is designed so that the rate of flow of water through the valve is proportional to the difference

FIRST-ORDER SYSTEMS

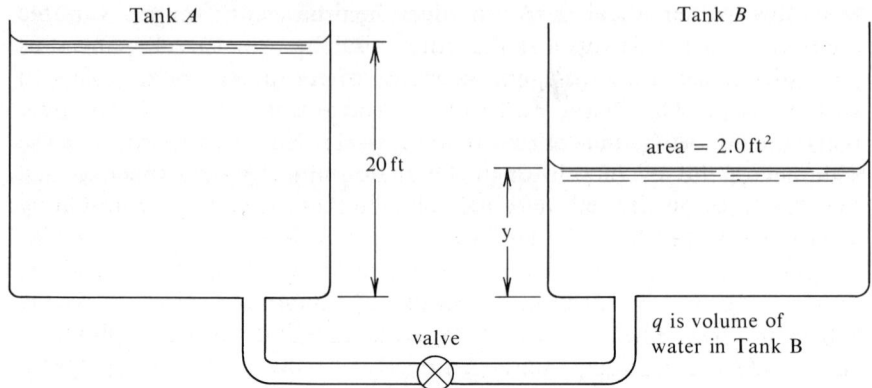

FIG. 5-1
Hydraulic System.

in pressure on the two sides of the valve. This difference in pressure can be considered as proportional to the difference in the level of the water in the two tanks. Let q represent the quantity of water in Tank B and let y represent the height of water in Tank B. Eq. (5-2a) relates q to y and the area of Tank B.

$$q = A_B * y = 2.0 * y \qquad (5\text{-}2a)$$

The time rate of flow of water into Tank B, dq/dt, is related to the time rate of change of the quantity of water in the tank by Eq. (5-2b).

$$\frac{dq}{dt} = 2.0 * \frac{dy}{dt} \qquad (5\text{-}2b)$$

The time rate of flow of water into Tank B is also related to the difference in the level of the water in the two tanks by Eq. (5-2c).

$$\frac{dq}{dt} = K * (20.0 - y) \qquad (5\text{-}2c)$$

The proportionality constant, K, has units of cu ft/sec-ft or sq ft/sec. Eliminating dq/dt by equating Eq. (5-2b) and Eq. (5-2c) gives the mathematical model for the system in terms of depth of water in Tank B as the dependent variable.

$$2.0 * \frac{dy}{dt} = K * (20.0 - y) \qquad (5\text{-}2d)$$

HYDRAULIC SYSTEM 75

Since this mathematical model involves derivatives, it is called a differential equation. This form of the differential equation is convenient to program on the analog computer, and the relation of this equation to the physical system being studied is easy to see. Differential equations are frequently written in canonical form, that is, standard from a mathematician's point of view, with all terms in the dependent variable and its derivatives on the left side and all other terms on the right side as shown in Eq. (5-2e).

$$2.0 * \frac{dy}{dt} + (K * y) = 20.0 * K \qquad (5\text{-}2\text{e})$$

STEP 2. Scaling of the Mathematical Model

For this problem the maximum value for y occurs when the derivative is equal to zero, and hence the maximum value of y is 20 ft. For the TR-20 analog computer the value of Cm is 10.0 volts. The amplitude scale factor for the TR-20 computer is therefore as follows:

$$K_y = \frac{20.0 \text{ ft}}{10.0 \text{ volts}} = 2.0 \text{ ft/volt} \qquad (5\text{-}2\text{f})$$

The general relation between depth, y, on the real system and the voltage, Y, representing depth on the computer model is:

$$y \text{ ft} = (K_y \text{ ft/volt}) * Y \text{ volts} \qquad (5\text{-}2\text{g})$$

Substitution of Eq. (5-2f) and (5-2g) into Eq. (5-3d) produces:

$$2.0 \text{ ft}^2 * \frac{d[(K_y \text{ ft/volt}) * (Y \text{ volts})]}{dt}$$

$$= K \text{ ft}^2/\text{sec} * [(K_y \text{ ft/volt}) * 10.0 \text{ volts} - (K_y \text{ ft/volt}) * Y \text{ volts}] \qquad (5\text{-}2\text{h})$$

The units on each quantity were carried to show the dimensional consistency of the equation, and when the units are consolidated the result is cubic ft/sec for all the terms. Since K_y is a constant, the differentiation on the left side yields

$$\frac{d[(K_y \text{ ft/volt}) * Y \text{ volts}]}{dt} = (K_y \text{ ft/volt}) * \frac{dY}{dt} \text{ (volts/sec)} \qquad (5\text{-}2\text{i})$$

Eq. (5-2h) can be simplified by dividing through by K_y to give

$$2.0 * \frac{dY}{dt} = K * (10.0 - Y) \qquad (5\text{-}2\text{j})$$

76 FIRST-ORDER SYSTEMS

For the range of values of K from 4.0 to 1.0, there is no need for us to consider time scaling of the problem, since the time required for the real system to function, that is, to fill Tank B, ranges from 2.5 to 10.0 sec. This fact is demonstrated by the trial solution of the next section. Values of K such that time scaling is required will be considered at the end of this example.

STEP 3. Implementing the Scaled Model

The next step in creating the analog computer model of the actual system is to solve for the highest-ordered derivative, which in this case is (dY/dt), since a first-order differential equation represents the system.

$$\frac{dY}{dt} = \frac{K}{2} * (10.0 - Y) \qquad (5\text{-}2k)$$

If the output of an analog integrator is defined as $-Y$, then the input is (dY/dt). The connection of an integrator, a summer, an inverter, and a potentiometer as shown in the block diagram of Fig. 5-2 produces the

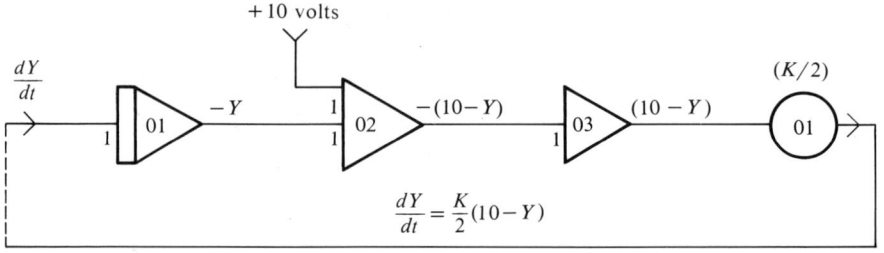

FIG. 5-2
Block Diagram of Analog Computer Model of Hydraulic System.

terms required to compute the quantity Y. If necessary refer to Chapter 2 or 3 for details on the operation of these components. The output of Potentiometer 01 is the quantity (dY/dt), and since this is the input required for Amplifier 01, the connection shown by the dotted line completes the analog model of the system of tanks and valves. The range of values of the constant, K, which can be accommodated with the amplifier gains of unity as shown is from 0 to 2.0, since the maximum coefficient which can be set on the potentiometer is 1.0. If the quantity (dY/dt) is not of interest, then the computer model can be simplified as shown in Fig. 5-3 by combining the operation of summation with integration and eliminating the two inverters which remain. If Y is desired rather than $-Y$, the desired result is obtained by changing from $+10$ to -10 volts as

HYDRAULIC SYSTEM 77

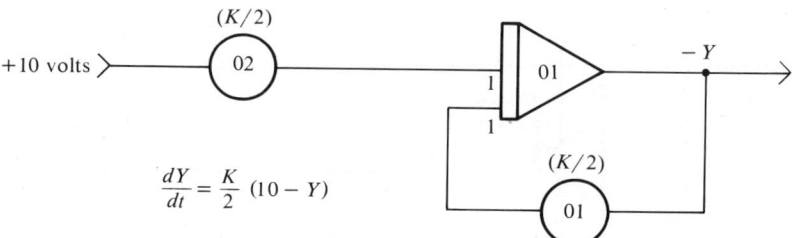

FIG. 5-3
Analog Model Using One Amplifier, $-Y$ Output.

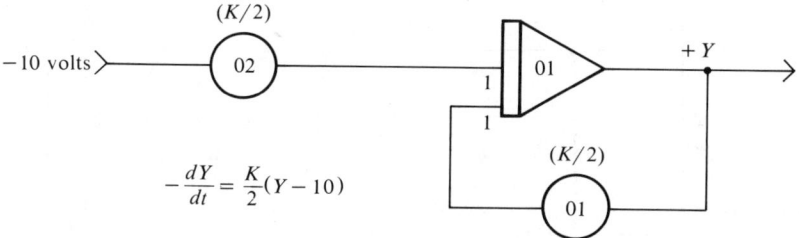

FIG. 5-4
Analog Model Using One Amplifier, $+Y$ Output.

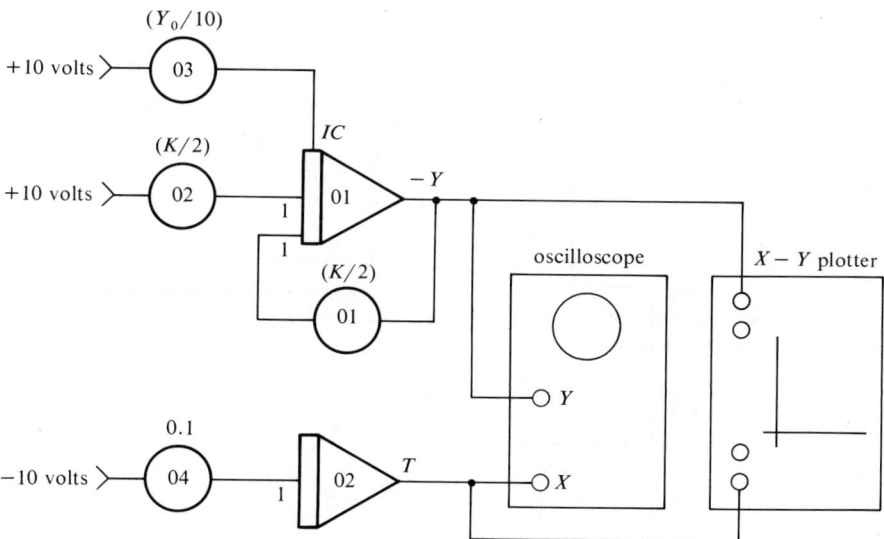

FIG. 5-5
Block Diagram of Complete Analog Computer Set-up.

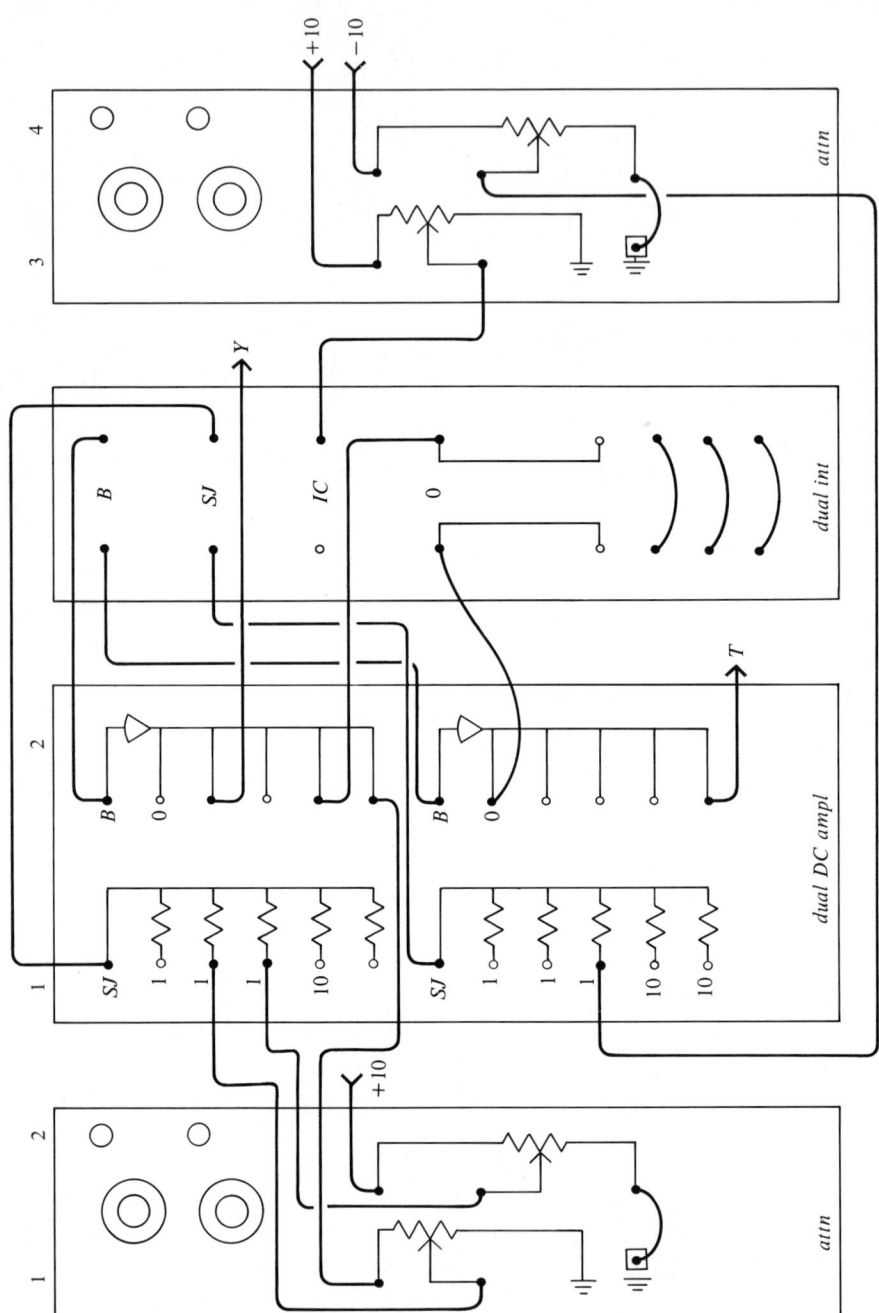

FIG. 5-6
Panel Connections on TR-20 for Analog Model of Hydraulic System.

shown in Fig. 5-4. The model of Fig. 5-2 has more amplifiers but is easier to use since the ratio ($K/2$) occurs only once, rather than twice as with the alternative models shown in Fig. 5-3 and Fig. 5-4. The block diagram for the complete analog computer setup including the time base generator and the X-Y plotter is shown in Fig. 5-5. Potentiometer 04 provides an input of -1.0 volt to integrator 02. The output of amplifier 02 is a ramp voltage with a slope of $+1.0$ volt per sec. Potentiometer 03 has been added to provide an initial condition on the depth of the water in the tank. Since the output voltage of amplifier 01 is $-Y$, a positive voltage is used for the initial condition. This block diagram is now complete, and the analog model can be implemented on the analog computer by making the indicated connections. The connections on a TR-20 computer for an analog model based on Fig. 5-5 is shown in Fig. 5-6.

STEP 4. Running a Trial Solution

After making the connections shown in Fig. 5-6, a trial solution was run for the value of $K = 1$. When observed on the oscilloscope display with the computer running in the repetitive mode, the solution had the expected form. The initial value of Y was 0, and the final value was -10 volts. The time required for the tank to fill up was approximately 10 sec. When the value of K was increased (POT 01 and POT 02) corresponding to opening up the valve, the tank filled up faster as expected.

STEP 5. Solving the Problem

The analog computer model was operated in the normal mode and solutions recorded for three values of K on the X-Y plotter. The results are shown in Fig. 5-7. The axes are marked both in voltage units for the computer variables Y and T, and in problem units, ft and sec, for the variables y and t.

Curves were also run for two nonzero initial conditions for a value of $K = 1$. The initial height is adjusted by setting potentiometer 03. These results were plotted on the X-Y plotter and are shown in Fig. 5-8. The case for zero initial height of water was rerun here for comparison. These curves show the interesting fact that the time to fill the tank is independent of the initial depth of water in the tank. The reason for this perhaps unexpected result is the specification that the rate of flow of water is proportional to the difference in the depth of water in the two tanks.

When the mathematical model is expressed as follows:

$$\frac{dy}{dt} = \frac{1}{\tau} * (y_f - y) \tag{5-21}$$

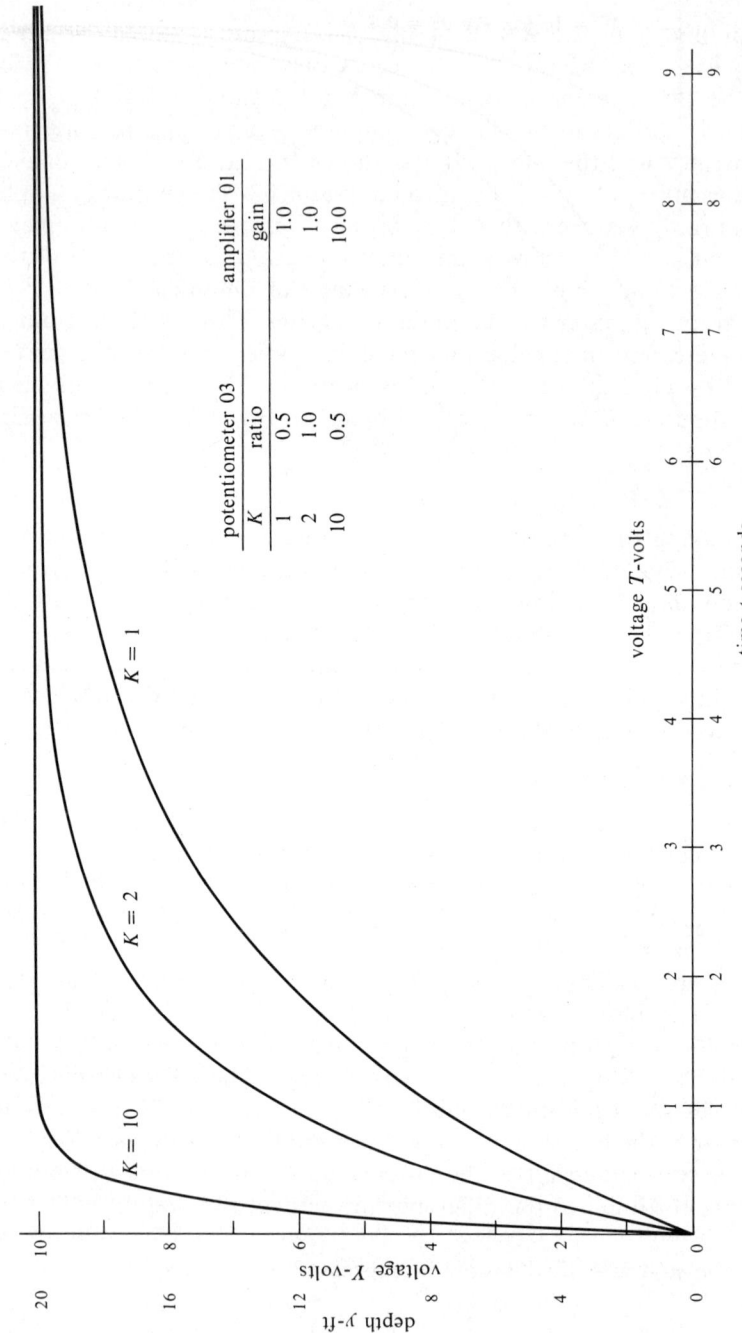

FIG. 5-7 Depth of Water vs. Time for Several Valve Openings.

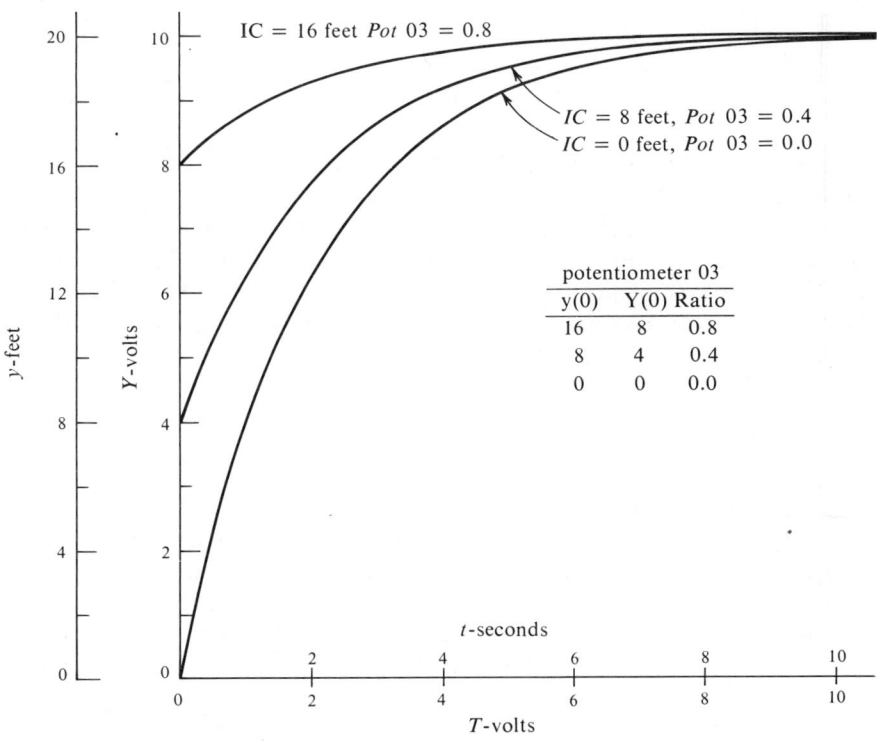

FIG. 5-8

Height of Water vs. Time for Several Initial Heights.

then the time required for y to attain its final value is approximately 5τ. The constant, τ, is called the time constant. The general solution to Eq. (5-2l) is shown in courses in differential equations to be as follows:

$$y = y_0 + (y_f - y_0)(1 - \epsilon^{-t/\tau}) \qquad (5\text{-}2m)$$

The constants y_0 and y_f are the initial and final depth of the water in the tank. The correctness of this solution can be easily demonstrated by differentiating Eq. (5-2m) and substituting y and dy/dt into Eq. (5-2l). When t is zero, the exponential term ϵ^0 equals one, and y is equal to the initial value of y or y_0. When the exponent t/τ is greater than five, the exponential term $\epsilon^{-t/\tau}$ is less than 0.00674. Under these conditions the value of y is very nearly equal to the final value y_f, and the solution is said to have attained a steady-state or static condition. Comparison of Eq. (5-2d) and Eq. (5-2l) shows that

$$\frac{1}{\tau} = \frac{K}{2.0} \qquad (5\text{-}2n)$$

82 FIRST-ORDER SYSTEMS

This equation can be solved for τ:

$$\tau = \frac{2.0}{K} \tag{5-2o}$$

When K equals one, τ equals 2.0 sec, and the solution is expected to attain steady-state in 5 * 2.0 or 10.0 sec. When K equals 2.0, τ equals 1.0 sec, and the solution is expected to attain steady-state in 5 * 1.0 or 5.0 sec. The solutions plotted in Fig. 5-7 demonstrate these ideas. The value of the time constant provides an indication of whether time scaling will be required. For systems with values of τ from 0.5 to 10 sec, no time scaling is needed for recording with electromechanical X-Y plotters.

5-3 Time Scaling

Let us consider some other values for the parameter K in the water tank example in order to see the process of time scaling. If the value of K were 0.05 sq ft/sec, then the time constant for this system would be (2/0.05), or 40 sec, and the tank would require 200 sec to fill. See Fig. 5-9 for the block diagram. This period of time poses no problems from a computational point of view, since the time-base generator could be

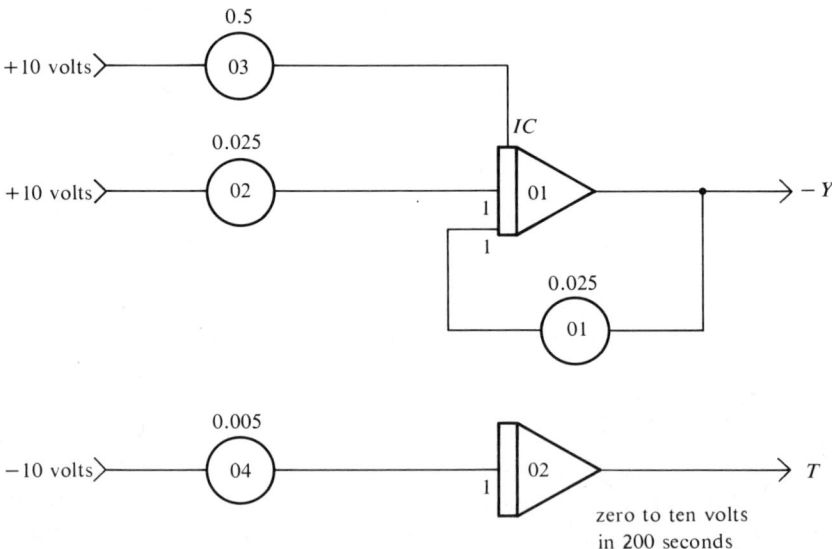

FIG. 5-9

Block Diagram for Analog Model of Tank Problem with $K = 0.05$ and no Time Scaling.

slowed down, but since the model on the computer can "fill the tank" in 10 sec, the additional 190 seconds of computer time are wasted. Furthermore, the accuracy of the potentiometer settings is low for low ratios. Let T represent time on the analog computer model of the system and let t represent time on the actual system. In a manner consistent with the definition of amplitude scale factors, K_t is defined as the ratio of the maximum time for the physical system, t_m, to the maximum time desired on the model, T_m, that is,

$$K_t = \frac{t_m}{T_m} \qquad (5\text{-}3a)$$

If the desired model time runs to 10 sec when the system time runs to 200 sec, then $K_t = 20.0$ and has units of sec per sec. Problem time, t, and computer time, T, are related by the scale factor K_t in the following ways:

$$t = K_t * T$$

or

$$T = \frac{1}{K_t} * t \qquad (5\text{-}3b)$$

The time rate of change of a variable Y with respect to these two time bases are related in the following way:

$$\frac{dY}{dt} = \frac{dY}{dT} * \frac{dT}{dt}$$

$$\frac{dY}{dt} = \frac{dY}{dT} * \frac{1}{K_t} \qquad (5\text{-}3c)$$

Substitution of Eq. (5-3c) into Eq. (5-2k) and solving for (dY/dT) gives the time-scaled equation:

$$\frac{dY}{dt} = \frac{K * K_t}{2.0} * (10.0 - Y) \qquad (5\text{-}3d)$$

Since in the present example the value of K is 0.05, and the tank on the model is to be filled in 10.0 sec, the value of K_t would be chosen to be 20 (the student should check this), and the time axis of the plot produced on the X-Y plotter would be labeled to show 10.0 in. as representing 200 sec of time on the real system. Since the settings on potentiometers 01 and 02 are $[(K * K_t)/2]$ for the mathematical model after the time scaling

84 FIRST-ORDER SYSTEMS

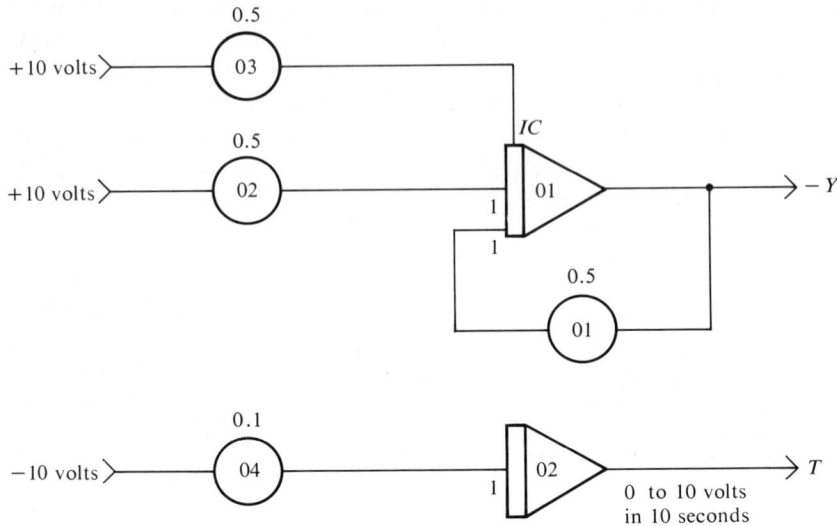

FIG. 5-10

Block Diagram for Analog Model of Tank Problem with $K = 0.05$ and Time Scaling $K_t = 20$.

has been performed, the time scaling is accomplished on the analog computer model by multiplying the original integrator gains by the factor K_t. Note the changes in potentiometers 01, 02, and 04 in Fig. 5-10 from those in Fig. 5-9. Note also that the setting of the potentiometer 03 that establishes the initial height of the water in the tank is not changed. The initial condition is not affected by changing the time scale on the integrators.

The need for time scaling in the other direction may also arise. Suppose that the value of K for the hydraulic system was 20 sq ft/sec. The tank on the real system would now fill in 0.5 sec, but the X-Y plotter could not accurately follow the results produced by the analog computer model. If the model tank is to fill in 10 sec, a value of $K_t = 0.05$ is chosen, and potentiometer settings are multiplied by this factor. The time axis of the X-Y plotter is labeled to show 10.0 inches as being 0.5 sec.

5-4 Freely Falling Body

STEP 1. Formulation of Mathematical Model

Consider a body with mass M falling under the influence of gravity. Assume for simplicity that the friction of the atmosphere is negligible.

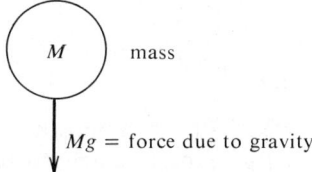

FIG. 5-11
Freely Falling Body.

This would not be a bad assumption at high altitudes. This situation is shown pictorially in Fig. 5-11. Newton's second law states that the rate of change of momentum is proportional to the impressed force and takes place in the direction of that force. The momentum of a body is the product of the mass and the velocity, or

$$\text{momentum} = Mv \tag{5-4a}$$

Since mass is assumed constant, the rate of change of momentum with respect to time is as follows:

$$\frac{d(Mv)}{dt} = M\frac{dv}{dt} \tag{5-4b}$$

If the units are consistent, such as the meter-kilogram-second (MKS), then the factor of proportionality is one, and

$$\text{force} = M\frac{dv}{dt} \tag{5-4c}$$

For the present case the force is due to gravity, and therefore,

$$M\frac{dv}{dt} = Mg \tag{5-4d}$$

After dividing both sides by the mass, M, we find:

$$\frac{dv}{dt} = g \tag{5-4e}$$

This result is the mathematical proof of Galileo's famous experiment at the Leaning Tower of Pisa. The acceleration experienced by a body as a result of gravity is independent of its mass.

STEP 2. Scaling the Mathematical Model

Assume that this problem is to be worked on an analog computer with a reference voltage of ± 10 volts. If this experiment is to be performed around the earth, the maximum acceleration is 32.2 ft per sec². For convenience assume $\max|a| = 40$ ft per sec².

$$K_a = \frac{\max|a|}{Cm} = \frac{40 \text{ ft/sec}^2}{10 \text{ volts}} = 4 \text{ ft/sec}^2\text{-volts} \tag{5-4f}$$

Assume that the problem is to run for 25 sec. The velocity will be 25 sec times 32 ft per sec² or 800 ft per sec. Therefore, assume $\max|v| = 800$ ft/sec.

$$K_v = \frac{800 \text{ ft/sec}}{10 \text{ volts}} = 80 \text{ ft/sec-volt} \tag{5-4g}$$

Assume that a computer voltage G represents the problem variable g, therefore,

$$g = K_a G \tag{5-4h}$$

Assume that a computer voltage V represents the problem variable v, therefore,

$$v = K_v V \tag{5-4i}$$

Substitution of Eq. (5-3h) and (5-3i) into Eq. (5-3e) yields

$$\frac{d(K_v V)}{dt} = K_v \frac{dV}{dt} = K_a G \tag{5-4j}$$

Division by K_v yields

$$\frac{dV}{dt} = \frac{K_a}{K_v} G \tag{5-4k}$$

STEP 3. Implementing the Scaled Model

The computer voltage G which represents g is computed by using Eq. (5-4h).

$$G = \frac{g}{K_a} = \frac{32.0 \text{ ft/sec}^2}{4.0 \text{ ft/volt-sec}^2} = 8 \text{ volts} \tag{5-4l}$$

Alteration of Eq. (5-3k) by multiplying both sides by −1 yields:

$$-\frac{dV}{dt} = -\frac{K_a}{K_v} G \qquad (5\text{-}4\text{m})$$

Assume that the output of an integrator is V. Then the input is $-dV/dt$. Hence the appropriate block diagram representation of the amplitude scaled analog computer model is as shown in Fig. 5-12. The computer

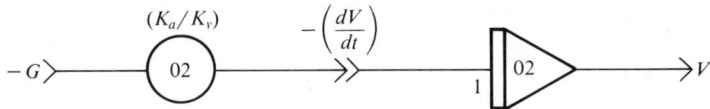

FIG. 5-12
Block Diagram Relating $-G$ and V.

voltage G should be obtained from a potentiometer followed by an inverter to eliminate loading. Therefore, the complete block diagram is as shown in Fig. 5-13. A ramp function generator has been added to provide a voltage going from 0 to 10 volts in 25 sec.

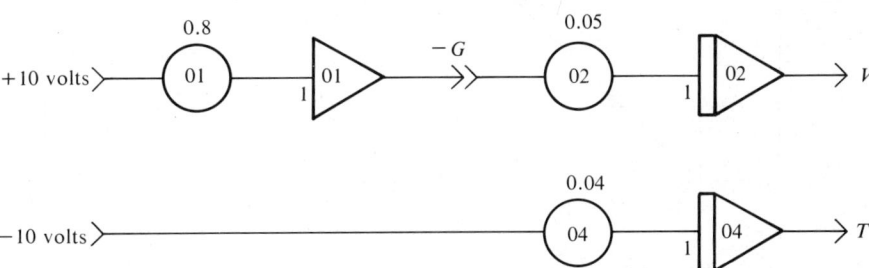

FIG. 5-13
Complete Block Diagram.

STEP 4. Running a Trial Solution

The trial solution verifies that the variable V goes from 0 to 10 volts in 25 sec and that T goes from 0 to 10 volts in 25 sec. Can you see from the block diagram that $V = T$ as would be expected from the nature of the scaling?

STEP 5. Solving the Problem

The solution produced by the analog computer was recorded on the X-Y plotter and is shown in Fig. 5-14.

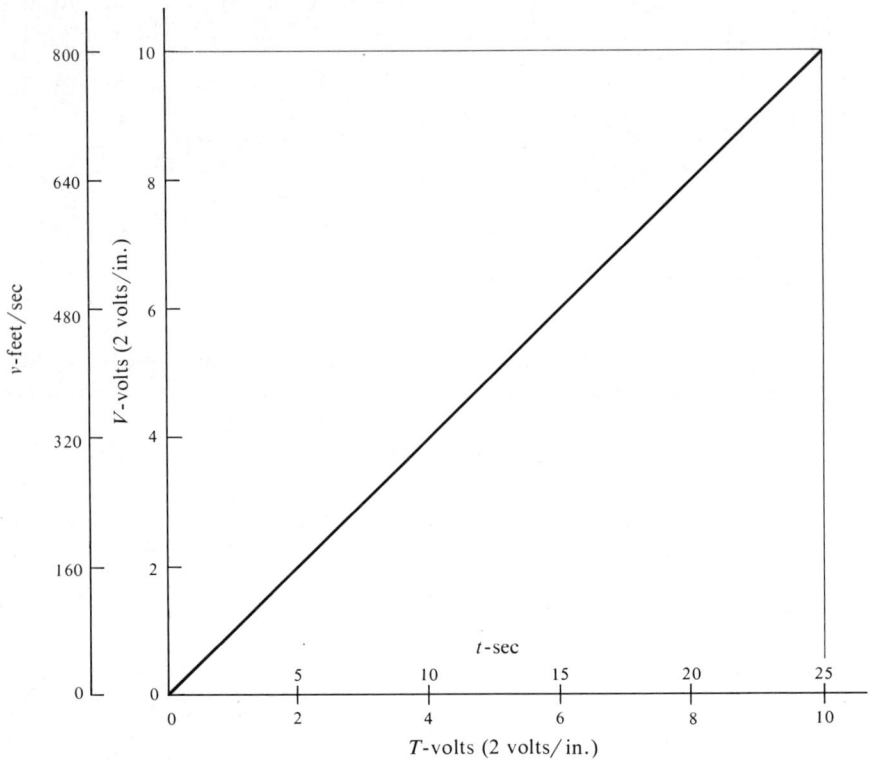

FIG. 5-14

Plot of Velocity vs. Time for Freely Falling Body.

5-5 Falling Body with Viscous Drag

STEP 1. Formulation of Mathematical Model

Consider that there is opposition to the motion of the falling body considered in the previous section. This opposition to motion is called damping or friction. In some cases this damping may be deliberately increased by adding a parachute. The functional relationship between

FALLING BODY WITH VISCOUS DRAG

the velocity of the object and the opposing force may be very complex. In some cases the frictional force may be considered proportional to the velocity and is computed as

$$f = Dv \tag{5-5a}$$

If the force is a linear function of velocity, the drag or friction is called viscous. The direction of this force is opposite to the direction of motion of the body. The parameter D is the damping coefficient. The force acting on the body is now the difference between the force of gravity and the damping force.

$$M \frac{dv}{dt} = Mg - Dv \tag{5-5b}$$

The velocity of the body in the previous example increased without bound. Eq. (5-5b) shows that the object in this case will attain a limited velocity because the impressed force decreases as the velocity increases. Ultimately the damping force, Dv, approaches the force of gravity, Mg, and the acceleration of the body approaches zero. This limiting value of velocity is called terminal velocity.

STEP 2. Scaling the Mathematical Model

Assume that the mass, M, is 20 kg and that the damping coefficient D is 10 newtons per (m per sec). The mathematical model then becomes:

$$20 \frac{dv}{dt} = 20\,g - 10\,v \tag{5-5c}$$

The limiting velocity is obtained by setting $dv/dt = 0$.

$$20 * g = 10\,v$$

$$v = 2 * g = 2 * 9.8 = 19.6 \text{ m/sec}$$

For convenience assume max $|v| = 20$ m per sec. The amplitude scale factor K_v is for a 10 volt analog computer

$$K_v = \frac{\max |v|}{Cm} = \frac{20 \text{ m/sec}}{10 \text{ volts}}$$

$$= 2 \text{ m/volt-sec} \tag{5-5d}$$

FIRST-ORDER SYSTEMS

The amplitude scale factor K_a is as follows (assuming 10 m per sec² as the maximum acceleration):

$$K_a = \frac{\max |a|}{Cm} = \frac{10 \text{ m/sec}^2}{10 \text{ volts}} = 1 \text{ m/volt-sec}^2$$

$$G = \frac{g}{K_a} = \frac{9.8 \text{ m/sec}^2}{1 \text{ m/volt-sec}^2} = 9.8 \text{ volts} \qquad (5\text{-}5e)$$

The amplitude scaled model is therefore:

$$M \frac{d(K_v V)}{dt} = M K_a G - D K_v V$$

$$K_v \frac{dV}{dt} = K_a G - \frac{D}{M} K_v V$$

$$\frac{dV}{dt} = \frac{K_a}{K_v} G - \frac{D}{M} V \qquad (5\text{-}5f)$$

STEP 3. Implementing the Scaled Model

Assume that the output of an integrator is $+V$; then the input to that integrator is $-dV/dt$. Therefore, an appropriate block diagram representing the analog computer model is as shown in Fig. 5-15. The output of amplifier 04 provides the voltage needed as the input for amplifier 01. If the voltage dV/dt is not needed, this block diagram can be simplified as shown in Fig. 5-16. This block diagram also includes a ramp function generator to produce a voltage changing from 0 to 10 volts in 20 sec.

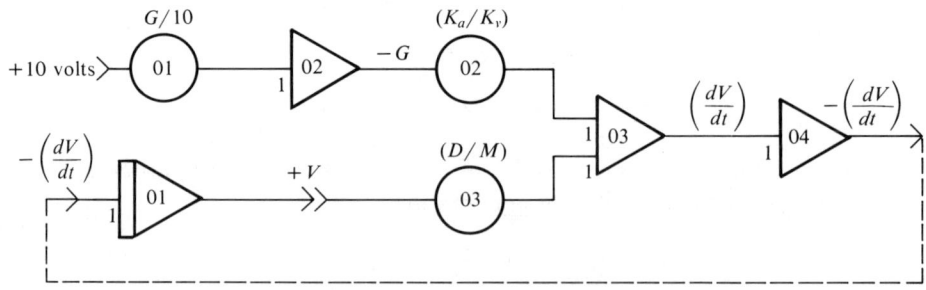

FIG. 5-15
Block Diagram for Falling Body with Viscous Drag.

FALLING BODY WITH VISCOUS DRAG

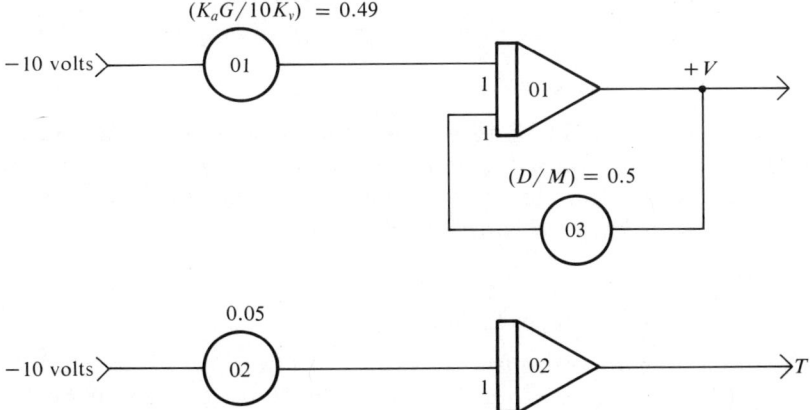

FIG. 5-16
Simplified Block Diagram for Falling Body with Viscous Drag.

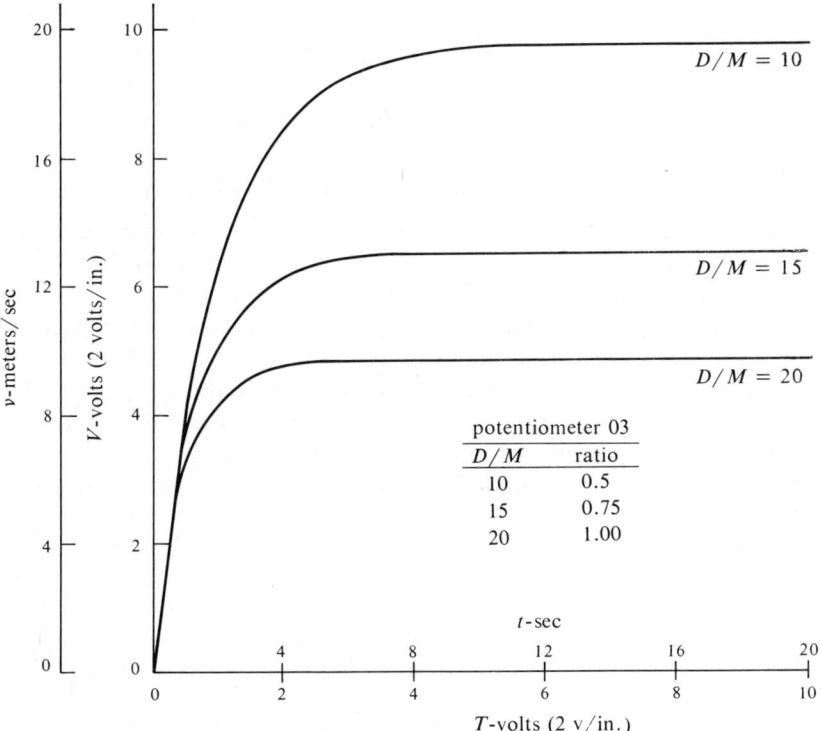

FIG. 5-17
Plot of Velocity vs. Time for Falling Body with Viscous Drag.

STEP 4. Running a Trial Solution

When the circuit of Fig. 5-16 is connected. The voltages V and T behave as expected. If the ratio set on potentiometer 03 is made larger, the terminal velocity decreases as it should when either the damping D is increased, or the mass M is decreased.

STEP 5. Solving the Problem

Solutions run for various settings of potentiometer 03 are shown in Fig. 5-17. The terminal velocity decreases by 50 per cent as the ratio set on potentiometer 03 is increased to 1.0. This ratio corresponds to reducing the mass by 50 per cent or doubling the amount of damping. Notice that the axes are marked both in terms of computer variables V and T in volts, and in terms of problem variables v and t in m per sec. and sec.

5-6 Thermal Behavior of a Semiconductor Device

STEP 1. Formulation of the Mathematical Model

The current which most electrical devices can safely carry is limited by the resulting temperature rise of the device. The rate at which heat is produced is measured for direct current devices by the product of voltage and current, which is called electric power. When voltage is measured in volts, and current is measured in amps, the power is given in watts. The thermal capacity of a device is a measure of the quantity of heat energy absorbed by the body per unit change in temperature. The thermal resistance of the device is a measure of the rate at which heat energy is lost by the device per unit temperature difference. The ideas are expressed mathematically as

$$q = C_t \theta \qquad (5\text{-}6a)$$

$$p_c = \frac{dq}{dt} = \frac{\theta}{R_t} \qquad (5\text{-}6b)$$

θ is the difference between the temperature of the device and its surroundings (°C)

q is the amount of heat energy stored (watt-sec)

THERMAL BEHAVIOR OF A SEMICONDUCTOR DEVICE

C_t is the thermal capacity (watt-sec/°C)

R_t is the thermal resistance (°C/watt)

$p_c = \dfrac{dq}{dt}$ is the rate of transfer of heat energy by thermal conduction (watts)

Consider the problem of determining the time for a semiconductor device to attain a critical temperature for a fixed power input. Assume the following parameters for the device:

$$C_t = 20 \text{ watt-sec/°C}$$

$$R_t = 4 \text{°C/watt}$$

Also assume that the maximum permissible temperature for this device is 85°C and that the ambient temperature is 25°C. The difference between the thermal power supplied and the thermal power conducted serves to raise the temperature of the device. Thus:

$$p_s - p_c = \frac{d(C_t\theta)}{dt}$$

$$C_t \frac{d\theta}{dt} = p_s - \frac{\theta}{R_t} \tag{5-6c}$$

The temperature attains equilibrium when the thermal power conducted away is equal to the thermal power supplied. Hence the device can continuously handle a thermal power input:

$$\frac{\max |\theta|}{R_t} = \frac{(85-25)°C}{4°C/\text{watt}} = 15 \text{ watts} \tag{5-6d}$$

STEP 2. Scaling the Mathematical Model

Since the temperature difference over which the device can operate is limited to 60°C, an appropriate value for K_θ is as follows:

$$K_\theta = \frac{\max |\theta|}{C_m} = \frac{60°C}{10 \text{ volts}}$$

$$= 6°C/\text{volt} \tag{5-6e}$$

Assume that the maximum thermal power of interest will be 100 watts. Thus the amplitude scale factor K_p is as follows:

$$K_p = \frac{\max |p|}{Cm} = \frac{100 \text{ watts}}{10 \text{ volts}}$$

$$= 10 \text{ watts/volt} \qquad (5\text{-}6f)$$

The general relations between problem variables and computer variables are as follows:

$$\theta = K_\theta * \Theta$$

$$p = K_p * P \qquad (5\text{-}6g)$$

Substitution of these scale factor equations into Eq. (5-6c) yields the amplitude scaled equation:

$$C_t \frac{d(K_\theta \Theta)}{dt} = K_p P_s - \frac{K_\theta \Theta}{R_t}$$

$$C_t K_\theta \frac{d\Theta}{dt} = K_p P_s - \frac{K_\theta}{R_t} \Theta$$

$$\frac{d\Theta}{dt} = \frac{K_p P_s}{C_t K_\theta} - \frac{1}{R_t C_t} \Theta \qquad (5\text{-}6h)$$

STEP 3. Implementing the Amplitude Scaled Model

Assume that the voltage $- d\Theta/dt$ is available. Integrate this to obtain Θ, and create additional terms to form $- d\Theta/dt$. An appropriate block diagram representing the analog computer model is as shown in Fig. 5-18. As shown before, the analog model can be simplified as shown in

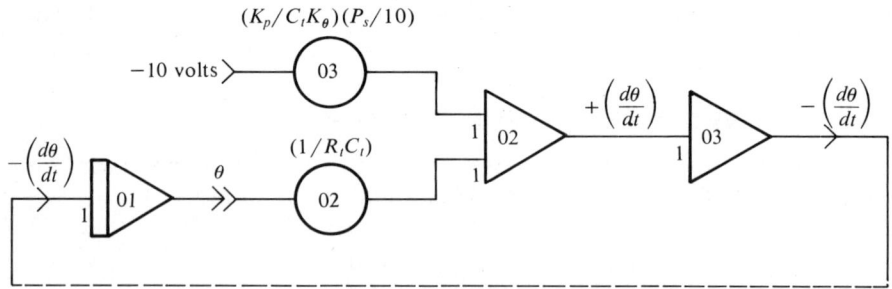

FIG. 5-18

Block Diagram of Amplitude Scaled Model.

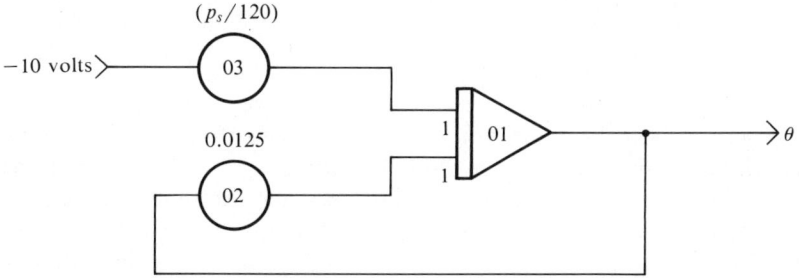

FIG. 5-19

Block Diagram of Simplified Analog Model.

Fig. 5-19 if the variable $d\theta/dt$ is not needed. The potentiometer settings are computed as:

$$\text{POT } 02 = \frac{1}{R_t C_t} = \frac{1}{(4°C/\text{watt})(20 \text{ watt-sec}/°C)}$$
$$= 0.0125/\text{sec}$$

$$\text{POT } 03 = \frac{K_p}{C_t K_\theta} \frac{P_s}{10} = \frac{(10 \text{ watts/volt})(P_s \text{ volts})}{(20 \text{ watt-sec}/°C)(6°C/\text{volts})(10 \text{ volts})}$$
$$= (P_s/120)/\text{sec}$$

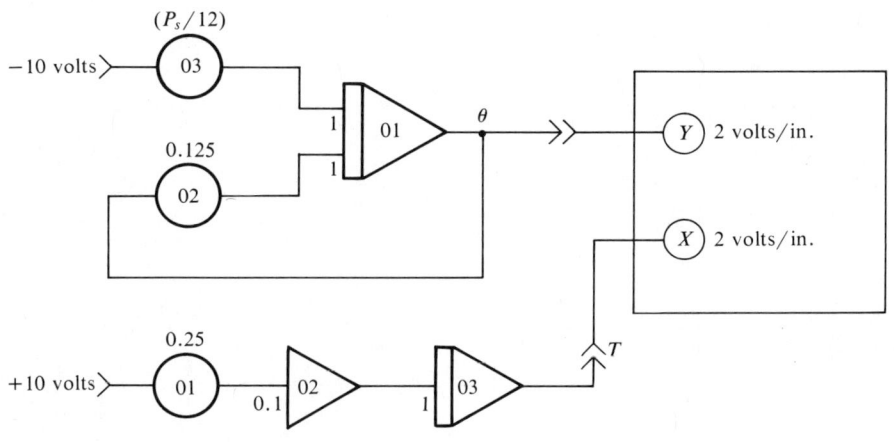

FIG. 5-20

Block Diagram After Time Scaling.

96 FIRST-ORDER SYSTEMS

STEP 4. Trial Solution

When a trial solution is run, the temperature is found to change very, very slowly. This fact is evident from the very low gains on the inputs to the integrator 01. Multiplying all integrator gains by 10.0 causes the solution to be generated 10 times faster. Thus one second of computer time is 10 sec of problem time. The block diagram of the analog model after time scaling is shown in Fig. 5-20. The time-base generator has been chosen to produce a voltage T that changes from 0 to 10 volts in 40 seconds. Since this would have required a gain of 0.025 on potentiometer 01, an inverter with a gain of 0.1 was used to reduce the voltage.

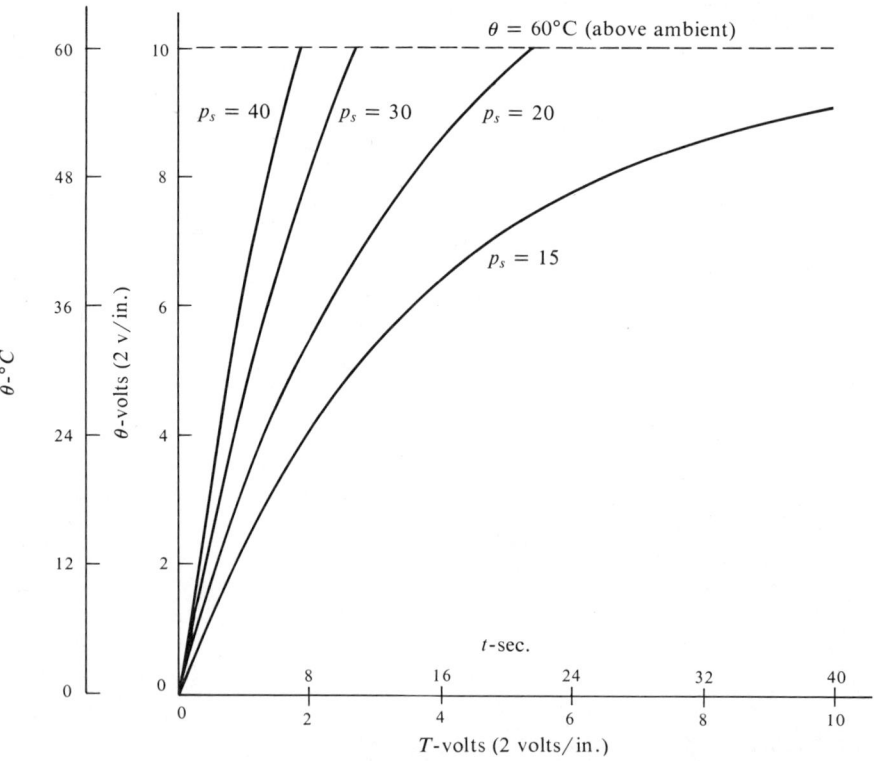

FIG. 5-21

Plot of Temperature vs. Time as a Function of Power Dissipation.

THERMAL BEHAVIOR OF A SEMICONDUCTOR DEVICE

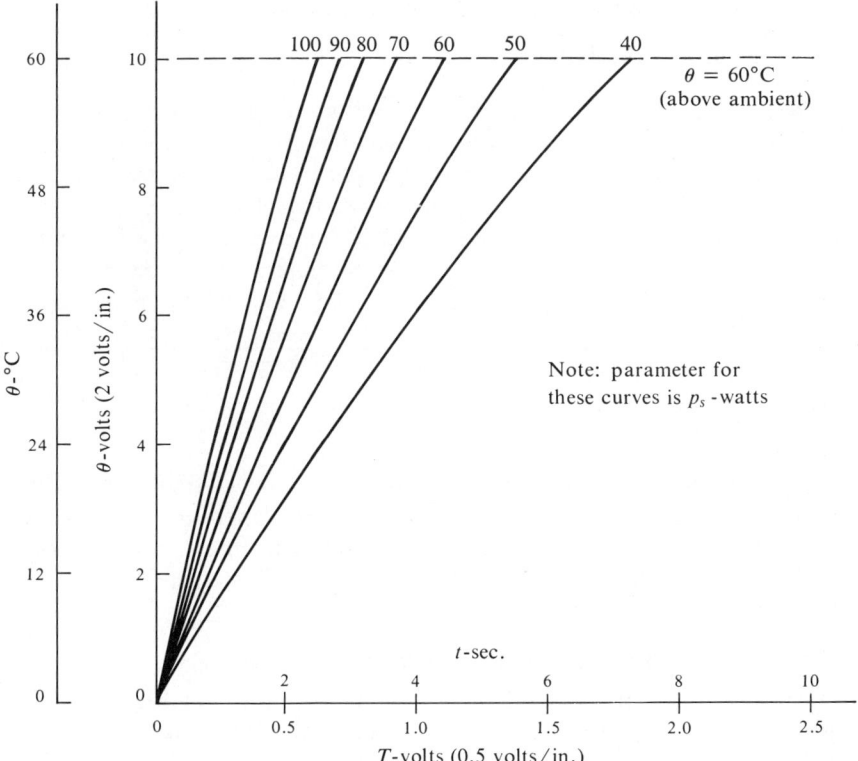

FIG. 5-22

Plot of Temperature vs. Time as a Function of Power Dissipation.

STEP 5. Solving the Problem

The parameter of interest is the power input P_s. Solutions are shown in Fig. 5-21 and Fig. 5-22 for various values of p_s. Table 5.1 lists the values of p_s in problem units, the corresponding value of the model variable P_s, and the potentiometer settings. The dotted line is drawn for $\theta = 60°C$ or $\Theta = 10$ volts. The time required for the solution to reach this value is the time interval over which the power can be held at the indicated level without overheating. For example, this semiconductor device can dissipate 50 watts for 5.5 sec before the temperature rise exceeds the permissible 60°C rise.

TABLE 5-1. POTENTIOMETER SETTINGS FOR STUDY OF THERMAL BEHAVIOR OF SEMICONDUCTOR DEVICE

p_s WATTS	P_s VOLTS	$P_s/12$ = RATIO OF 03
100	10	.833
90	9	.750
80	8	.667
70	7	.583
60	6	.500
50	5	.417
40	4	.333
30	3	.250
20	2	.167

5-7 Hydraulic System of Three Tanks

The examples considered thus far have involved a single dependent variable. Some situations require two or more dependent variables to define the system. These dependent variables are interrelated in some fashion. Such systems are referred to as coupled systems.

STEP 1. Formulation of the Mathematical Model

Consider the hydraulic system of three tanks shown in Fig. 5-23. The rate of transfer of liquid out of Tank A and into Tank B is proportional to the difference in depths, $(y_a - y_b)$.

$$q_1 = K_1(y_a - y_b) \tag{5-7a}$$

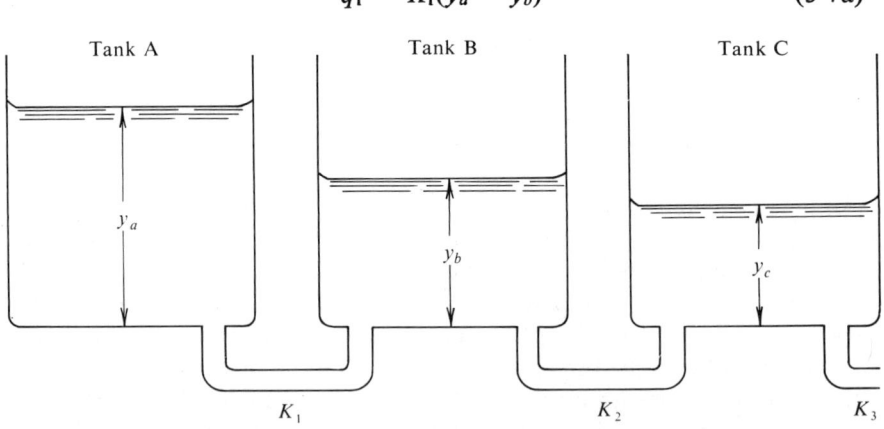

FIG. 5-23
Hydraulic System with Three Tanks.

HYDRAULIC SYSTEM OF THREE TANKS

Similarly the rate of transfer out of Tank B into Tank C is proportional to the difference in depths y_b and y_c.

$$q_2 = K_2(y_b - y_c) \tag{5-7b}$$

The rate of transfer out of Tank C is proportional to depth y_c.

$$q_3 = K_3 y_c \tag{5-7c}$$

The rate of change of height is related to the net rate of flow out of the tanks in general terms as

$$A \frac{dy}{dt} = q_{in} - q_{out} \tag{5-7d}$$

This relation becomes for each tank:

$$A_a \frac{dy_a}{dt} = -q_1 = -K_1(y_a - y_b) \tag{5-7e}$$

$$A_b \frac{dy_b}{dt} = q_1 - q_2 = K_1(y_a - y_b) - K_2(y_b - y_c) \tag{5-7f}$$

$$A_c \frac{dy_c}{dt} = q_2 - q_3 = K_2(y_b - y_c) - K_3 y_c \tag{5-7g}$$

These equations can be solved for the derivatives of the height of water in each of the tanks.

$$\frac{dy_a}{dt} = -\frac{K_1}{A_a} y_a + \frac{K_1}{A_a} y_b \tag{5-7h}$$

$$\frac{dy_b}{dt} = \frac{K_1}{A_b} y_a - \left(\frac{K_2}{A_b} + \frac{K_1}{A_b}\right) y_b + \frac{K_2}{A_b} y_c \tag{5-7i}$$

$$\frac{dy_c}{dt} = \frac{K_2}{A_c} y_b - \left(\frac{K_2}{A_c} + \frac{K_3}{A_c}\right) y_c \tag{5-7j}$$

These three equations constitute the mathematical model of the system of three tanks.

STEP 2. Amplitude Scaling the Mathematical Model

The parameters of the problem are as follows:

Area of Tanks
$A_a = 100$ sq ft
$A_b = 75$ sq ft
$A_c = 50$ sq ft

Flow Coefficients
$K_1 = 40$ sq ft/sec
$K_2 = 30$ sq ft/sec
$K_3 = 20$ sq ft/sec

Height of all the tanks is 50 ft.

Initial Conditions
$y_a(0) = 50$ ft
$y_b(0) = 10$ ft
$y_c(0) = 5$ ft

The scale factor for y is appropriately chosen to be the same for all tanks since the depth of the tanks is the same. Assume $Cm = 10$ volts.

$$K_y = \frac{\max |y|}{Cm} = \frac{50 \text{ ft}}{10 \text{ volts}} = 5 \text{ ft/volt} \tag{5-7k}$$

Assume that computer voltages Y_a, Y_b, and Y_c represent the problem variables y_a, y_b, and y_c.

$$y_a = K_{ya}Y_a$$
$$y_b = K_{yb}Y_b$$
$$y_c = K_{yc}Y_c \tag{5-7l}$$

Then the equations of the mathematical model become

$$\frac{dY_a}{dt} = -\frac{K_1}{A_a}Y_a + \frac{K_1}{A_a}Y_b \tag{5-7m}$$

$$\frac{dY_b}{dt} = \frac{K_1}{A_b}Y_a - \left(\frac{K_2}{A_b} + \frac{K_1}{A_b}\right)Y_b + \frac{K_2}{A_b}Y_c \tag{5-7n}$$

$$\frac{dY_c}{dt} = \frac{K_2}{A_c}Y_b - \left(\frac{K_2}{A_c} + \frac{K_3}{A_c}\right)Y_c \tag{5-7o}$$

Note that because $K_{ya} = K_{yb} = K_{yc}$ that the equations are unchanged.

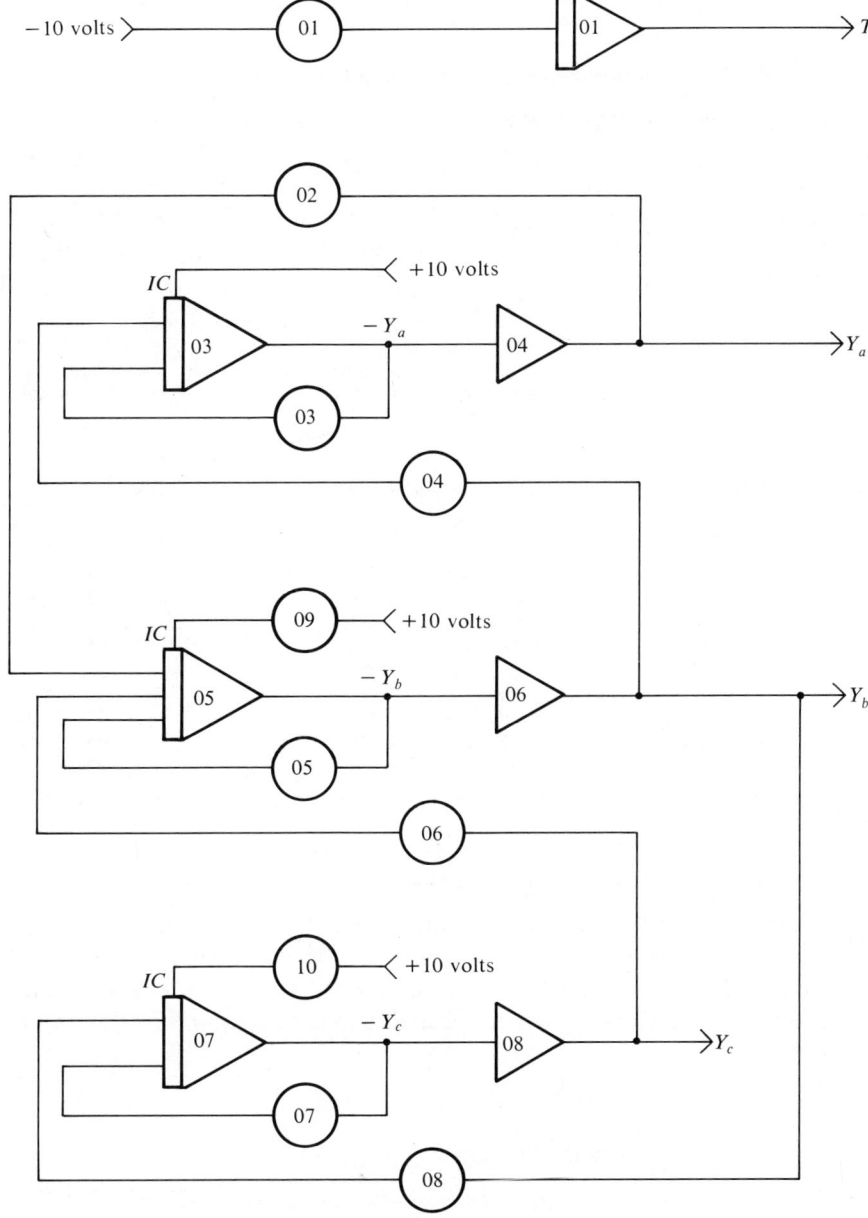

Note: See Table 5-2 for potentiometer settings and amplifier gains

FIG. 5-24

Block Diagram of Analog Model for System of Three Tanks.

STEP 3. Implementing the Scaled Model

The computer voltages $-Y_a$, $-Y_b$, and $-Y_c$ will be produced by integrating dY_a/dt, dY_b/dt, and dY_c/dt. The block diagram is shown in Fig. 5-24. The derivatives are formed by summing the appropriate terms as defined by the mathematical model. Table 5-2 shows the ratios to be set on each potentiometer and the amplifier gain to be used with each potentiometer.

TABLE 5-2. POTENTIOMETER RATIOS AND AMPLIFIER GAINS FOR ANALOG COMPUTER MODEL SHOWN IN FIG. 5-24.

POTENTIOMETER	COEFFICIENT		GAIN	AMPLIFIER
01		.05	1	01
02	(K_1/A_b)	0.533	1	05
03	(K_1/A_a)	0.400	1	03
04	(K_1/A_a)	0.400	1	03
05	$(K_2/A_b)+(K_1/A_b)$	0.933	1	05
06	(K_2/A_b)	0.400	1	05
07	$(K_2/A_c)+(K_3/A_c)$	1.00	1	07
08	(K_2/A_c)	0.600	1	07
09	$(Y_b/10)$	0.200	IC	05
10	$(Y_c/10)$	0.100	IC	07

STEP 4. Running a Trial Solution

The analog model was tested using the REP-OP mode and the CRO display. The water level in Tank C was found to go below zero, which is not physically possible. When the computer model was checked, the high side of potentiometer 08 was found connected to amplifier 05 rather than 06.

STEP 5. Solving the Problem

The voltages Y_a, Y_b, and Y_c were plotted using the X-Y plotter. The results are shown in Fig. 5-25. Notice that the water level in Tank C is always less than that in Tank B, which in turn is less than that in Tank A. This is as expected since water is flowing from Tank A to Tank B to Tank C.

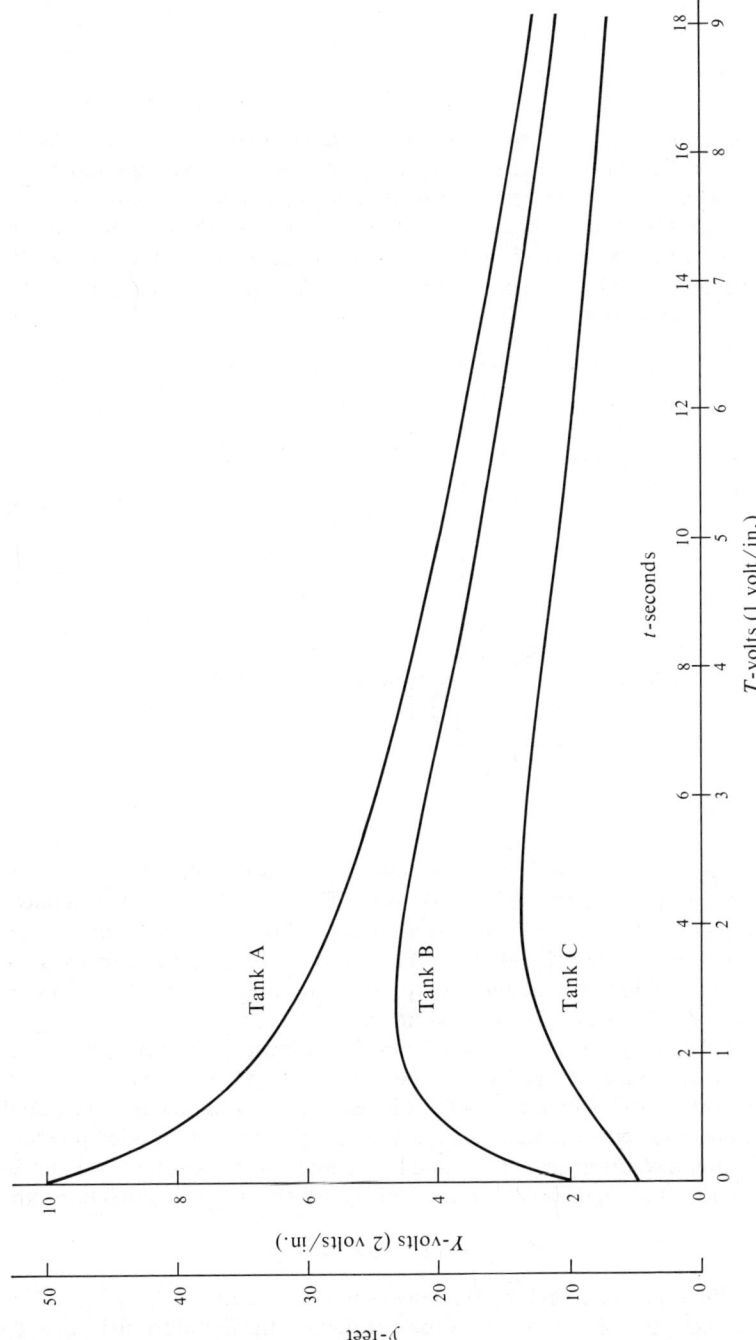

FIG. 5-25 Plot of Water Level in the Three Tanks.

5-8 Exercises

1. A water tank is in the shape of a right circular cylinder with the circular cross section in the horizontal plane. The tank is 100 ft high and has a diameter of 20 ft. Water is initially 80 ft deep. The discharge of water through a pipe in the bottom is found to be proportional to the depth of the water in the tank. The proportionality factor is 20 cu ft per sec-ft. Create a suitable mathematical model (differential equation) which describes this system.

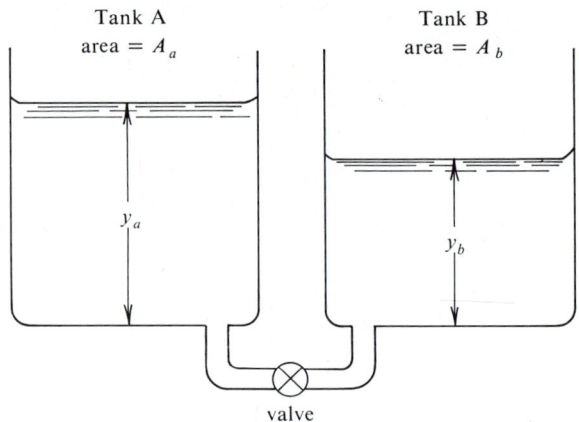

FIG. 5-26

2. One portion of an industrial process involves two tanks, A and B, connected by piping and a valve as shown in Fig. 5-26. After Tank A is filled, the valve is opened and liquid is allowed to flow into Tank B until equilibrium is attained. Create a mathematical model describing this system on the assumption that the rate of flow is proportional to the difference of the depth of liquid in the two tanks.
3. In order to speed up the transfer of liquid from Tank A to Tank B in Exercise 2, a pump is added to the system to pump the liquid from Tank A to Tank B as shown in Fig. 5-27. It is reasonable to assume that the liquid will be transferred at a greater rate initially because of the added pressure difference resulting from the liquid being deeper in Tank A than in Tank B. Assume that the transfer rate is given by the following relationship:

$$q = [K_1 + K_2(y_a - y_b)] \text{ cu ft/sec}$$

Create a mathematical model describing this system.
4. Another possible arrangement for transferring the liquid from Tank A to Tank B would be that shown in Fig. 5-28. Create a mathematical model

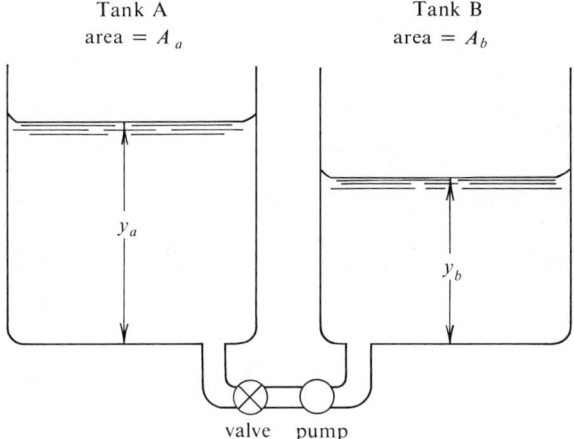

FIG. 5-27

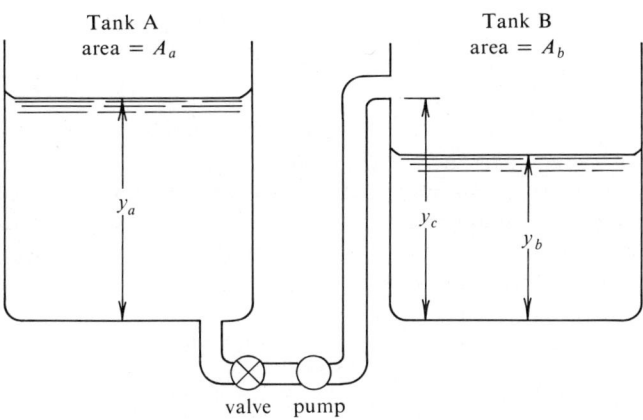

FIG. 5-28

describing this system. Assume that the pump is the same one used in Exercise 3. Is this model valid for $y_b > y_c$?

5. Will the system of Exercise 4 transfer the fluid faster than the system of Exercise 3? Explain why or why not on a qualitative basis.

6. Assume the parameters listed below for the system of Exercise 2. The mathematical model for this system then becomes:

$$\frac{dy_a}{dt} = -0.60(y_a - y_b)$$

$$\frac{dy_b}{dt} = +0.50(y_a - y_b)$$

106   FIRST-ORDER SYSTEMS

   a. Check your results for Exercise 2.
   b. Amplitude scale these equations for solution on an analog computer which has reference voltages ± 100 volts.
   c. Draw the block diagram of the amplitude scaled analog computer model for this system.

$$K = 30 \text{ sq ft/sec} \qquad y_a(0) = 70 \text{ ft}$$

$$A_a = 50 \text{ sq ft} \qquad y_b(0) = 5 \text{ ft}$$

$$A_b = 20 \text{ sq ft}$$

7. Assume that Exercise 3 has the parameters listed below. The mathematical model for the system becomes

$$\frac{dy_a}{dt} = -2.0 - 0.1(y_a - y_b)$$

$$\frac{dy_b}{dt} = +5.0 + 0.25(y_a - y_b)$$

   a. Verify the correctness of your model for Exercise 3.
   b. Can Tank B overflow? Explain quantitatively.
   c. Amplitude scale the model to fit on an analog computer with reference voltages of ± 100 volts.
   d. Draw the block diagram for the amplitude scaled analog computer model for this system.

$$K_1 = 100 \text{ cu ft/sec} \qquad y_a(0) = 70 \text{ ft}$$

$$K_2 = 5 \text{ sq ft/sec} \qquad y_b(0) = 5 \text{ ft}$$

$$h_a = 80 \text{ ft}$$

$$h_b = 100 \text{ ft}$$

8. Assume that the height y_c for Exercise 4 is 60 ft. The mathematical model for the system is then

$$\frac{dy_a}{dt} = -2 - 0.1(y_a - 60)$$

$$\frac{dy_b}{dt} = 5 + 0.25(y_a - 60)$$

a. Verify the correctness of your answer for Exercise 4.
b. What is the maximum possible depth of water in Tank B? Explain your answer qualitatively.
c. Draw the block diagram of the amplitude scaled analog computer model for this system. Assume that the analog computer used has a reference voltage of ± 100 volts.

9. Make an analog computer study of the effect of varying the parameters of the pump for Exercise 7. Make two series of tests. Present the results on two graphs.
    a. For $K_1 = 100$ cu ft/sec
       $K_2 = 0, 5, 10, 20$ sq ft/sec
    b. For $K_2 = 5$ cu ft/sec
       $K_1 = 0, 50, 100, 200$ sq ft/sec

   Note: The parameter K_1 is a measure of the volume of water which this pump delivers at zero pressure difference. The parameter K_2 is a measure of the rate of back flow through the pump as a function of pressure rise across the pump. The ratio of K_1 to K_2 is a number with units of feet. Thus the ratio (K_1/K_2) is the pressure measured in feet of water at which the net flow through the pump is 0.

10. A projectile weighs 2 kg and is launched vertically with an initial velocity of 20 m per sec. Assume that the drag resulting from air friction is viscous and that the coefficient is 10^{-11} newton-sec per m.
    a. Produce the block diagram representation for the amplitude scaled analog model for this system. Scale the model for an analog computer with reference voltages of ± 100 volts (or to fit the computer which you are going to use for Part c).
    b. A simple modification of the analog computer model will permit the vertical height to be displayed. What modification is required?
    c. Set up the analog model, and determine the time the projectile will be in the air and the maximum height that it will attain.

11. A cannon has a barrel 8 m long and a bore (internal diameter) of 15 cm. The projectile weighs 12 kg. Assume that the gas pressure in the barrel is constant at 5×10^4 kg per sq m. Assume the friction of the projectile in the barrel to be viscous with a coefficient of 2 newton-sec per m. One other assumption is needed.
    a. Produce the block diagram representation for the amplitude scaled analog model for this system. Scale the model for an analog computer with reference voltages of ± 10 volts (or to fit the computer available to you if you are going to do Part b).
    b. Set up the analog computer model to determine the velocity of the projectile as a function of time until the projectile reaches the muzzle (the end of the barrel). What is the velocity of the projectile as it leaves the end of the barrel?

12. Consider the electrical circuit shown in Fig. 5-29. The rectangular box at the left is the current generator which develops a constant current in-

FIRST-ORDER SYSTEMS

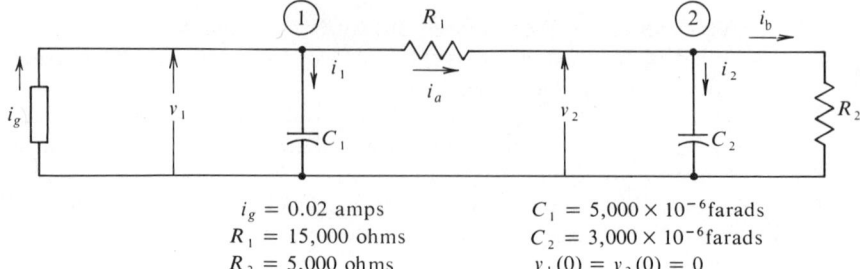

$i_g = 0.02$ amps
$R_1 = 15,000$ ohms
$R_2 = 5,000$ ohms

$C_1 = 5,000 \times 10^{-6}$ farads
$C_2 = 3,000 \times 10^{-6}$ farads
$v_1(0) = v_2(0) = 0$

FIG. 5-29

dependent of the potential difference across it. By Kirchhoff's Current Law the sum of the currents flowing out of a junction is equal to the sum of the currents flowing into that junction. The application of Kirchhoff's Current Law to junction 1 yields

$$i_1 + i_a = C_1 \frac{dv_1}{dt} + \frac{v_1 - v_2}{R_1} = i_g$$

Application to junction 2 yields

$$i_2 + i_b = C_2 \frac{dv_2}{dt} + \frac{v_2}{R_2} = \frac{v_1 - v_2}{R_1}$$

$i_g = 0.02$ amp

$R_1 = 15,000$ ohms

$R_2 = 5000$ ohms

$C_1 = 5000 \times 10^{-6}$ farad

$C_2 = 3000 \times 10^{-6}$ farad

$v_1(0) = v_2(0) = 0$

a. Create the block diagram representation for the amplitude scaled analog computer model of this electrical network. Amplitude scale for an analog computer with reference voltages of ± 100 volts or for the analog computer which you will use for part b.
b. Set up the analog model, and obtain plots of v_1 and v_2 which show the time from $t = 0$ until equilibrium is attained.

CHAPTER 6 SECOND-ORDER SYSTEMS

Some physical processes involve not only the first derivative of a variable, but also the second derivative of this variable. Such a system is called a second-order system. This situation arises when there are two different forms of energy storage. For example, in a mechanical system with a spring, mass, and dashpot, mechanical energy is stored as kinetic energy in the motion of the mass, and as potential energy in the deformation of the spring. In an electrical system consisting of a resistor, inductor, and capacitor, electrical energy is stored as potential energy in the form of electrical charge in the capacitor, and as kinetic energy in the motion of electrical charge through the inductor. Examples of several second-order systems will be considered to demonstrate the procedure of creating analog computer models for second-order systems. An alternate procedure consists of defining a set of two first-order differential equations which are equivalent to the second-order differential equation and then handling them by methods discussed in the previous chapter for sets

SECOND-ORDER SYSTEMS

of first-order differential equations. Both of these procedures will be demonstrated. The five steps of the previous chapter are used in both cases.

6-1 Spring-Mass-Dashpot System

STEP 1. Formulation of the Mathematical Model

Let us consider the spring-mass-dashpot system shown in Fig. 6-1. This system can store mechanical energy as kinetic energy in the motion of the mass. Mechanical energy is stored as potential energy, energy of position, in the displacement of the spring. Energy is dissipated by virtue of the viscous friction in the dashpot. An example of a dashpot is the shock absorber on an automobile. The shock absorber converts mechanical energy into heat when there is motion, and so reduces the oscillation caused by bumps in the road. The mathematical model for this system is formed by summing up the three forces as defined by physical laws and equating

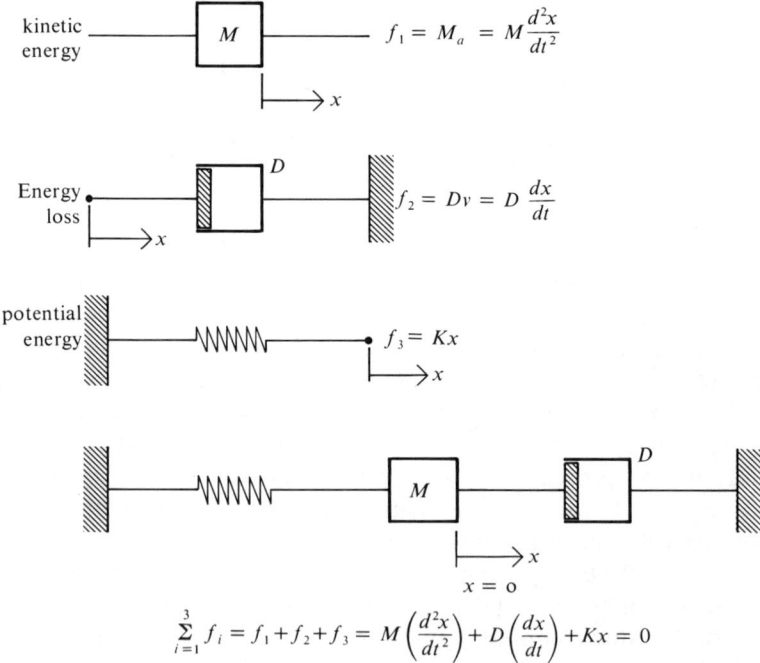

FIG. 6-1

Spring-Mass-Dashpot System and Differential Equation.

SPRING-MASS-DASHPOT SYSTEM

the sum to zero by virtue of the structure of the system. The inertial force is proportional to the product of the mass and the acceleration experienced by the mass. In equation form this force is as follows:

$$f_1 = M\frac{dv}{dt} = M\frac{d^2x}{dt^2} \tag{6-1a}$$

The frictional force is proportional to the velocity of the mass when the friction is viscous. The equation form of this force is f_2 where D is the damping force coefficient.

$$f_2 = Dv = D\frac{dx}{dt} \tag{6-1b}$$

The force resulting from stretching or compressing the spring is proportional to the displacement of the spring from its zero force position, which is taken for convenience to be zero. In equation form the spring force is f_3 where K is the spring force coefficient.

$$f_3 = K * x \tag{6-1c}$$

Consider first the case where the external applied force is zero and the mass is given an initial displacement from the zero position but no initial velocity. For this case the sum of the forces is zero:

$$f_1 + f_2 + f_3 = M\frac{d^2x}{dt^2} + D\frac{dx}{dt} + Kx = 0 \tag{6-1d}$$

For convenience take the following numerical values for the constants and the initial conditions:

$$M = 2.5 \text{ kg}$$
$$D = 4.0 \text{ newtons/(m/sec)}$$
$$K = 5.0 \text{ newtons/m}$$
$$x(0) = 0.5 \text{ m}, v(0) = 0 \tag{6-1e}$$

Substitution of these constants into Eq. (6-1f) yields the differential equation for this particular system.

$$2.5\frac{d^2x}{dt^2} + 4.0\frac{dx}{dt} + 5.0x = 0 \tag{6-1f}$$

112 SECOND-ORDER SYSTEMS

The following integral relations result from the definition of the process of integration and are useful in setting up the analog computer model.

$$x = \int \frac{dx}{dt} dt + c_1 \qquad (6\text{-}1g)$$

$$\frac{dx}{dt} = \int \frac{d^2x}{dt^2} dt + c_2 \qquad (6\text{-}1h)$$

STEP 2. Scaling the Mathematical Model

The displacement x will never be greater than the initial displacement because the mass has no initial velocity and therefore the stored energy in the system must decrease, and the displacement when the mass is at rest is proportional to the square root of the stored energy. An appropriate scale factor for displacement is therefore as follows:

$$k_x = \frac{\max |x|}{Cm} = \frac{0.5 \text{ m}}{10 \text{ volts}} = 0.05 \text{ m/volt} \qquad (6\text{-}1i)$$

Assume that U is the computer voltage which represents the displacement x. The displacement x relates to the voltage U by

$$x \text{ m} = 0.05(\text{m/volt}) * U \text{ volts} \qquad (6\text{-}1j)$$

For lack of information on the range of velocity, let us assume initially the same scale factor on velocity as on displacement and that V is the computer voltage which represents the velocity, dx/dt. The velocity, v, relates to this voltage, V, by

$$v = \frac{dx}{dt} \text{ m/sec} = 0.05(\text{m/sec-volt}) * V \text{ volts} \qquad (6\text{-}1k)$$

The initial value of the acceleration will be the largest encountered because, as before, the energy in the system will be decreasing. Therefore substitute the initial conditions into Eq. (6-1f) and solve for d^2x/dt^2.

$$\left(\frac{d^2x}{dt^2}\right)_{t=0} = -1.6(0) - 2.0(0.5)$$

$$= -1.0 \text{ m/sec}^2 \qquad (6\text{-}1l)$$

The appropriate scale factor for acceleration is, therefore,

$$k_a = \frac{\max [d^2x/dt^2]}{Cm} = \frac{1.0 \,(\text{m/sec}^2)}{10 \text{ volts}}$$

$$= 0.1 \text{ m/sec}^2\text{-volts} \qquad (6\text{-}1\text{m})$$

Assume that W is the computer voltage that represents the acceleration, dv/dt or d^2x/dt^2. The acceleration, dv/dt, relates to this voltage, W, by

$$\frac{d^2x}{dt^2} = 0.1W \qquad (6\text{-}1\text{n})$$

Substitution of Eq. (6-1j), (6-1k), and (6-1n) into Eq. (6-1f) and solving for W yields

$$0.1W = -1.6(0.05V) - 2.0(0.05U)$$
$$W = -0.8V - U \qquad (6\text{-}1\text{o})$$

This equation in the computer variables U, V, and W comes from the differential equation for the system. Since there are three variables, two additional mathematical relationships are needed between the computer voltages U, V, and W. These relations are obtained from the integral Eqs. (6-1g) and (6-1h) by substitution of the amplitude scaling Eqs. (6-1j), (6-1k), and (6-1n) as follows:

$$0.05U = x = \int \frac{dx}{dt} dt + c_1 = \int 0.05V \, dt + 0.05U(0)$$

$$0.05V = \frac{dx}{dt} = \int \frac{d^2x}{dt^2} dt + c_2 = \int 0.1W \, dt + 0.05V(0) \qquad (6\text{-}1\text{p})$$

Simplifying these equations yields the following relationships:

$$U = \int V dt + U(0) \qquad (6\text{-}1\text{q})$$

$$V = \int 2W dt + V(0) \qquad (6\text{-}1\text{r})$$

STEP 3. Implementing the Analog Computer Model

The last two integral equations provide the starting point for creating the analog computer model for the given differential equation. Because of the sign inversion associated with the process of integration, the equations

114 SECOND-ORDER SYSTEMS

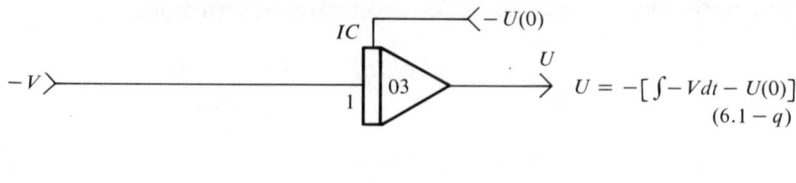

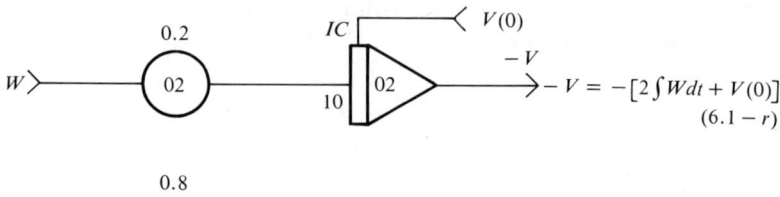

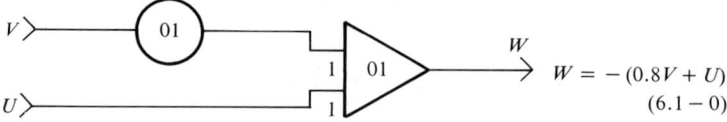

FIG. 6-2

Analog Computer Block Diagrams for Individual Equations.

are rewritten as shown in Fig. 6-2. From this form of the equations, the three block diagram segments can be easily drawn. The output W from amplifier 01 provides the input needed for potentiometer 02. The output, $-V$, from amplifier 02 provides the input needed for amplifier 03. An inverter is needed to provide the $+V$ input for potentiometer 01. These connections are shown in Fig. 6-3. If the value of acceleration is not required, the summer amplifier 4 may be omitted as shown in Fig. 6-4. In this block diagram provision has been made for the initial condition on U by connecting potentiometer 3 to the IC terminal on integrator 3.

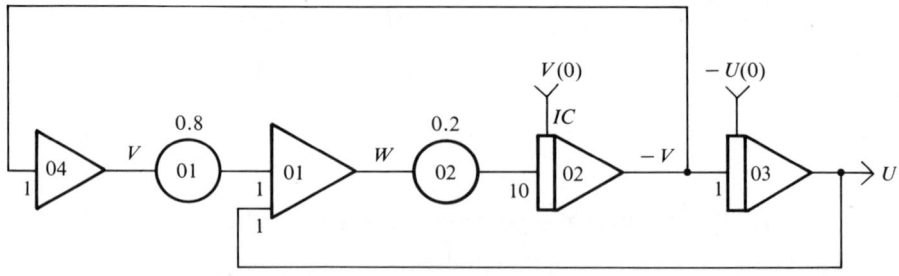

FIG. 6-3

Analog Computer Block Diagram for Second-Order System of Fig. 6-1.

SPRING-MASS-DASHPOT SYSTEM

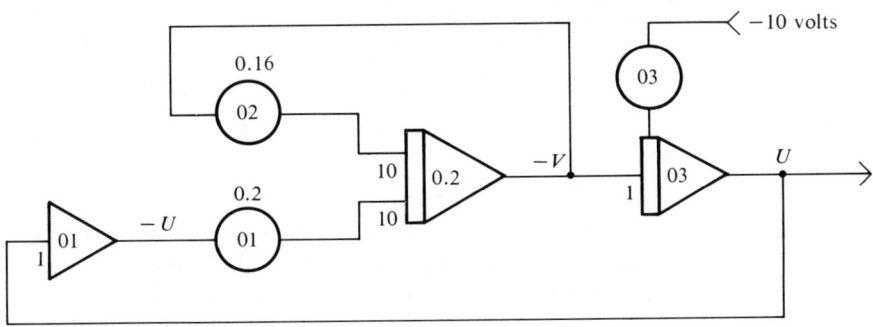

FIG. 6-4

Analog Computer Block Diagram Simplified by Elimination of W.

Note the changes in the ratios set on potentiometers 01 and 02. The ratio on 02 is set to the value which preserves the gain around the upper loop, that is, $-10(0.8)(0.2) = -1.6$. The ratio on 01 is set to the value which preserves the gain around the lower loop, that is, $-10(0.2) = -2.0$.

STEP 4. Trial Solution on the Computer

When the system shown in Fig. 6-4 is connected and operated on the computer, the solution changes too rapidly to be satisfactorily recorded

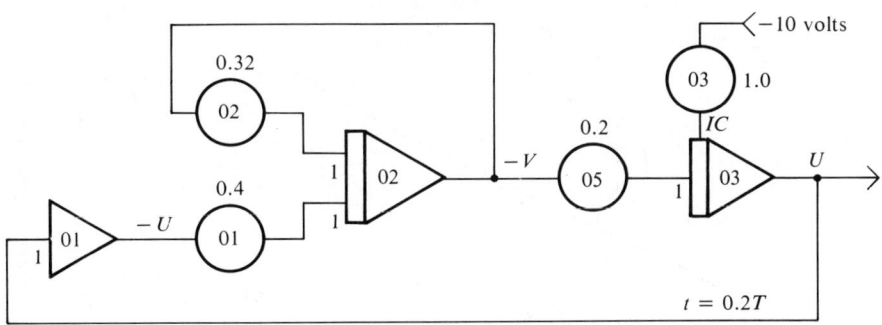

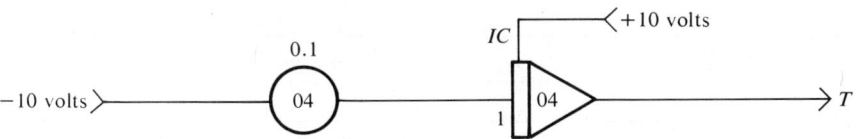

FIG. 6-5

Computer Block Diagram After Time Scaling.

116 SECOND-ORDER SYSTEMS

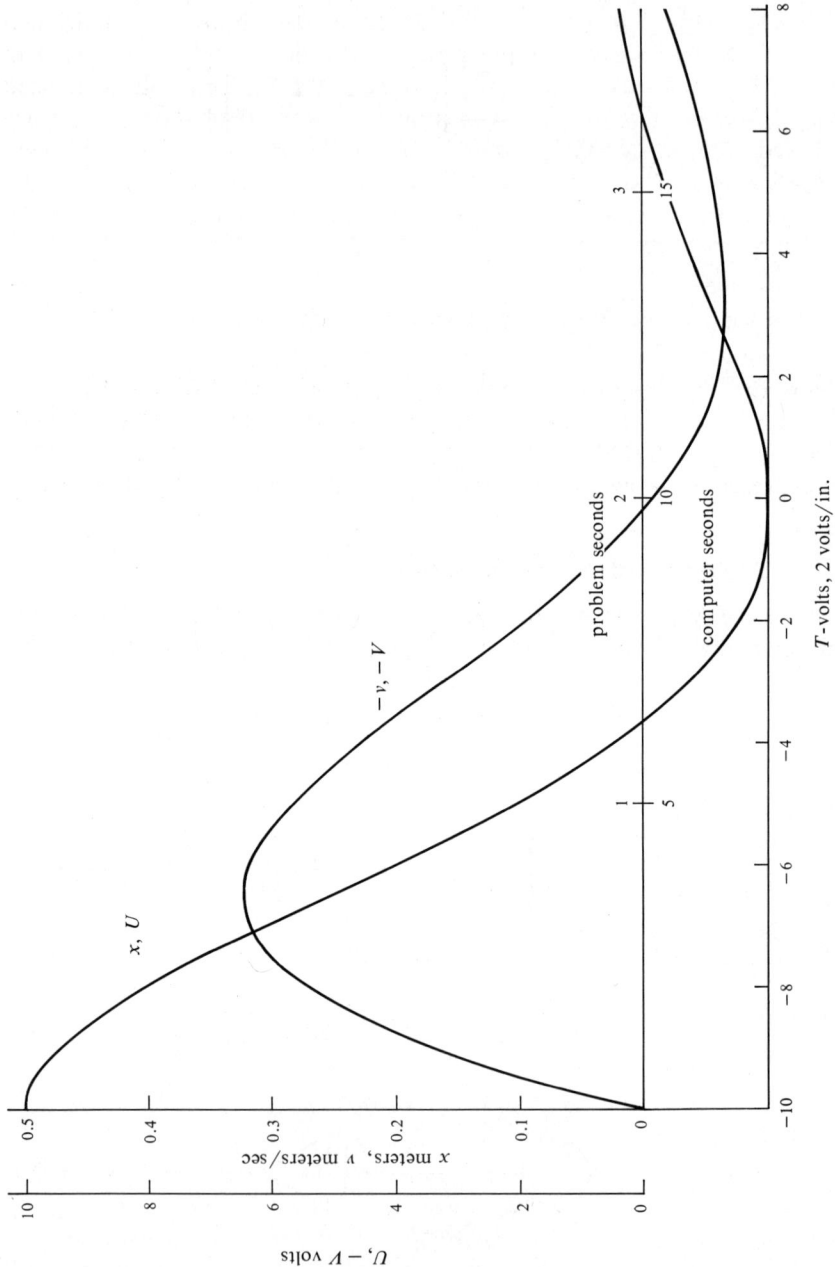

FIG. 6-6 Velocity and Displacement for Spring-Mass-Dashpot System.

on the X-Y plotter. Therefore, the time scale must be changed to slow down the generation of the solution. To cause the solution to be generated only 20 per cent as fast, the gains of all inputs to integrators are multiplied by 0.20. Now 5 sec of computer time correspond to 1 sec of problem time. The new block diagram is shown in Fig. 6-5. The results as plotted on an X-Y plotter are shown in Fig. 6-6. Note that vertical axes are marked in terms of both the computer variable in volts and the problem variables in m and m per sec. The time axes is marked in terms of the computer variable, T volts, the computer time variable in computer sec, and the problem variable t in problem sec.

6-2 Nonzero Forcing Function

The term or terms of a differential equation which do not involve the dependent variable are referred to as the forcing function, since such terms arise when a force is applied to a system as shown in Fig. 6-7. The differential equation then becomes

$$M \frac{d^2x}{dt^2} + D \frac{dx}{dt} + Kx = f \tag{6-2a}$$

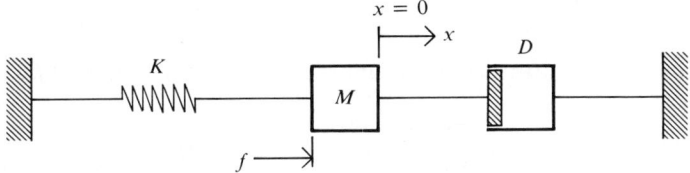

FIG. 6-7
Spring-Mass-Dashpot System with Applied Force.

When this is solved for d^2x/dt^2 the result is as follows:

$$\frac{d^2x}{dt^2} = \frac{f}{M} - \frac{D}{M}\frac{dx}{dt} - \frac{K}{M}x \tag{6-2b}$$

Suppose that the constants are the same as used in the previous example, that the force applied is 2.0 newtons, and that the initial displacement is zero. As time increases, the derivatives approach zero and the displacement approaches a limiting value which can be computed in the following way:

$$0 = \frac{f}{M} - \frac{D}{M}(0) - \frac{K}{M}x$$

$$x = \frac{f}{K} = \frac{2.0 \text{ newtons}}{5.0 \text{ newtons/m}}$$

$$x = 0.4 \text{ m}$$

Since this final displacement is less than the initial displacement of the previous example, the maximum acceleration will be less than for the previous example, and therefore the same k_a will be valid. The constant term f/M has a value of

$$\frac{f}{M} = \frac{2.0 \text{ newtons}}{2.5 \text{ kg}} = 0.8 \text{ m/sec}^2 \qquad (6\text{-}2c)$$

Since this term has units of acceleration, the acceleration scale factor should be used here. Assume that a voltage F on the computer represents the term f/M. Then the voltage F and the term f/M are related in the following way:

$$\frac{f}{M}(\text{m/sec}^2) = k_a(\text{m/sec}^2\text{-volt}) \, F(\text{volt}) \qquad (6\text{-}2d)$$

Solving for F and substitution of numerical values for f/M and k_a yields

$$F = \frac{0.8(\text{m/sec}^2)}{0.1(\text{m/sec}^2\text{-volt})} = 8.0 \text{ volts} \qquad (6\text{-}2e)$$

Substitution of the amplitude scaling equations into Eq. (6-2b) and solving for W yields

$$0.1W = 0.1F - 1.6(0.05V) - 2.0(0.05U)$$

$$W = F - 0.8V - U \qquad (6\text{-}2f)$$

The integral equations which relate the computer variables are not changed from the previous example because they depend on the relationships between displacement, velocity, and acceleration. The block diagram representation of the analog models for these three equations is

NONZERO FORCING FUNCTION

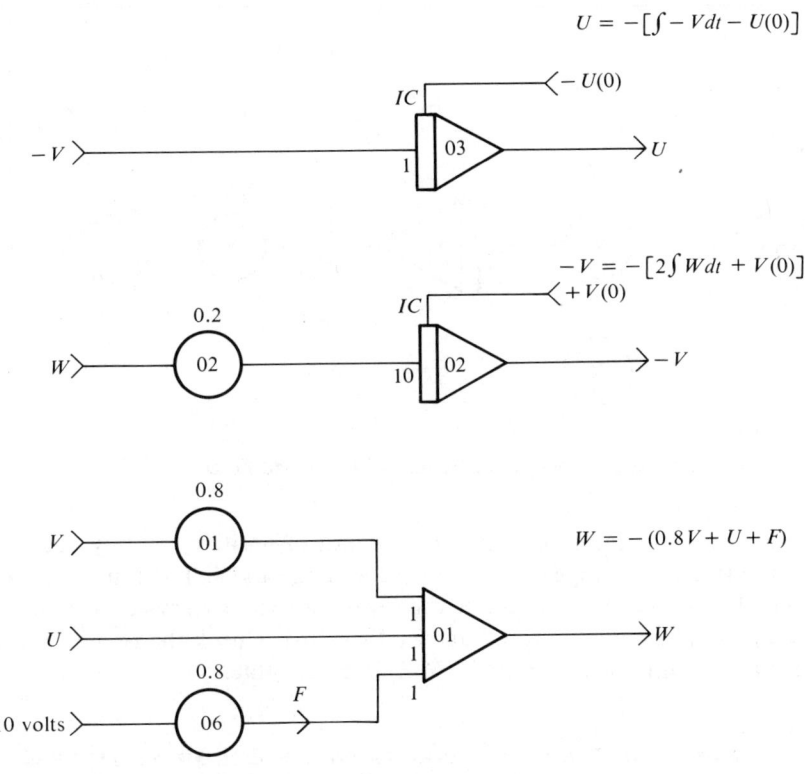

FIG. 6-8

Block Diagram of Analog Models for System with Force Applied.

shown in Fig. 6-8. Compare with Fig. 6-2 and note that the only change is the additional input F into amplifier 01.

These models can be combined as in the previous exercise. Since the solution will be generated too rapidly for plotting using an X-Y plotter, time scaling is again required. The Block diagram for the analog model is shown in Fig. 6-9 after all integrator gains have been multiplied by 0.2 to slow down the computer model. Again 5 sec of computer time is equal to 1 sec of system time.

Compare the block diagram of Fig. 6-5 for the previous example with Fig. 6-9 for this example. The solution curve for this problem is shown in Fig. 6-10. Compare the solution curves for these two examples. Notice that the velocity curve plotted in Fig. 6-6 is negative velocity. The velocity is negative initially in the actual system because the mass is moving from a positive displacement toward the origin or neutral position. The velocity

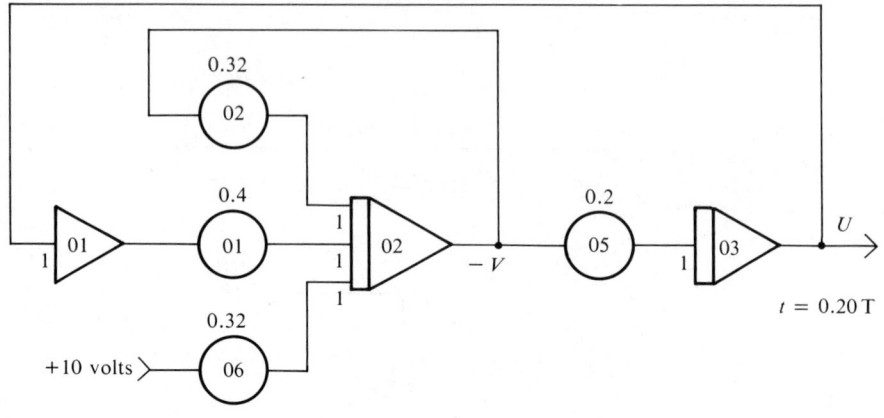

FIG. 6-9

Computer Block Diagram for System with Applied Force.

curve plotted for the second system is a plot of positive velocity obtained by inverting the voltage, $-V$, from the analog model. The time of occurrence of certain events should be the same for these two systems. Some of these pairs of events are tabulated in Table 6-1. Check the two curves to see that the times are identical. Complete the table.

TABLE 6-1. PAIRS OF EVENTS WHICH OCCUR AT THE SAME TIME FOR THE TWO EXAMPLES

FIG. 6-6	FIG. 6-10
maximum negative velocity	maximum positive velocity
zero velocity	zero velocity
zero displacement	$x = +0.8$
maximum negative displacement	?
?	$x = +0.4$

6-3 The Swinging Door System

Consider a swinging door that is 1.0 m wide and 2 m high and which weighs 8.0 kg. This swinging door is returned to the closed position by a torsional spring which has a torque constant of 0.3 newton-m per radian.

THE SWINGING DOOR SYSTEM 121

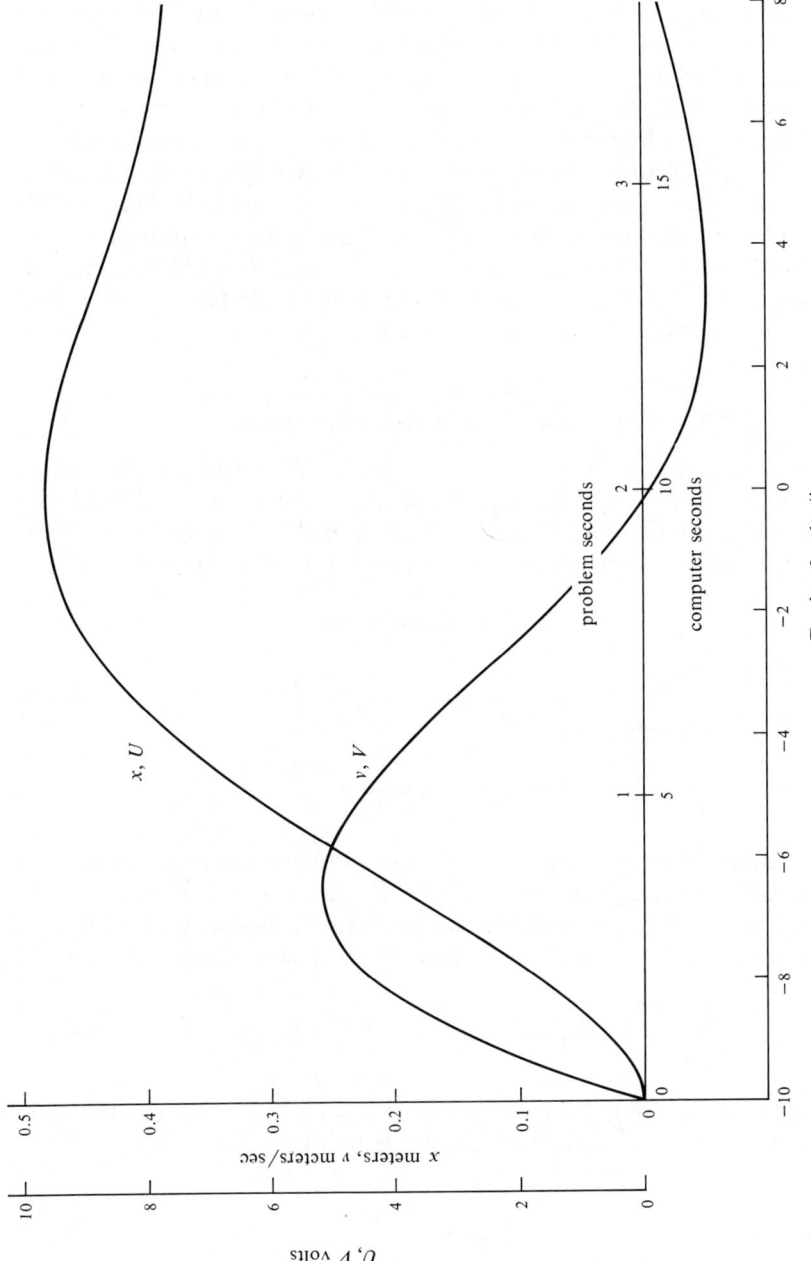

FIG. 6-10 Velocity and Displacement for Spring-Mass-Dashpot System with Applied Force.

The problem is to determine the amount of damping required to allow the door to close in the minimum possible time with a maximum overshoot of 0.1 radian. Overshoot is the amount the door swings past the equilibrium position of $\Theta = 0$. If the damping is too small, the door will close more rapidly but will have more overswing. If the damping is too large, the door will have less overswing but will require a longer time to close. The problem as stated is not completely defined. This situation frequently arises in practice where the problem is not fully defined. It is the engineer's responsibility to find the missing information, if the information exists, or to make reasonable assumptions for the missing information. In the latter case these assumptions should be explicitly called out. Consider what else needs to be specified.

STEP 1. Formulation of the Mathematical Model

Three torques will be present in this system: the spring torque tending to close the door, the damping torque proportional to the angular velocity of the door, and the inertial torque proportional to the angular acceleration of the door. These torques are expressed quantitatively as

$$\text{Spring torque} = K\Theta$$

$$\text{Damping torque} = D\frac{d\Theta}{dt} \tag{6-3a}$$

$$\text{Inertial torque} = J\frac{d^2\Theta}{dt^2}$$

The angular position of the door with respect to its equilibrium position is measured by the angle Θ. The sum of these three torques is equal to the applied torque which is zero for this problem. This condition yields the mathematical model for the structure of the system given as Eq. 6-3b.

$$\Sigma \text{ torques} = J\frac{d^2\Theta}{dt^2} + D\frac{d\Theta}{dt} + K\Theta \tag{6-3b}$$

The definitions of angular velocity and angular acceleration yield the two additional equations needed which are as follows:

$$\Theta = \int \frac{d\Theta}{dt}\,dt + \Theta(0) \tag{6-3c}$$

$$\frac{d\Theta}{dt} = \int \frac{d^2\Theta}{dt^2}\,dt + \left(\frac{d\Theta}{dt}\right)_{t=0} \tag{6-3d}$$

STEP 2. Amplitude Scaling the Mathematical Model

The point at which the problem is not completely specified becomes evident now, if it was not evident before. The initial displacement and initial velocity are needed. For the door in question the maximum displacement is 100°. Since the remainder of the problem is stated in terms of radians, consider for convenience that the maximum displacement of the door from its equilibrium position is 2.0 radians. The amplitude scale factor for displacement is, for an analog computer with a range of ±10 volts, found as follows:

$$K_d = \frac{\max |\Theta|}{Cm} = \frac{2 \text{ radians}}{10 \text{ volts}} = 0.2 \text{ radian/volt} \qquad (6\text{-}3e)$$

If a computer voltage U represents displacement, then

$$\Theta = K_d U = 0.2U \qquad (6\text{-}3f)$$

A consideration of our experience with swinging doors suggests that the door should require the order of 5 sec to close. If the door closes too rapidly, it may be dangerous to small children, and if it closes too slowly, its function to keep the hot air in in the winter and the cold air in in the summer will be impaired. An estimate of the average velocity would therefore be as follows:

$$v_{av} = 2 \text{ radians}/5 \text{ sec} = 0.4 \text{ radian/sec}$$

The maximum velocity may be three to four times the average velocity since the initial and final velocity are zero. This gives an estimate of 1.2 to 1.6 m per sec for the maximum velocity. For convenience assume initially that the maximum velocity is 2.0 radians per sec. The amplitude scale factor for velocity is therefore as follows:

$$K_v = \frac{\max \left|\frac{d\Theta}{dt}\right|}{Cm} = \frac{2 \text{ radians/sec}}{10 \text{ volts}} \qquad (6\text{-}3g)$$

$$= 0.2 \text{ radian/volt-sec}$$

If the computer voltage, V, represents the angular velocity of the door, then

$$\frac{d\Theta}{dt} = K_v V \qquad (6\text{-}3h)$$

The validity of the assumptions made in arriving at these amplitude scale factors will be tested by the trial solution run on the analog model. If they are not valid, the trial solution will provide insight as to the changes required. We will consider that the initial angular velocity of the door is zero. An estimate of the maximum angular acceleration can be made by substituting the initial displacement and angular velocity into Eq. (6-3b) and solving for the initial acceleration. Since the initial velocity is zero, the unknown value of D poses no problem. The numerical value for the moment of inertia J is needed before proceeding with the solution.

Consider that the door is hinged on the y-axis and that the door is in the x-y plane when at rest. The moment of inertia about the y-axis is then defined to be as follows:

$$J = \iiint r^2 \sigma \, dx \, dy \, dz \tag{6-3i}$$

If the door is thin compared to the width, then the distance r from the axis of rotation to the element of volume is approximately the x coordinate of the volume. If the density, σ, is uniform and the thickness Z constant, then the moment of inertia can be computed as

$$J = \sigma Z \int_0^Y \int_0^X x^2 \, dx \, dy \tag{6-3j}$$

See Fig. 6-11 for a sketch of the door and the element of area. Integration of Eq. (6-3j) yields

$$J = \frac{ZYX^3\sigma}{3} = \frac{(\sigma XYZ)X^2}{3} = \frac{MX^2}{3} \tag{6-3k}$$

The product of the dimensions X, Y, Z of the door and the density σ gives the mass M of the door. The original statement of the problem gave a value of 8.0 kg for the mass and 1.0 m for the width X of this door and, therefore, the inertia J is:

$$J = \frac{8}{3} = 2.67 \text{ kg-m}^2 \tag{6-3l}$$

Eq. 6-3b becomes upon substituting the known constants:

$$2.67 \frac{d^2\theta}{dt^2} + D\frac{d\theta}{dt} + 0.3 \, \theta = 0 \tag{6-3m}$$

THE SWINGING DOOR SYSTEM 125

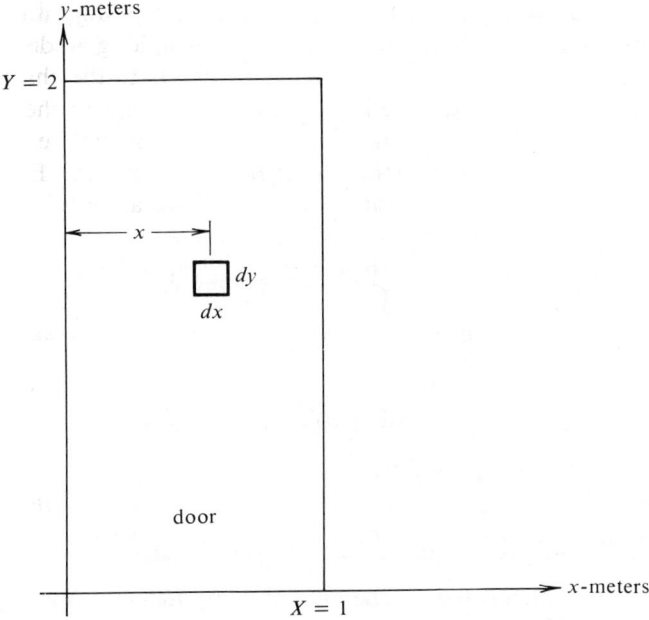

FIG. 6-11
Sketch of Swinging Door in an *X-Y* Coordinate System.

Solution of this equation for the initial value of angular acceleration remembering that $d\Theta/dt$ is zero initially yields:

$$\frac{d^2\Theta}{dt^2} = -\frac{(0.3)(100°)}{(2.67)}\left(\frac{\pi}{180} \text{ radian/degree}\right)$$

$$= 1.4 \text{ radians/sec}^2 \qquad (6\text{-}3n)$$

The nearest value that produces a convenient scale factor is 2.0 radian/sec², and therefore the scale factor for acceleration is as follows:

$$K_a = \frac{\max \left|\frac{d^2\Theta}{dt^2}\right|}{C_m} = \frac{2.0 \text{ radian/sec}^2}{10 \text{ volts}}$$

$$= 0.2 \text{ radian/volt-sec}^2 \qquad (6\text{-}3o)$$

Assume that the computer voltage, W, represents the angular acceleration:

$$\frac{d^2\Theta}{dt^2} = K_a W \qquad (6\text{-}3p)$$

SECOND-ORDER SYSTEMS

Substitution of the amplitude scaling equations into the model equations yields the following set of amplitude scaled equations, which the student should verify.

$$2.67W + DV + 0.3U = 0$$
$$U = \int V\,dt + U(0)$$
$$V = \int W\,dt \tag{6-3q}$$

The value of the initial condition, $U(0)$, is computed

$$U(0) = \frac{\Theta(0)}{K_d}$$
$$= 1.75 \text{ radian}/(0.2 \text{ radian/volt})$$
$$= 8.75 \text{ volts} \tag{6-3r}$$

STEP 3. Implementing the Analog Computer Model

Eq. (6-3q) are implemented on the analog computer by assuming that the voltage, W, is available as the output from a summer, by integrating

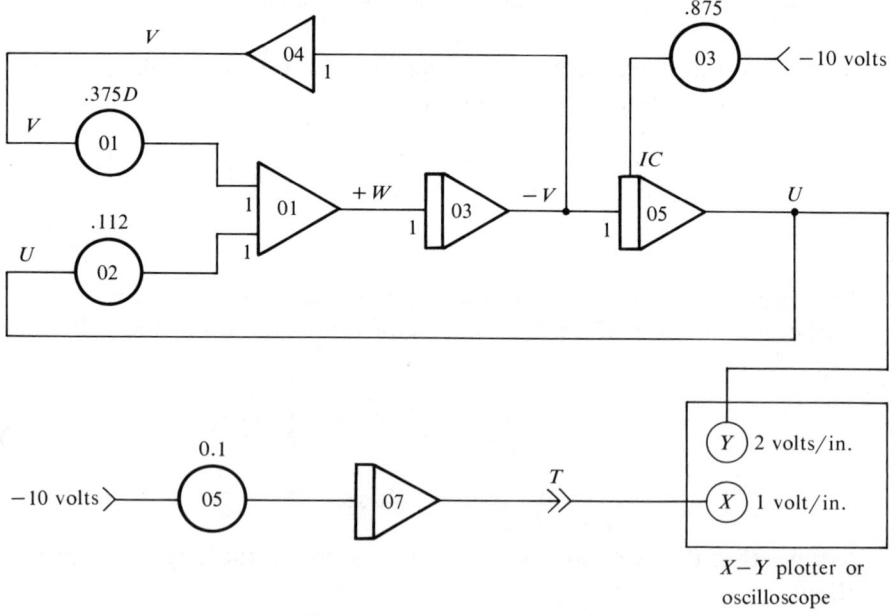

FIG. 6-12

Block Diagram of Analog Computer Model for Swinging Door.

THE SWINGING DOOR SYSTEM 127

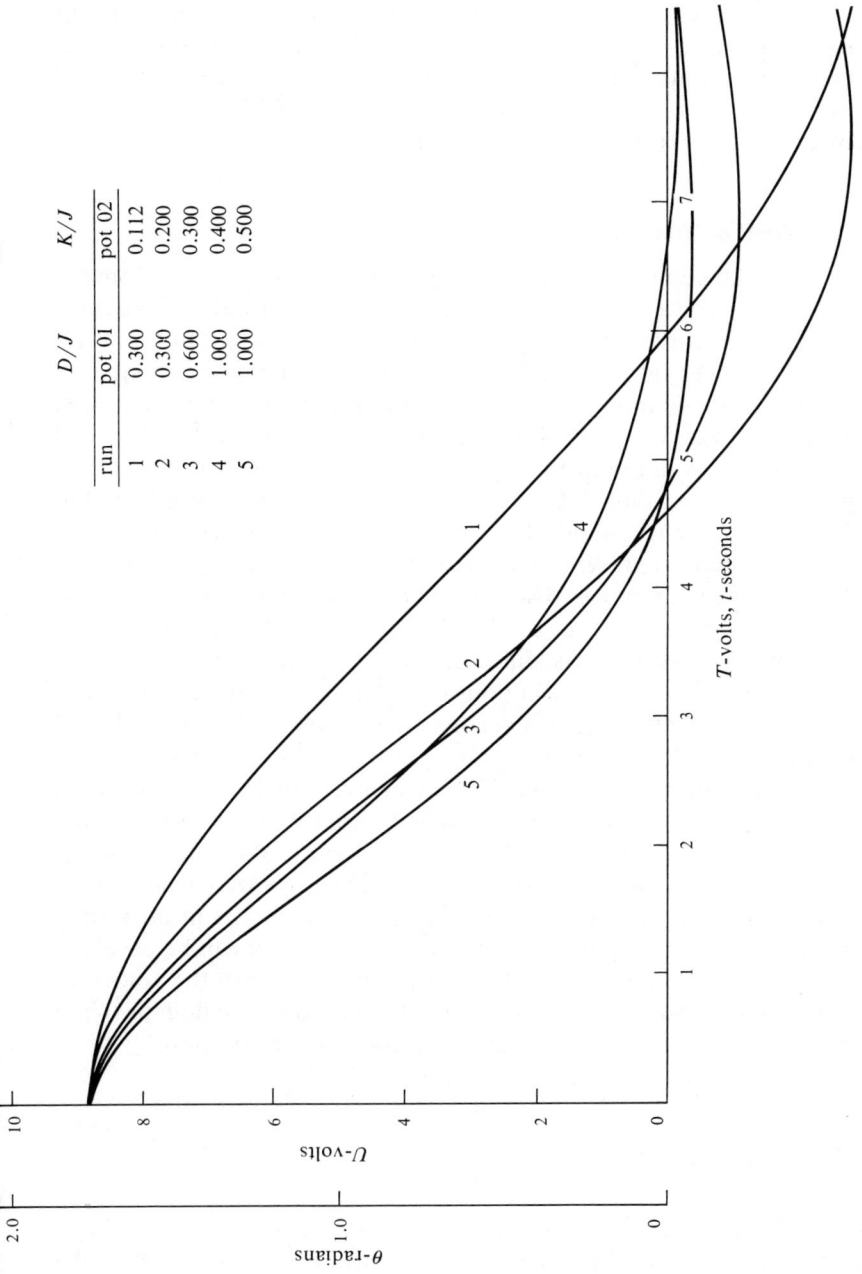

FIG. 6-13 Angular Position vs. Time for Swinging Door.

W to obtain $-V$, and then integrating $-V$ to obtain displacement, U. See Fig. 6-12. Inverter 04 is needed to provide $+V$ as required to make up the inputs for the summer 01. Potentiometer 03 produces the -8.75 volts required for the initial condition on the displacement, U. Integrator 07 provides a time-base voltage, T that goes from 0 to 10 volts in 10 sec, which covers the expected time for solution.

STEP 4. Trial Solutions

The first trial solution was run for a setting of 0.30 on potentiometer 01. This setting is the value of the product $0.375D$. Hence this value is for a damping constant less than 1.0. Solution Curve 1, plotted in Fig. 6-13, has too much overshoot, which suggests that more damping is required. However, if more damping is added, the door will close even more slowly, and it already takes in excess of 5 sec to close. Although a value, D, could be found which would limit the overshoot to the desired 0.1 radian with the given spring constant, such a solution would leave the door open too much of the time. The real problem then is to adjust both the damping, D, and the spring constant, K, to meet the condition of closing the door to less than ± 0.1 radian in less than 5 sec. Trial Run 2 was made for an increase in the torque constant of the closing spring. The closing time is reduced, but the overshoot is still excessive as would be expected. Trial Run 3 was run for an increase in both the spring constant and the damping. This curve is better, but the overshoot is still too large and the closing is too slow. Trial Run 4 was made for a further increase in the damping and the spring constant. Trial Run 5 is made for a further increase in the spring constant of 20 per cent and produces what appears to be a satisfactory closing of the door. This series of adjustments could be made much more rapidly using the REP-OP mode. The plots were made on the X-Y plotter to show the process of adjusting the parameters in the system to obtain the desired response. The behavior of the door can be observed very nicely by watching the needle on the voltmeter when the voltmeter is measuring the voltage, U. The position of the needle is analogous to the position of the door if you look down on the door from above.

6-4 Simple Pendulum

A simple pendulum consists of a rigid rod whose moment of inertia is negligible compared to the inertia of the weight or bob which is attached at the lower end of the rod. This rod is usually pivoted at the upper end in such a way that the friction of rotation of the rod and bob about the support is quite small. A diagram of such a pendulum is shown in Fig. 6-14.

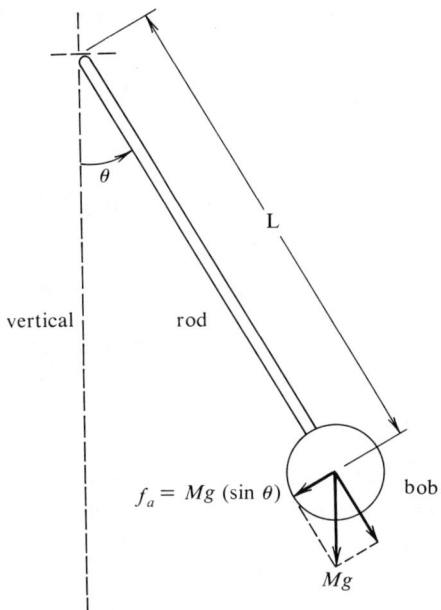

FIG. 6-14
Diagram of a Simple Pendulum.

The distance from the point of support to the center of gravity of the bob is represented by the symbol L. The mass of the bob is represented by the symbol M, and the angle between the supporting rod and vertical is represented by the angle θ measured in radians.

STEP 1. Formulating the Mathematical Model

Gravity acting on the bob produces a downward force equal to the product of the mass, M, of the bob and the acceleration of gravity, g. This force can be resolved into two components: one that is parallel to the axis of the supporting rod and a second one that is perpendicular to the supporting rod. Both of these forces act through the center of the bob. The force perpendicular to the rod is as follows:

$$f_a = Mg \sin \theta \qquad (6\text{-}4a)$$

130 SECOND-ORDER SYSTEMS

This force tends to cause the pendulum to move to the equilibrium position where $\Theta = 0$. The pendulum also experiences an inertial force, f_i, which can be calculated as

$$f_i = M \frac{dv}{dt} \qquad (6\text{-}4\text{b})$$

The velocity, v, is related to the angular velocity ω by Eq. (6-4c)

$$v = L\omega \qquad (6\text{-}4\text{c})$$

The inertial force can be expressed in terms of angular velocity as

$$f_i = M \frac{d(L\omega)}{dt} = LM \frac{d\omega}{dt} \qquad (6\text{-}4\text{d})$$

The third force acting on the bob is the damping force, which is assumed to be proportional to velocity,

$$f_d = DL\omega \qquad (6\text{-}4\text{e})$$

The sum of these three forces is equal to zero, since there is no externally applied force in this system. Thus the mathematical model that results from the structure of the system is obtained by summing the forces as follows:

$$f_i + f_d + f_a = LM \frac{d\omega}{dt} + LD\omega + Mg(\sin \Theta) = 0 \qquad (6\text{-}4\text{f})$$

The following relation is used to further simplify the equation based on the assumption that the angle is sufficiently small.

$$\sin \Theta \approx \Theta \qquad (6\text{-}4\text{g})$$

The substitution of this relation into Eq. (6-4f) yields

$$LM \frac{d\omega}{dt} + LD\omega + Mg\Theta = 0 \qquad (6\text{-}4\text{h})$$

This equation can be further simplified by dividing through by LM.

$$\frac{d\omega}{dt} + \frac{D\omega}{M} + \frac{g\Theta}{L} = 0 \qquad (6\text{-}4\text{i})$$

The angular velocity ω is related to the angle Θ by

$$\omega = \frac{d\Theta}{dt} \qquad (6\text{-}4\text{j})$$

SIMPLE PENDULUM   131

These latter two equations constitute a set of simultaneous first-order differential equations representing the dynamics of the pendulum, which is a second-order system because there are two forms of energy storage, kinetic and potential. These two equations can be organized in a manner similar to that for simultaneous algebraic equations as follows:

$$\frac{d\omega}{dt} + \frac{D}{M}\omega \quad\quad + \frac{g}{L}\theta = 0 \qquad (6\text{-}4\text{k})$$

$$-\quad \omega + \frac{d\theta}{dt} \quad\quad = 0 \qquad (6\text{-}4\text{l})$$

These two equations can be solved together to eliminate one or the other of the variables. If ω is eliminated, the following second-order differential equation results:

$$\frac{d^2\theta}{dt^2} + \frac{D}{M}\frac{d\theta}{dt} + \frac{g}{L}\theta = 0 \qquad (6\text{-}4\text{m})$$

This process is clearly reversible and demonstrates the process of representing a second-order differential equation by a set of two first-order differential equations. The analog computer model that results will be the same for either approach. The following equations are needed along with Eq. (6-4m) to complete the mathematical model:

$$\theta = \int \omega\, dt + \theta(0) \qquad (6\text{-}4\text{n})$$

$$\omega = \int \frac{d^2\theta}{dt^2}\, dt + \omega(0) \qquad (6\text{-}4\text{o})$$

STEP 2. Amplitude Scaling the Mathematical Model

For purposes of this example take the following as parameters for the pendulum to be studied:

$L = 1.0$ m

$M = 2$ kg

$D = 0.06$ newton-sec/m

$-0.1 \leq \theta \leq +0.1$ radian

$\theta(0) = 0.1$ radian

$g = 9.81$ m/sec^2

132 SECOND-ORDER SYSTEMS

These constants are comparable to that for the pendulum of a typical grandfather clock. Substitution of these constants into Eq. (6-4m) yields the following:

$$\frac{d^2\theta}{dt^2} + 0.03 \frac{d\theta}{dt} + 9.81\theta = 0 \tag{6-4p}$$

For a reference voltage of ± 100 volts, the amplitude scale factor for displacement is as follows:

$$K_d = \frac{\max |\theta|}{Cm} = \frac{0.1 \text{ radian}}{100 \text{ volts}}$$

$$= 0.001 \text{ radian/volt} \tag{6-4q}$$

The pendulum of the typical grandfather clock makes a complete cycle from one side to the other and returns in 2 sec. The average velocity is therefore 0.4 radian divided by 2 sec, or 0.2 radian per sec. The maximum velocity will be greater than the average velocity, since the velocity is zero twice each cycle. Select a value of 0.5 radian per sec to give a convenient scale factor.

$$K_v = \frac{\max \left|\frac{d\theta}{dt}\right|}{Cm} = \frac{0.5 \text{ radian/sec}}{100 \text{ volts}}$$

$$= 0.005 \text{ radian/volt-sec} \tag{6-4r}$$

The maximum acceleration will occur when the displacement is maximum and the velocity is zero. Therefore, the maximum acceleration can be computed from Eq. (6-4p) as

$$\max \left|\frac{d^2\theta}{dt^2}\right| = 0.981 \text{ radian/sec}^2 \tag{6-4s}$$

Select a value of 1 radian per sec^2 to give a convenient scale factor.

$$K_a = \frac{\max \left|\frac{d^2\theta}{dt^2}\right|}{Cm}$$

$$= \frac{1 \text{ radian/sec}^2}{100 \text{ volts}}$$

$$= 0.01 \text{ radian/volt-sec}^2 \tag{6-4t}$$

The problem variables can be expressed in terms of computer variables U, V, W as:

$$\Theta = K_d U = 0.001U$$

$$\omega = \frac{d\Theta}{dt} = K_v V = 0.005V$$

$$\frac{d\omega}{dt} = \frac{d^2\Theta}{dt^2} = K_a W = 0.010W \qquad (6\text{-}4u)$$

Substitution of the amplitude scaling of Eq. 6-4u into the equations for the mathematical model, Eqs. (6-4n), (6-4o), and (6-4p), yields the amplitude scaled equations:

$$0.001U = \int (0.005V)dt + 0.001U(0)$$
$$0.005V = \int (0.010W)dt + 0.005V(0)$$
$$(0.010W) + 0.03(0.005V) + 9.81(0.001U) = 0 \qquad (6\text{-}4v)$$

These equations can be solved for the three computer variables $W, U,$ and V:

$$U = \int 5.0V dt + U(0)$$
$$V = \int 2.0W dt + V(0)$$
$$W = -0.015V - 0.981U \qquad (6\text{-}4w)$$

The initial velocity is assumed to be zero, and therefore $V(0) = 0$. The initial displacement is 0.1 radian and therefore $U(0) = 100$ volts.

STEP 3. Implementing the Amplitude Scaled Model

The amplitude scaled equations are implemented as shown in Fig. 6-15. A convenient place to start is to form the voltage, W, by summing appropriate fractions of U and V. The voltage, $-V$, is then formed by integrating the voltage $2W$. The voltage U is formed by integrating the voltage $-5V$. An inverter is required to invert $-V$ to obtain $+V$. A time-base generator is included to provide a voltage increasing at 10 volts per sec. The IC on integrator 07 creates a voltage, T, which starts at -100 volts. Thus a period of 20 sec is available for recording solutions.

STEP 4. Running Trial Solutions and STEP 5. Solving the Problem

These steps are left as an exercise for the student.

134   SECOND-ORDER SYSTEMS

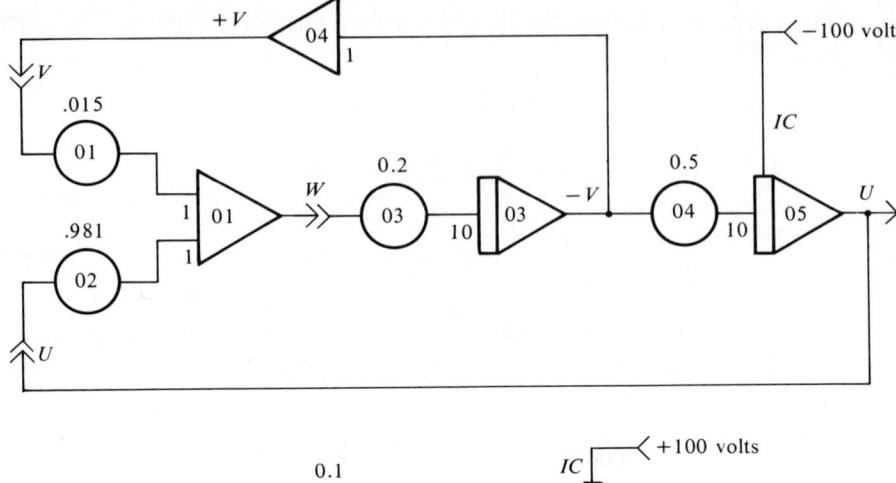

FIG. 6-15
Block Diagram of Analog Model for Grandfather Clock Pendulum.

6-5 Exercises

1. a. Connect the analog model for the pendulum of the grandfather clock and determine the period of oscillation, that is, the time required for one complete cycle. This can best be obtained by recording the displacement for at least ten cycles. Check the computer variables V and W to verify that the scaling is satisfactory.
    b. Reduce the damping to zero and observe the period of oscillation. As long as the damping is small enough, the damping should not much influence the period of oscillation.
2. a. Adjust the length of the pendulum to obtain a period as near to 2.0 seconds as possible.
    b. In physics books it is shown that the frequency of oscillation in radians per sec of a simple pendulum is $\sqrt{g/L}$. The frequency in cycles per sec is obtained by dividing the frequency in radians per sec by 2π. The period of an oscillation is the reciprocal of the frequency in cycles per sec. Using this series of calculations, check to see that the length which you determined does indeed have a period of 2 sec.

3. An assumption was made in the formulation of the mathematical model for the simple pendulum that the sin θ was approximated by the angle θ in radians for small angles. Reduce the initial displacement to 0.05 radians and run a solution for comparison with the solution for an initial displacement of 0.1 radian. A convenient way to compare the solutions is to change the sensitivity of the recorder so that the two curves will be coincident.

4. Consider a Blackburn Double Pendulum which consists of a weight suspended on a string attached to the midpoint of a second string. This second string is attached to two points at the same horizontal elevation. The particular pendulum of interest for this problem has a string 100 cm long attached to two points on a bar which are 60 cm apart. A string 40 cm long is attached by a knot to the midpoint of the first string. Consider that the support is arranged parallel to the x-axis as shown in Fig. 6-16. If the

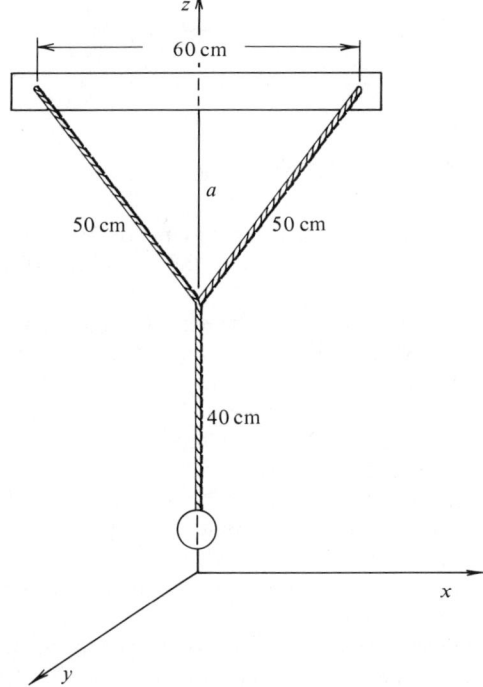

FIG. 6-16
Blackburn Double Pendulum.

pendulum swings only in the y-z plane, the length of the pendulum is effectively 40 cm plus the distance a. If the pendulum swings in the x-z plane, the length is only 40 cm. If it swings in both planes, the total motion is simply the sum of the individual motions.

136   SECOND-ORDER SYSTEMS

    a. Produce an amplitude scaled block diagram representation for an analog computer model for this pendulum. The initial displacement in the x-z plane should be 0.08 radian, and the initial displacement in the y-z plane should be 0.04 radian.

    b. Set the analog model up on an analog computer and study its behavior. *Hint:* You will need to use small angle approximation to convert from analog model variables for the angles with respect to the z-axis into displacements along the x and y axis for plotting.

5. Consider the problem of stopping a rolling freight car such as occurs at the end of a spur track on the railroad. A schematic representation of this system is shown in Fig. 6-17. The mass of the car is 20,000 kg. The rolling

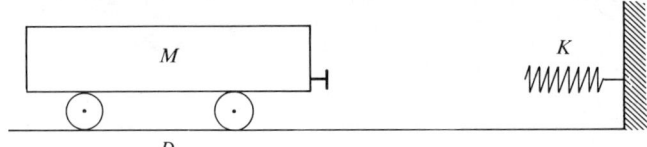

FIG. 6-17
Schematic Representation for Stopping a Rolling Freight Car.

friction of the car at low velocities is 1000 newton-sec per m. The spring coefficient is 5000 newtons per m. The velocity of the car as it strikes the bumper is 0.5 m per sec.

    a. Create a block diagram of the amplitude scaled analog computer model for this system. Chose scaling appropriate to the analog computer which you have available.

    b. Run the analog simulation and determine
        (1) the position of the car vs. time after impact.
        (2) the velocity vs. time after impact.
        (3) the acceleration of the car vs. time after impact.

    c. What is the maximum deflection of the spring, and what is the maximum deceleration of the car?

    d. Based on the results of your analog simulation, should more damping be added to reduce the rebound?

    e. For the system as modeled, determine by trial and error the maximum initial velocity with which the car can strike the bumper for a maximum deceleration of 0.2 g.

6. Modify the model of Exercise 5 and determine how far the car would roll on level track in the absence of the bumper for initial velocities of
    a. 2 m/sec.
    b. 1 m/sec.
    c. 0.5 m/sec.

7. In what way can the analog model of Fig. 6-12 for the swing door be simplified to use less equipment? Draw the simplified block diagram.

CHAPTER 7 NONLINEAR OPERATIONS

The assumption that systems are linear makes the mathematical analysis much simpler. Many real life systems however are not linear, and hence the analysis may be quite difficult without the assistance of computers. If the analog computer is to be of aid in these situations, means must be found to model nonlinear phenomena. The electrical diode is a nonlinear resistor and is very useful in creating analog models.

7-1 Diode Limiters

The electrical diode has the property that the resistance is very low for current flow in one direction, called the forward direction. The resistance to current flow in the opposite direction, called the reverse direction, is very high. Symbols for diodes are shown in Fig. 7-1. The

138   NONLINEAR OPERATIONS

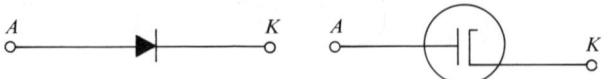

FIG. 7-1

Symbols for Electrical Diodes.

symbol on the left is that commonly used for semiconductor diodes and the symbol on the right is that used for vacuum diodes. Semiconductor diodes are widely used in analog computers today because they have adequate ratios of backward to forward resistance and they do not have the heaters of the vacuum diodes. The forward direction is that indicated by the arrow. It is customary to mark the cathode end with a *K*, or perhaps just with a band. The operation of diodes in a simple circuit is illustrated in Fig. 7-2. In the left circuit the current is flowing in the re-

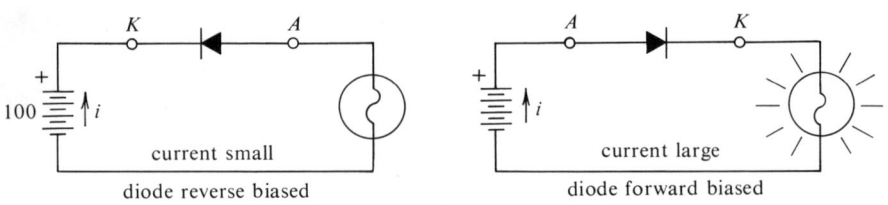

FIG. 7-2

Simple Diode Circuits.

verse direction through the diode, and hence the diode exhibits a very high resistance. Since the back resistance of the diode is very large compared to the resistance of the lamp, the lamp does not light. The diode is said to be reverse biased. The connection of the diode has been reversed in the circuit on the right; and the current now is flowing in the forward direction of the diode, which is the low resistance direction. Since the forward resistance of the diode is small compared to the resistance of the lamp, the lamp lights. The diode is now said to be forward biased. The diode thus functions as a switch in an electrical circuit. If the current tries to flow in the preferred direction, the switch is closed. When the current tries to flow in the reverse direction, the diode acts as an open switch.

Consider now the analog computer circuit shown in Fig. 7-3. A diode has been connected in series with the feedback resistor. When the input voltage is positive, the output voltage is negative, and the diode is conducting current in the forward direction. The forward resistance of the

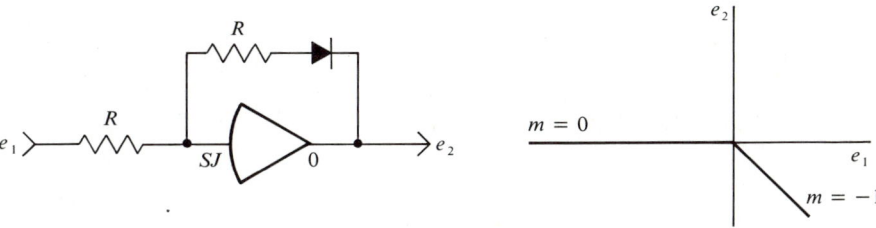

FIG. 7-3
Inverter with the Diode in the Feedback Path.

diode is small compared to the resistance, R, and hence the inverter functions in the usual manner. However when the input voltage becomes negative, the output voltage tries to go positive and the current in the feedback resistor is now trying to flow through the diode in the reverse direction. The reverse resistance of the diode is very large compared to the feedback resistor, R, and hence the voltage gain of the inverter is very low. A plot of the output voltage, e_2, vs. the input voltage, e_1, is also shown in Fig. 7-3. Such a plot of an output variable vs. an input variable is called a transfer characteristic. The circuit functions as a limiter since the output voltage is limited to negative values of voltage. The switching point of actual diodes may be a few tenths of a volt positive, rather than zero voltage as is the case for an ideal diode. If the diode is placed in parallel with the feedback resistor as shown in Fig. 7-4, the nature of the

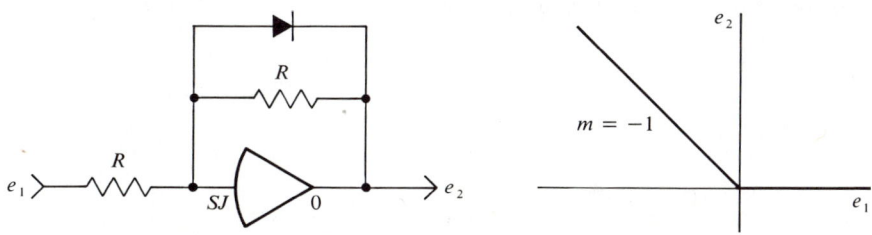

FIG. 7-4
Inverter with Diode in Parallel with the Feedback System.

limiting is reversed. When the output voltage is positive, the diode is reverse biased, and the circuit functions as a normal inverter with unity gain. When the input voltage goes positive, the output tries to go negative, but the diode is then forward biased and hence has a low resistance. Since the gain is the ratio of the feedback resistance to the input resistance, the

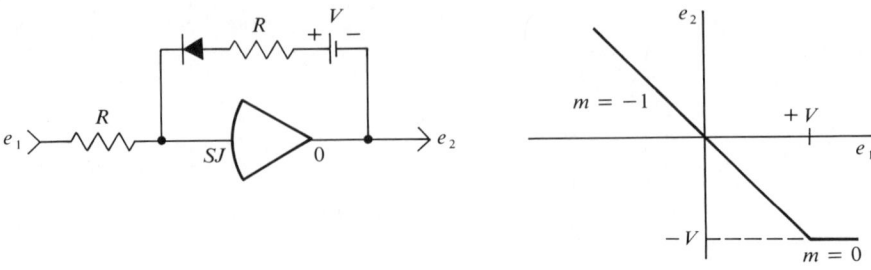

FIG. 7-5

Inverter with a Diode and Battery in the Feedback Path.

gain becomes very small, and the output voltage, e_2, is constrained from going negative.

Consider now the circuit shown in Fig. 7-5, which has added a battery in series with the diode and the feedback resistor. This battery is assumed to have a voltage, V, and to have an internal resistance that is negligibly small compared to R. As long as the output voltage, e_2, is positive, the diode will be forward biased and so will have a very low resistance. When the output voltage is equal to $-V$, the voltage across the diode will be zero because the summing junction is at a potential very near to zero. When the input becomes more positive, the diode is reverse biased, and the output voltage is prevented from going more negative than $-V$. Although this circuit is simple to understand, it is not convenient to supply the voltage, V. Therefore, the circuit that is usually used is that shown in Fig. 7-6. This circuit is a variation of that of Fig. 7-4 where the diode

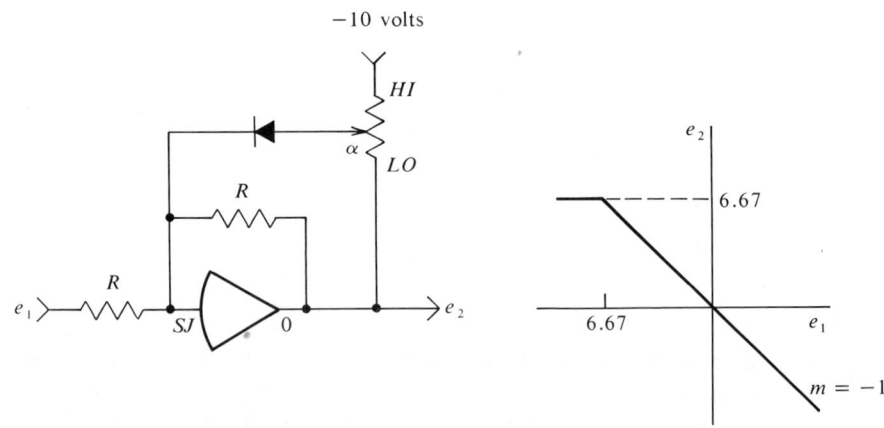

FIG. 7.6

Practical Limiting Circuit for Positive Voltages.

was in parallel with the feedback resistor. Assume that the potentiometer is set for a ratio of $\alpha = 0.40$. The voltage at the ARM of the potentiometer would be -4.0 volts when $e_2 = 0$, and therefore the diode is reverse biased.

The diode will be reverse biased as long as the potential at the arm of the potentiometer is negative. When the voltage, e_2 has become sufficiently positive, there will be a potential difference of ten volts across the upper portion of the potentiometer, and the voltage at the arm will be zero. Under these conditions the voltage across the diode is zero, and any further increase in the voltage, e_2, will cause the diode to be forward biased. The voltage across the entire potentiometer is $e_2 + 10$. The voltage across the upper part is:

$$(1 - \alpha)(e_2 + 10) \tag{7-1a}$$

The switching point, or zero voltage condition on the diode, occurs when this voltage is equal to 10 volts. This condition gives Eq. (7-1b).

$$(1 - \alpha)(e_2 + 10) = 10 \tag{7-1b}$$

Substitution of 0.4 for α and solving for e_2 yields

$$e_2 = +6.67 \tag{7-1c}$$

For any input voltage more negative than -6.67, the diode will be forward biased, the feedback resistance will be very low, and the output voltage is constrained to be not more than $+6.67$ volts. Rather

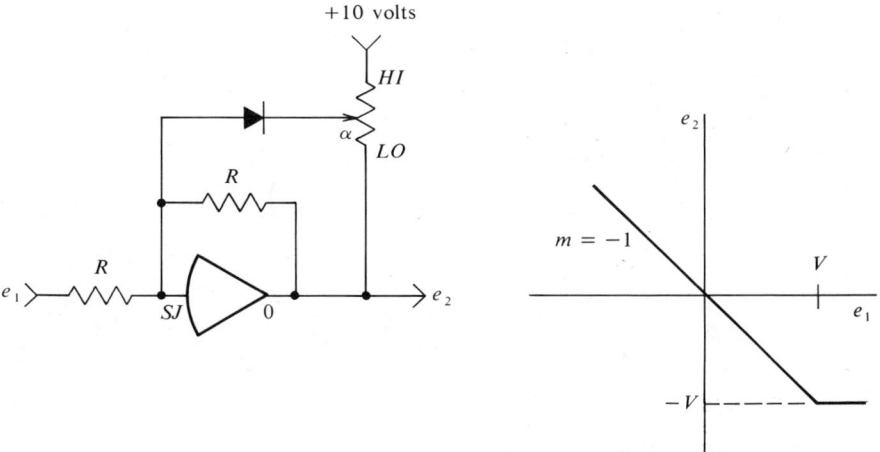

FIG. 7-7
Limiting Circuit for Negative Output Voltages.

142   NONLINEAR OPERATIONS

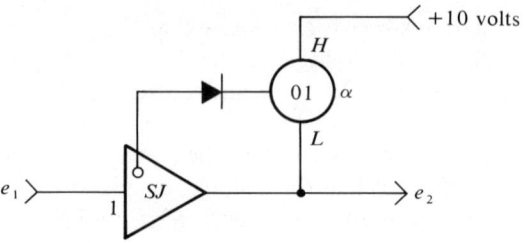

FIG. 7-8

Block Diagram Representation of Limiting Circuit.

than computing the ratio to be set on the potentiometer, the usual procedure is to connect the circuit, supply a -10 volts for e_1, and adjust the potentiometer to give the desired output voltage. The circuit would be set up as shown in Fig. 7-7 to limit in the other quadrant. The block diagram representation of such a circuit is shown in Fig. 7-8. These circuits demonstrate an application for the potentiometers that have the lower end ungrounded. Note that the anode end of the diode is connected to the summing junction, SJ, rather than to an input resistor.

Consider now the functional relationship between y and x that is described by the graph of Fig. 7-9. This function is to be modeled on a 10-volt analog computer. This function can be broken into two parts called y_1 and y_2 as shown in Fig. 7-10. If y_1 is added to y_2, the result

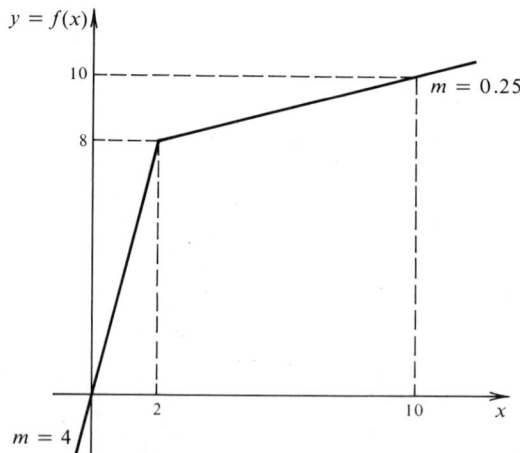

FIG. 7-9

Graphical Definition of $y = f(x)$.

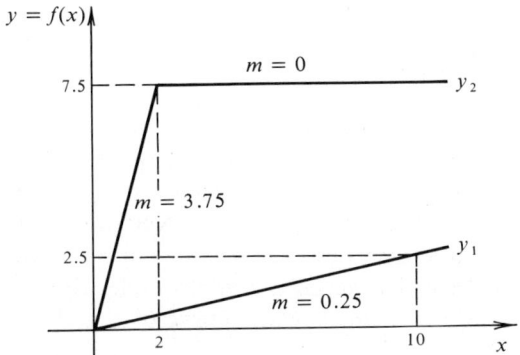

FIG. 7-10

Decomposition of $f(x)$ into Two Functions: y_1 and y_2.

will be the desired function. When x equals 2.0, y_1 equals 0.5, and y_2 equals 7.5, these two values add to give the desired value of 8.0 as required by Fig. 7-9. When x equals 10.0, y_1 equals 2.5, y_2 equals 7.5, and the sum of y_1 and y_2 equals 10.0 as required. These functions can be created as shown by the block diagram of Fig. 7-11. Inverter 01 produces $-x$, which is converted to $-y_1$ by potentiometer 03. Amplifier 03 inverts this $-y_1$ to produce the $+y_1$ component of y. The inverter 02 with a gain of 10.0 produces $-y_2$ with a slope of -3.75. The diode and potentiometer 02 constrains y_2 to be not more negative than -7.5 volts. Amplifier 03 inverts this $-y_2$ to produce the $+y_2$ component of y.

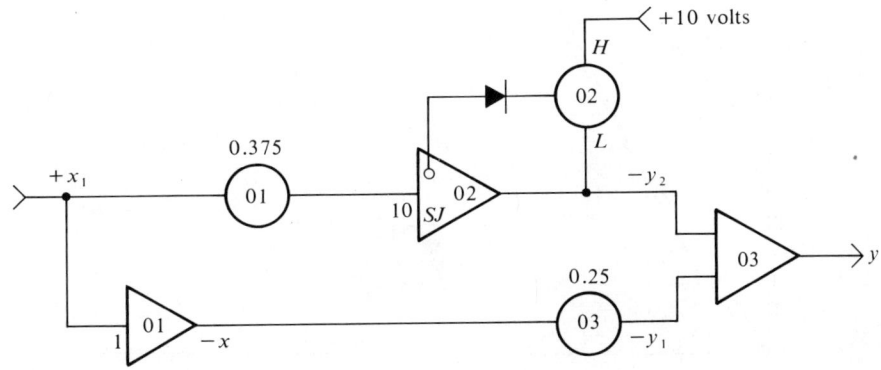

FIG. 7-11

Generation of $f(x)$ by Summing Negative y_1 and Negative y_2.

7-2 Diode Function Generators

Although it would be possible to approximate functions by using a number of simple diode limiter circuits discussed in the previous section, this would not be particularly convenient. Collections of diodes, resistors, and potentiometers are assembled into units called diode function generators. Some of these units are designed to be adjustable so that the user can approximate special functions. For example, the relation between the variables x and y is defined by the curve of Fig. 7-12. This

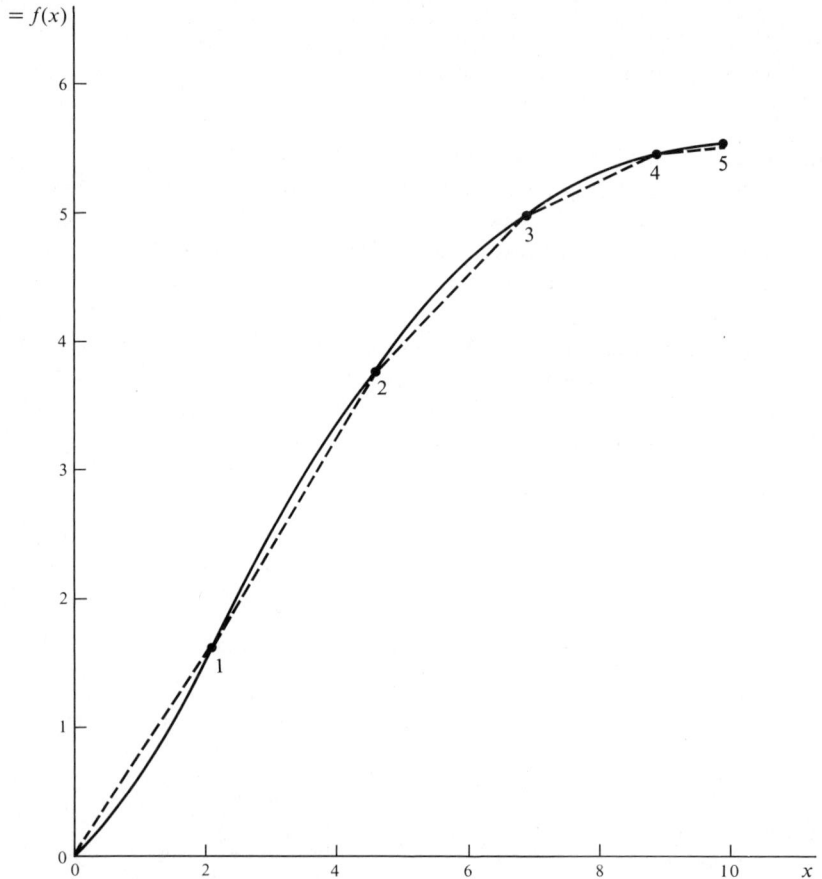

FIG. 7-12
Variable Diode Function Generator.

curve can be approximated by a series of straight lines such as the dashed lines shown. In this example five straight line segments are used to approximate the actual function. The general procedure for setting up a diode function generator is the following:

a. Move all break points to the upper limit.
b. Adjust the slope and intercept of the first segment.
c. Move the first breakpoint in to the proper location.
d. Adjust the slope of the second segment.
e. Continue until all of the segments have been set properly.

The manuals for your computer should be consulted for specific details on patching and adjusting the diode function generators on your computer.

7-3 Multipliers

The operation of multiplying two variables together is frequently desired. This process has been implemented in at least three different ways on analog computers: quarter-square multipliers, time-division multiplication, and servo multipliers. With the development of economical diode function generators for producing the square of a voltage, the quarter square multiplier has become very popular. This multiplier is based on the algebraic identity

$$XY = \frac{[(X+Y)^2 - (X-Y)^2]}{4} \qquad (7\text{-}3a)$$

This equation can be implemented in principle by the block diagram shown in Fig. 7-13. This circuit requires five summer-inverters. The

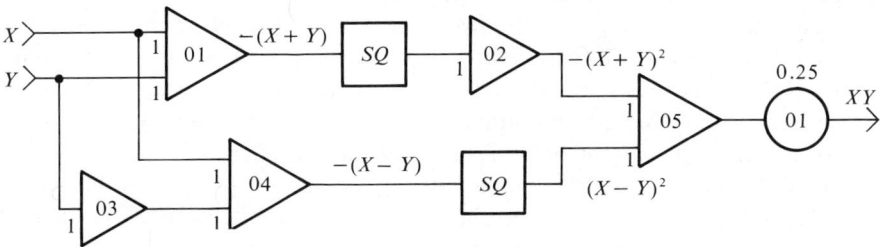

FIG. 7-13
Block-Diagram of Principle of Quarter Square Multiplier.

scheme is implemented somewhat more efficiently in practice by combining some of these operations. A multiplier may still require three operational amplifiers unless both the positive and the negative representation of both variables is available. The block diagram representation for quarter-square multipliers such as used by EAI on the TR-20 is shown in Fig. 7-14. The patch panel connections are shown on the right

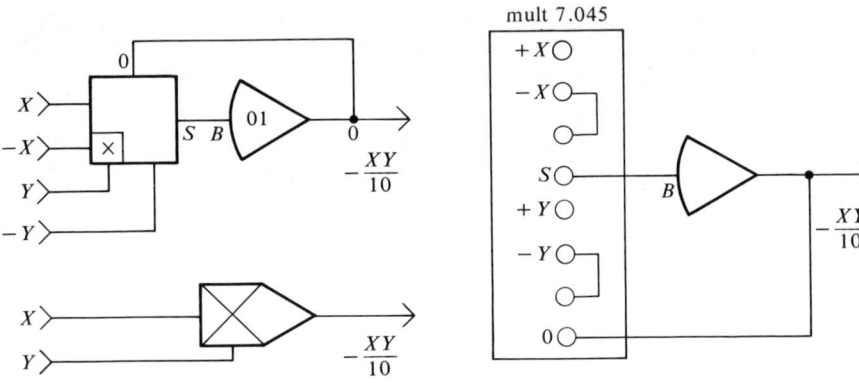

FIG. 7-14

Block Diagram of Actual Multipliers.

side of this figure. Inverters are required to produce the inverted signals if they are not otherwise available. The simplified block diagram representation is often used to show multipliers, but all of the detail is required for actually connecting the multiplier. The connections for the BURR-BROWN Model 600 multiplier is shown in Appendix I-B.

Notice that the multipliers when implemented as a unit for the TR-20 or the BB-600 have a factor of 10 included in the design. This is done to permit two voltages of 10 volts to be multiplied together without going beyond the range of the computing equipment. This factor of ten must be taken into account in creating the analog model. If the computer was designed for 100 volt reference voltages, the dividing factor would be 100 so that two voltages of 100 volts would produce a product which was 100 volts. The quarter square multiplier units can obviously be used to produce the square of a variable by making $Y = X$. Diode function generators are available for producing the square of a variable. These special units may be more economical for some applications. The quarter square multipliers can also be used to implement the process of division as shown in Fig. 7-15.

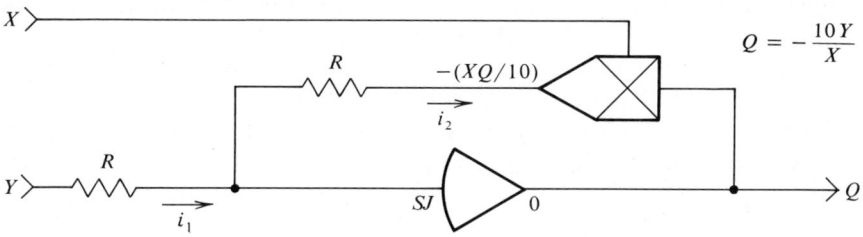

FIG. 7-15

Block Diagram of Analog Division Circuit Using a Multiplier.

The operation of the circuit is evident from the constraint that the current, i_2, is equal to the current, i_1.

$$i_1 = \frac{Y}{R} = i_2 = -\frac{QX}{10R}$$

$$Q = -10\frac{Y}{X} \qquad (7\text{-}3b)$$

This process of division has the property that the quotient of two voltages which are 10 volts will be a voltage which is also 10 volts. This amplitude scaling must also be taken into account when the analog model is created. The division process is implemented on the TR-20 computer as shown in the diagram of Fig. 7-16. The nature of the process requires that the

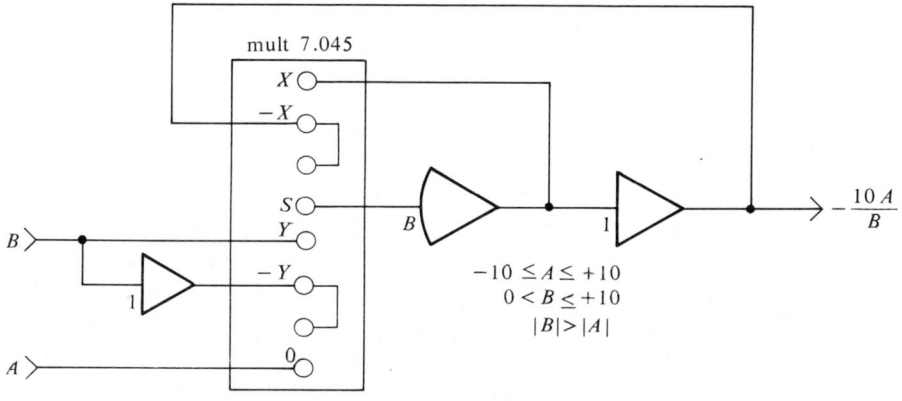

FIG. 7-16

Circuit for Division on the TR-20 Analog Computer.

indicated limitations be placed on the variables. See the manual for your analog computer for details of this and other applications such as square root of the quarter-square or other multipliers available to you. The principles outlined here for the applications of the quarter-square multiplier also apply to time-division multipliers and to servo multipliers. An example showing the use of the multiplier will be considered after the sine-cosine generator is presented in the next section.

7-4 Sine-Cosine Generator

The problem of the pendulum involved the need for a sine function in order to model the pendulum for other than small deflections. Sine and cosine functions arise in many places where forces or motions must be broken into components. Special diode function generators are made for this purpose. These functions can also be generated by electromechanical servo type devices with special potentiometers which have an output voltage proportional to the sine or the cosine of the angle of rotation of the shaft of the potentiometer. The diode type generators are generally preferred today because they can operate at much higher speeds than the servo type generators. This process also must be scaled to produce the reference voltage when the angle is 90°. The generation of sine and cosine functions can be represented as shown in Fig. 7-17

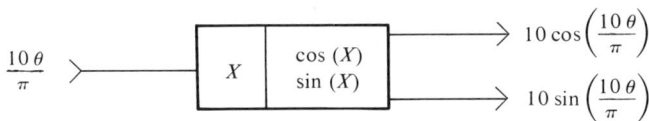

FIG. 7-17

Generation of Sine and Cosine Functions.

for a computer with reference voltage of 10 volts. The angle must be scaled according to the reference voltage of the computer and the range of the input angle for which the generator is designed. Typically the range of input angle is $\pm 180°$ or expressed in radians $\pm \pi$. The implementation of the sinc-cosine generator usually requires the use of several summer-inverters in a manner similar to that for the multiplication and division circuits previously considered. Consult the manuals for your particular computer for details on patching the sine-cosine generator.

SINE-COSINE GENERATOR

EXAMPLE 7-1

Consider the problem of computing the position or a vehicle in terms of the speed and bearing of the vehicle. The parameters of the problem are as follows:

> Speed: 0 to 1800 knots
> Bearing: $\pm 180°$ relative to north
> Distance: N-S $\pm$ 100 nautical miles
> E-W $\pm$ 70 nautical miles

The knot as a unit of speed is one nautical mile per hour. For convenience take the same scale factor on distance in both the E-W and N-S direction.

$$K_x = K_y = \frac{100 \text{ miles}}{10 \text{ volts}} = 10 \text{ miles/volt} \qquad (7\text{-}4a)$$

The amplitude scale factor for speed is as follows:

$$K_s = \frac{1800 \text{ knots}}{10 \text{ volts}} = 180 \text{ knots/volt} \qquad (7\text{-}4b)$$

The amplitude scale factor for the angle β is determined by the construction of the sine-cosine generator. Let us assume that a 10-volt input corresponds to 180°.

$$K_\beta = \frac{\max |\beta|}{Cm} = \frac{180 \text{ degrees}}{10 \text{ volts}}$$

$$= 18 \text{ degrees/volt} \qquad (7\text{-}4c)$$

Assume that the computer voltages X, Y, S, and B represent problem variables x, y, speed, and bearing. Then the amplitude scale factors relate problem variables to the analog model variables as follows:

$$x = 10X$$
$$y = 10Y$$
$$s = 180S$$
$$\beta = 18B \qquad (7\text{-}4d)$$

150 NONLINEAR OPERATIONS

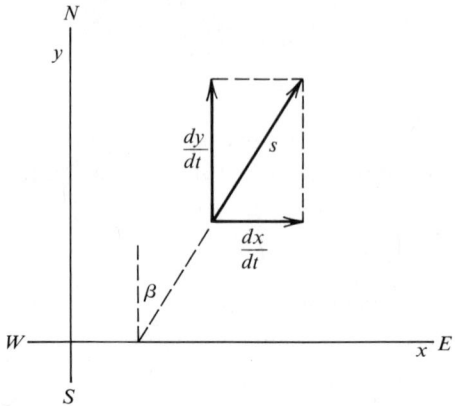

FIG. 7-18

Geometry of Relations Between Speed, Bearing, and Velocity Components.

The speed s can be resolved into components as shown in Fig. 7-18. The components dx/dt and dy/dt of the speed, s, of the vehicle are computed as follows:

$$\frac{dx}{dt} = s \sin \beta$$

$$\frac{dy}{dt} = s \cos \beta \tag{7-4e}$$

The x and y coordinates of the vehicle are computed by integrating these components:

$$x = \int \frac{dx}{dt} dt + x(0) = \int (s \sin \beta)dt + x(0)$$

$$y = \int \frac{dy}{dt} dt + y(0) = \int (s \cos \beta)dt + y(0) \tag{7-4f}$$

Substitution of the amplitude scaling Eqs. (7-4d) into Eqs. (7-4e) and dividing by ten yields the equations for the analog model.

$$X = \int 18S \sin (18B)dt + X(0)$$

$$Y = \int 18S \cos (18B)dt + Y(0) \tag{7-4g}$$

SINE-COSINE GENERATOR

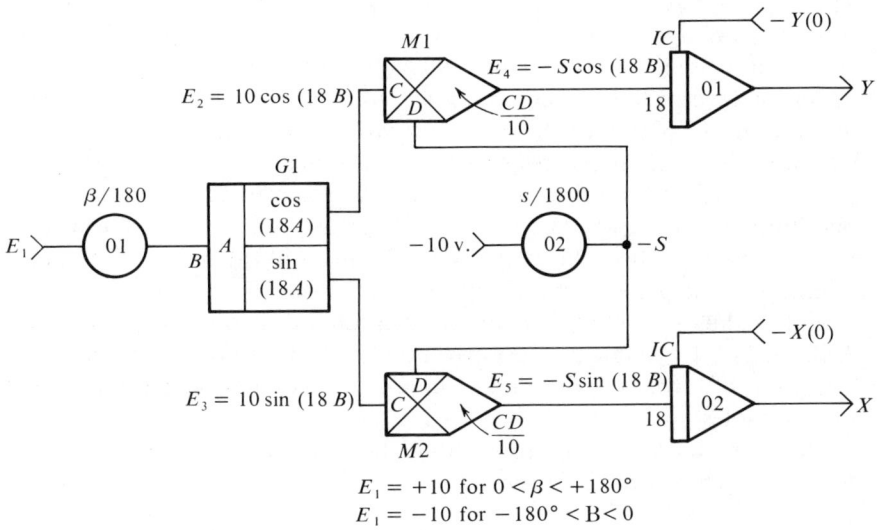

$E_1 = +10$ for $0 < \beta < +180°$
$E_1 = -10$ for $-180° < B < 0$

FIG. 7-19

Block Diagram of Analog Computer Model Demonstrating the Use of Multipliers and Sine-Cosine Generator.

The block diagram of Fig. 7-19 shows how the analog computer model is connected. The polarity, plus or minus, of the voltage E connected to the input side of potentiometer 01 determines whether the bearing β is east of north or west of north. The sine-cosine generator G1 produces the functions of $18B$ degrees multiplied by the reference voltage of 10 volts. Notice that this factor of ten and the divisor of ten on the multipliers, M1 and M2, cancel to give the inputs shown for the integrators 01 and 02. Gains of 18 are used on the integrators to meet the conditions specified by Eqs. (7-4g).

As a check on the analog model assume that the vehicle is moving at a speed of 900 knots at a bearing of 90° East of North. Further assume, for simplicity, that $x(0) = y(0) = 0$. The ratio set on potentiometer 01 is 0.50 and the voltage B is 5 volts. This 5 volts input to the sine-cosine generator G1 produces functions of 90°, and hence E_2 equals zero and $E_3 = 10$ volts. The voltage S is minus 5 volts. The voltage E_4 is zero because the voltage E_2 is zero. The voltage E_5 is as follows:

$$E_5 = \frac{CD}{10} = \frac{10(-5)}{10} = -5.0 \text{ volts} \qquad (7\text{-}4\text{h})$$

The voltage Y remains at zero because the input to the integrator 01 is zero. The voltage X increases at the rate of 90 volts per second since the input voltage is $18(-5)$ or -90 volts. Thus after one second of operation (except that the computer would overload after approximately 0.1 second of operation) the voltage X would have increased from 0 to 90 volts. This voltage corresponds to a distance of 900 nautical miles. A distance of 900 nautical miles should be reached at 900 knots after one hour, not one sec. The error arose because the unit of speed, the knot is based on the hour as the unit of time, and the unit of time used to compute the gains of the integrators is the sec. The analog computer model is thus running 3600 times faster than real time. One hour or 3600 seconds of problem time corresponds to one sec of computer time. This kind of error is easy to make unless care is taken with the units of rate variables.

The gains on the integrators should be reduced by a factor of 3600 to 0.005 as shown by Eq. (7-4i)

$$\frac{18}{3600} = \frac{1}{200} = 0.005 \tag{7-4i}$$

This value will make 1 sec of problem time equal 1 sec of computer time. A more appropriate scaling might be to make 1 minute of problem time equal to 1 sec of computer time. Such scaling gives integrator gains of 0.30, which are more feasible than either of the previous values of 0.005 or 18.

7-5 Comparators

In some problems it is necessary to compare two variables. For example, suppose that we were interested in creating an analog model for a sump pump operation. Water collects in the sump until the level of the water reaches a depth, U, at which time the pump is turned on and water is pumped out. When the water level falls to a depth, L, the pump is turned off. The operation of a comparator can be thought of as that of a polarized relay. An ordinary relay operates when a sufficient current flows through the winding in either direction. A polarized relay, however, operates only when there is sufficient current flowing in a particular direction. The symbol frequently used on the patch panel of analog computers for comparators is a relay symbol. The two input terminals are distinguished by polarity marks, + or −, or perhaps by different numbers. See Fig. 7-20. If the voltage applied to the terminal

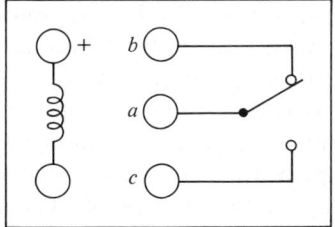

FIG. 7-20

Representation of Analog Comparator.

marked + is indeed positive with respect to the other terminal, then the relay in the comparator is energized and the circuit is completed through the normally open contacts from *a* to *c*. If the voltage applied to the terminal marked + is negative with respect to the other terminal, then the relay is not energized and the circuit is completed through the normally closed relay contacts from *a* to *b*. Comparators may have more than one set of contacts, and some comparators are all solid state, that is, these comparators do not have electromechanical relays to perform the switching. These solid state comparators operate much faster than

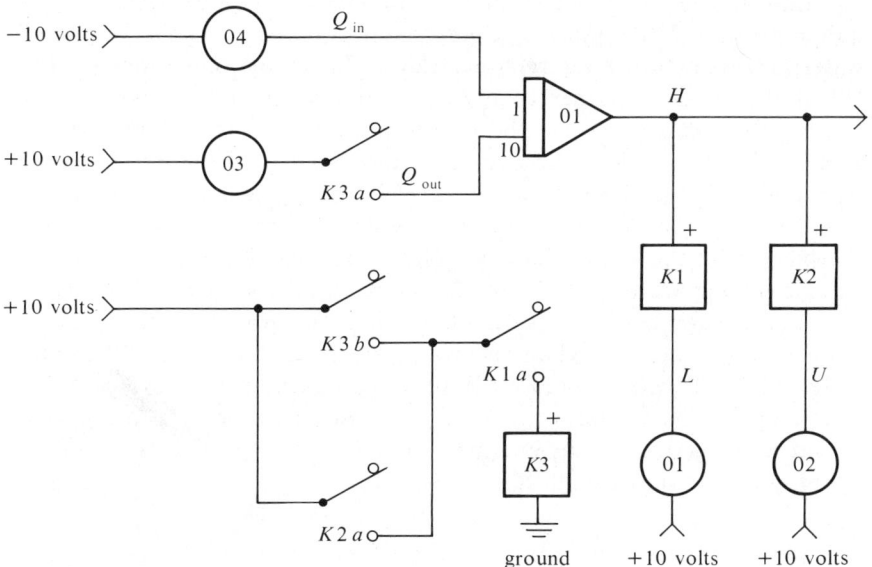

FIG. 7-21

Analog Model for Sump Pump Problem.

154 NONLINEAR OPERATIONS

relays and so are particularly desirable for REP-OP type solutions. Consult the manual on your computer for details on the terminal marking of the comparators you are using. It is also important to note the particular limitations that may exist as to the amount of current that the contacts can safely carry. For example, in the analog model shown in Fig. 7-21, it may not be desirable to place the contacts on comparator $K3$ between the $+10$ reference voltage and the HI end of POT 03 although the switching effect would be the same. The current to the HI terminal is much greater than is the current which flows in the ARM of the potentiometer.

EXAMPLE 7-2

Consider the problem of the sump pump proposed earlier. A block diagram of the analog model is shown in Fig. 7-21. Potentiometer 04 regulates the rate at which water flows into the tank and potentiometer 03 regulates the rate at which water is pumped out of the tank. When the contacts $K3a$ are in the position shown, the pump is turned off because the ARM of potentiometer 03 is not connected to the integrator input. When the contacts $K3a$ shift to the other position, a positive voltage is applied to the integrator input that will reduce the voltage, H, representing the depth of water in the sump. Three comparators are required to model this system. Comparator $K1$ compares the height of water, H, with the lower reference level, L, set by potentiometer 01. When the water is deeper than L, the comparator energizes its relay causing the contacts to take the position opposite to that shown on the sketch. The comparator $K2$ compares the depth of the water, H, with the upper reference level, U, which is set by potentiometer 02. When the water is above the level, U, both $K1$ and $K2$ are energized. This completes the path from the $+10$ reference voltage through $K2a$ and $K1a$ which energizes comparator $K3$. When $K3$ is energized, the "pump" is turned on and the water level begins to fall. The contacts $K3b$ prevent the pump from being turned off when the water level falls below U. When the water level falls below the lower limit, L, comparator $K1$ is de-energized which opens the circuit through $K1a$ to comparator $K3$. When this circuit is opened, $K3$ is de-energized and the "pump" is turned off by opening the circuit through $K3a$.

7-6 Exercises

1. Sketch the transfer characteristic for the analog circuit shown in Fig. 7-22.
2. Sketch the block diagram for an analog circuit that will provide the transfer characteristic shown in Fig. 7-23.

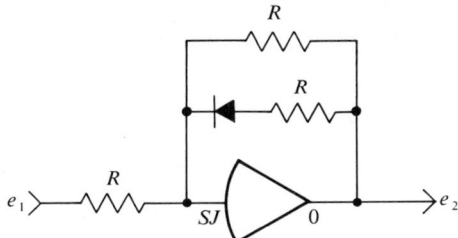

FIG. 7-22

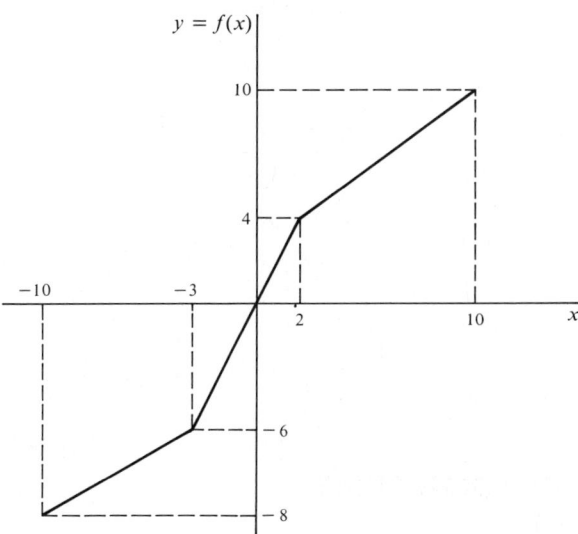

FIG. 7-23

3. Check the manuals for your computer and sketch the panel connections for
   a. forming the product of two variables,
   b. forming the square of a variable which is always positive,
   c. forming the square of a variable which is always negative,
   d. forming the sine and cosine function of a variable,
   e. forming the quotient of two variables for which the divisor is always positive,
   f. forming the absolute value of a variable.
4. Connect up the analog model of the sump pump and observe how the cycling of the pump is influenced by the rate at which water runs into the sump. Also investigate the effect of reducing the difference between the turn-on level, L, and the turn-off level, U.

BIBLIOGRAPHY

Textbooks

1. Ashley, J. Robert, *Introduction to Analog Computation*, John Wiley & Sons, New York, 1965.
2. Jenness, Roger R., *Analog Computation and Simulation: Laboratory Approach*, Allyn and Bacon, Boston, 1965.
3. Korn, G. A.; Korn, T. M., *Electronic Analog Computers*, McGraw-Hill Book Co., New York, 1956.
4. Peterson, Gerald R., *Basic Analog Computation*, The Macmillan Company, New York, 1967.
5. Rekoff, Michael G. Jr., *Analog Computer Programming*, Charles E. Merrill Publishing Co., Columbus, Ohio, 1967.
6. Stice, James E.; Swanson, Bernet S., *Electronic Analog Computer Primer*, Blaisdell Publishing Co., Waltham, Mass., 1965.
7. Warfield, John N., *Introduction to Analog Computers*, Prentice-Hall, Englewood Cliffs, N.J., 1959.

Periodicals

IEEE Transactions on Education, Institute of Electrical and Electronic Engineers, 345 E. 47th St., New York, N.Y. 00017.

IEEE Transactions on Electronic Computers, Institute of Electrical and Electronic Engineers, 345 E. 47th St., New York, N.Y. 10017.

Newsletter, Analog/Hybrid Computer Users Group, P.O. Box 582, Princeton, New Jersey 08540.

Simulation, Simulation Councils, Inc., P.O. Box 2228, La Jolla, California, 92037.

APPENDIX I

A. BASIC OPERATION OF THE ELECTRONIC ASSOCIATES TR-20 ANALOG COMPUTER

I-A-1 General Description

The Electronic Associates TR-20 is an all solid-state (transistorized) analog computer. The reference levels are ± 10 volts. The standard computer has ten chopper stabilized operational amplifiers, four integrator networks, ten potentiometers, a reference potentiometer, a volt meter, a set of overload indicators, and a mode control switch. This basic unit can be expanded up to a total of twenty operational amplifiers and twenty potentiometers. Integrator networks, comparators, function generators, multiplier networks, and other special functions can also be added. All of these additional functions can be added without any additional wiring in the console because the connectors into which these modules plug are wired at the factory when the computer is manufactured. The integrator networks may be obtained with provisions for REP-OP (repetitive operation) for an additional charge. A REP-OP control unit must also be added to provide for this type of operation. All of the components for the computing networks are contained inside the computing modules. The connections are made by plugging patch cords in an appropriate manner between terminals on the front panel, or by plugging in special jumper plugs. A prepatch panel can be added to permit programs to be patched together away from the computer, and then the panel is inserted to connect the units on the computer as desired. This prepatch capability permits wired programs to be saved, and the computer can be used for other problems by using a different prepatch panel. The sections which follow describe how the patching (connecting) of the modules is done on the TR-20 analog computer and how the computer is operated.

I-A-2 Multiplication by a Constant

The potentiometers are mounted two to a panel, and the connections are shown in Fig. I-1. These potentiometers are multiturn potentiometers and are set to a desired ratio by comparison to a master potentiometer. The lower end of the potentiometer whose terminals are on the left side is internally connected to ground or zero reference. The lower end of the other potentiometer must be grounded by a shorting plug for normal operation. The ground terminal is located to the left of the terminal for the lower end of the right potentiometer. To set a ratio of 0.75 on potentiometer 1 proceed as follows:

 a. Set the switch on the master potentiometer to $+10$.
 b. Set the master potentiometer for a reading of 0.75.
 c. Turn the voltmeter function switch to POT BUS.
 d. Press the button beside the knob for potentiometer 1 and turn the potentiometer knob to obtain a zero reading on the voltmeter.

If the output of the potentiometer is connected to an input resistor, the effect of "loading" is automatically compensated. The upper knob controls the potentiometer connected to the left set of terminals and the lower knob controls the potentiometer connected to the right set of terminals. The voltmeter will deflect off scale unless the potentiometers are very nearly to the same ratio. If the meter deflects down scale, the knob on the potentiometer should be turned clockwise to equalize the

APPENDIX I-A

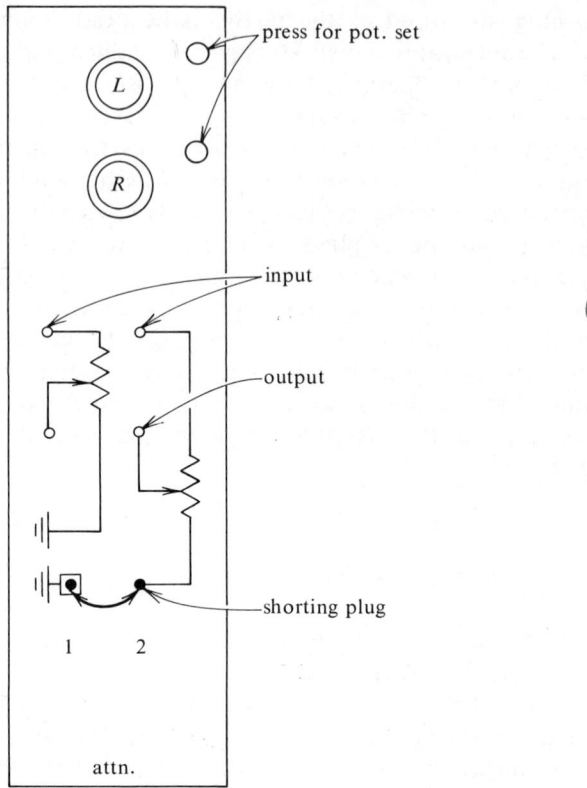

Note: Total resistance of the potentiometer is 5000 ohms

FIG. I-1

Potentiometer Panel on TR-20.

ratios. (Counterclockwise if the meter deflects up scale.) The meter is protected such that off-scale deflection does not damage the meter in the POT BUS mode of operation.

I-A-3 Inversion and Summation

The TR-20 computer is connected for summation or inversion as shown in Fig. I-2. The resistors connected to terminals marked "1" have a resistance of 100,000 ohms. The resistors connected to the terminals marked

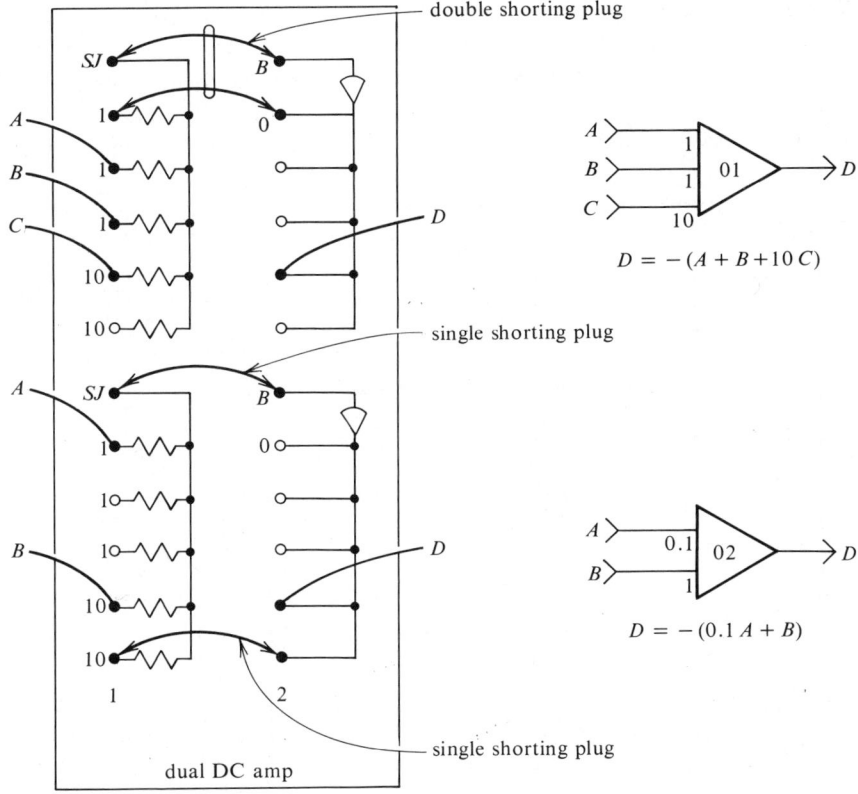

FIG. 1-2

Amplifier Panel on TR-20 With Connections for Summation.

"10" have a resistance of 10,000 ohms. The terminals in the red area of the panel are all connected together and are the output terminals of the operational amplifier. The upper amplifier, 1, has the summing junction connected to the input and the output connected to a feedback resistor by means of a double bottle plug. The numbers by the input terminals (green region on the panel) are the factors by which the input is multiplied in the process of summation. If only one input is used, then the operation is that of inversion. The lower amplifier, 2, has been connected by using two single bottle plugs. The feedback resistor is now one tenth the previous value, and so the gains are reduced by a factor of ten. The student should verify these gains from the principles of Chapter 2.

I-A-4 Integration

The integrating capacitors on the TR-20 are located in units named DUAL INT. The lower pair of terminals on the INT unit must be shorted by single bottle plugs as shown in Fig. I-3. These connections provide

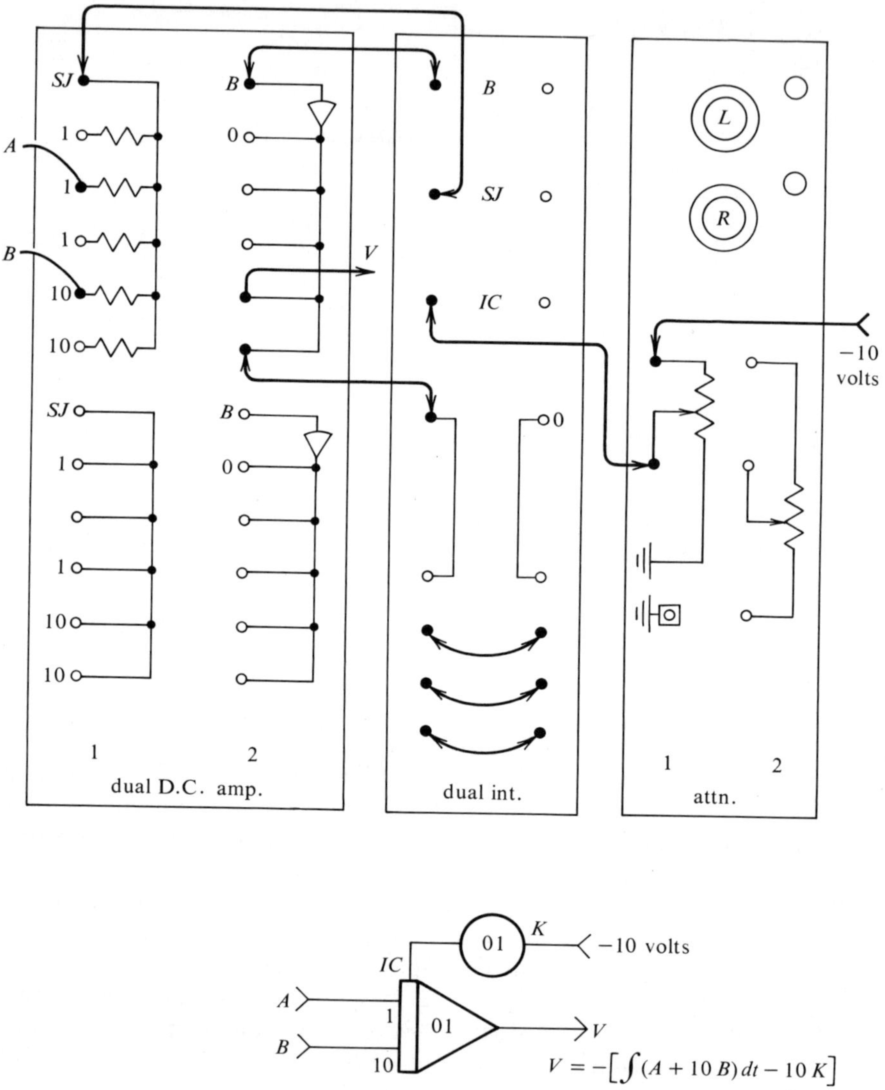

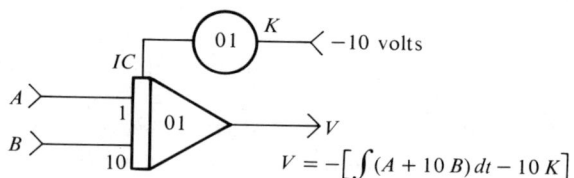

FIG. I-3

Block Diagram and Panel Connections for TR-20 for Integration.

for the operation of the relays which switch the computer from RESET to HOLD to OPERATE. Three connections must be made between the operational amplifier and the integrator unit. The pairs of terminals marked *B, SJ,* and *O* must be connected together as shown in Fig. I-3. The integrator gains are the numbers marked by the input terminals. The initial condition voltage is connected to the terminal marked *IC*. The sign change that is inherent in all analog operations occurs here also, and therefore, -5 volts connected to the *IC* terminal causes the initial condition to be $+5$ volts. The pair of terminals just below the output terminals must be connected by a single bottle plug for the repetitive mode of operation (REP-OP). The integrating capacitor has a value of 10 micro-farads when the computer operates in the normal mode. This value of capacitor and an input resistor of 100,000 ohms gives a gain of one as described in Chapter 3. When the computer is operated in the REP-OP mode, the value of all integrating capacitors is 0.02 micro-farad, and the gains of all integrators are multiplied by 500.

I-A-5 Normal Operation of TR-20

1. Be certain that feedback is provided on all amplifiers, that is, each amplifier should be connected for operation either as a summer with bottle plugs, or as an integrator by removing the bottle plug and patching to an integrator unit.
2. Make other connections as required for the problem.
3. Set the MODE control to RESET.
4. Set the COMPUTE TIME control to OFF.
5. Set the VOLTMETER range switch to 10.
6. Turn the POWER switch ON. The overload indicators will light temporarily, but should go out after a few sec.
7. Set the MASTER POT switch to $+10$.
8. Set the VOLTMETER function switch to POT BUS.
9. Adjust each potentiometer for a zero reading on the voltmeter with the POT BALANCE procedure described above.
10. Set the VOLTMETER function switch to AMPL.
11. Select the amplifier whose output is to be observed by setting the AMPL switch to the number of that amplifier.
12. Set the MODE control to OPER, and the computer solves the problem for which it is programmed. The solution is displayed by the voltmeter, or plotted by an attached plotter. After the desired solution has been generated, the MODE control should be placed in either HOLD or RESET. The HOLD mode stops the solution and the value of all voltages remains constant. The RESET mode re-initializes all initial conditions in preparation for another solution.

I-A-6 Repetitive Mode of Operation of TR-20

When the computer is operated in the REP-OP mode, the integrator gains are multiplied by 500, and therefore the solution which requires 10 sec in the normal mode is generated in (10/500) or 20 msec. The COMPUTE TIME control determines how long the computer will be in the OPERATE mode. Following this period of time, the computer is automatically placed in the RESET mode to prepare for generating the next solution, and the computer switched again automatically to the COMPUTE mode. Since the solutions are generated so rapidly, an oscilloscope type display unit must be used to display the solutions. Problem parameters can be adjusted while the computer is in operation and the effect of the change observed immediately. The overload indicators glow dimly when the computer is operated in the REP-OP mode. Any reading of amplifier output voltages by the voltmeter will be in error when the computer is in the REP-OP mode because the voltmeter cannot respond accurately to the rapidly changing voltages.

The steps 1 to 9 given for the normal mode of operation are the same for setting up the computer for REP-OP operation. Then proceed as follows:

10. Select the amplifier output to be observed and connect it to the display unit. With some display units several different voltages can be observed simultaneously.
11. Set the COMPUTE TIME control to 20 msec.
12. Set the MODE CONTROL to REP-OP and observe the solutions.
13. If a longer solution time is desired, select the appropriate time on the COMPUTE TIME control.
14. Potentiometers can be adjusted to give the desired form of solution while the computer is operating in the REP-OP mode. The numerical value of this ratio can be determined by setting up the POT BAL operation, but adjust the MASTER POT for a zero deflection while pressing the appropriate potentiometer button.

I-A-7 Reference

TR-20 Operator's Reference Manual, Electronic Associates Inc., Long Branch, N.J.

APPENDIX I

B. BASIC OPERATION OF THE BURR-BROWN MODEL 600 ANALOG COMPUTER

I-B-1 General Description

The Burr-Brown Model 600 is a solid-state, table-top size, analog computer. The reference levels are ±10 volts. This model has six operational amplifiers which may be patched either as summers or integrators. Four more amplifiers are required in conjunction with the two multiplier units, or if the multiplier units are not being used, these amplifiers may be used independently as unity gain inverters. The panel is laid out so that many connections can be made by a double-banana plug wired as a shorting plug. Other connections are made with banana plug patch cords. Ten coefficient setting potentiometers are provided with locking, calibrated dials. These potentiometers may be set with reference to a REFERENCE POTENTIOMETER by a NULL Balance method.

Five of the potentiometers may be operated with the lower end ungrounded if desired. The computer may be operated in the following modes: PATCH, RESET (this is also POT SET), COMPUTE, and HOLD. These modes are selected by pressing a pushbutton along the lower edge of the console. A red indicator marked DO NOT PATCH is lighted when the computer is in any mode but the PATCH mode. In the PATCH mode the reference voltages are removed from the front panel. A voltmeter is located in the center of the upper panel and has three ranges; NULL, $\times$ 1, and $\times$ 10. The desired range is selected by pressing the appropriate pushbutton. The pushbuttons that have been pressed remain lighted until another button in the group is pressed. A row of OVERLOAD INDICATOR lights are found on the left side of the upper panel. If any of the amplifiers one through six has an output voltage in excess of $+10$ volts, or less than -10 volts, the corresponding indicator light lights. This is an indication that the amplifiers are operating outside their ratings and that the problem solution may be in error. These lights will come on momentarily when the computer is first turned on, but should go out in a few seconds. If an overload indication persists, the associated amplifier probably does not have a proper feedback connection with either a resistor or a capacitor. Just below the OVERLOAD INDICATORS is a row of pushbuttons and jacks. The lower row of jacks connect to the ground terminal of the patch panel. The two upper terminals associated with the buttons marked AUX are connected to the voltmeter when the AUX button is pressed. The remaining jacks are connected to the output terminals of the amplifier having the same number. These jacks may be used to connect these output voltages to external equipment such as recorders. When the numbered pushbutton is pressed, the output of that amplifier is connected to the voltmeter circuit. The output terminal of each amplifier is also connected to the jacks on each side of the patch panel. The BUS 1 jacks on each side are connected together internally. The BUS 2 jacks are also connected together internally. These BUS jacks and output jacks are useful when two or more Model 600 computers are used jointly for solving larger problems. A control cable plugs in on the back to connect the mode control circuits of two or more Model 600 computers together. The patch panel is well laid out and diagramed in such a way that the proper patching of the elements is virtually obvious.

I-B-2 *Multiplication by a Constant*

A portion of the potentiometer panel is shown in Fig. I-4 below. The distance between adjacent jacks is $\frac{3}{4}$ in. so that adjacent terminals can be

"BURR-BROWN MODEL 600 ANALOG COMPUTER" 167

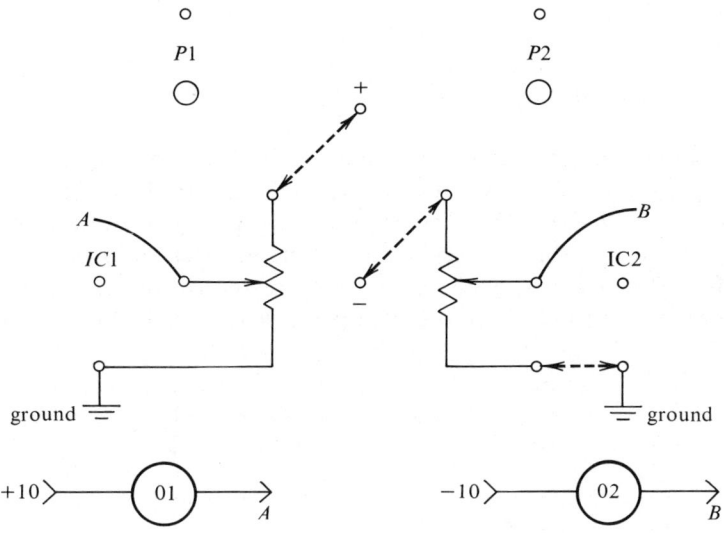

FIG. I-4

Panel Connections and Block Diagram Representation of Potentiometers.

connected together by inserting double banana shorting plugs. If shorting plugs are inserted as indicated by the dotted lines, the HI end of $P1$ is connected to $+10$ volts and the HI end of $P2$ is connected to -10 volts. The LO end of $P2$ must be grounded for normal operation as shown by the dotted line between the lower end and ground. The potentiometer can be set with reference to the master pot, NULL, by the following procedure:

1. Place the computer in the RESET mode.
2. Set the desired ratio on the NULL potentiometer.
3. Set the dial of the potentiometer to be adjusted to approximately the same reading.
4. Press the meter selector marked NULL.
5. Press the small button located above the potentiometer to be set.
6. Adjust the potentiometer to give zero deflection on the meter.

The potentiometer should be completely patched as it will be used in the analog model prior to these adjustments so that potentiometer loading will be properly compensated for. The lower end of the potentiometer must be connected to ground. If the potentiometer is to be used in some other fashion, this NULL BALANCE procedure cannot be used.

I-B-3 Inversion and Summation

The amplifiers associated with the multipliers may be used as inverters with a gain of one. The two resistors associated with the inverter symbol are connected together by plugging in a shorting plug. The left terminal of the left resistor is the input terminal for the inverter and is marked P in Fig. I-5. The output is available at either of the two jacks on the right. One of these jacks is just to the right of the vertex of the inverter symbol

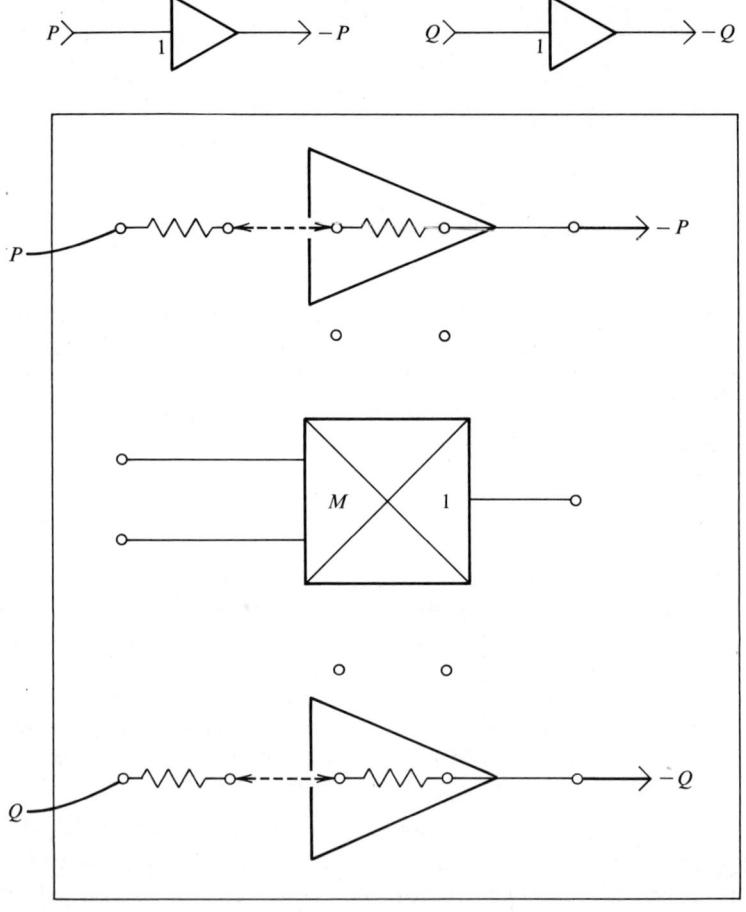

FIG. I-5

Panel Connections and Block Diagram Representation for Inverters.

and the other is just to the left. These two jacks are connected together internally. The lower inverter of the pair is connected in precisely the same manner. The corresponding block diagram is shown in the lower portion of Fig. I-5.

A sketch of the portion of the patch panel associated with a summer-integrator is shown in Fig. I-6. A shorting plug is connected between the jack marked *R* and the jack marked *SJ*. Note that these terminals are not marked on the panel of the actual computer. When this connection is made, the similarity between the appearance of the patch panel and the schematic diagram of a summer should be evident. Three variables, *P*, *Q*, and *R*, are shown connected to inputs of this summer. The output is labeled as *T*. The block diagram representation of this summer is shown at the bottom of Fig. I-6.

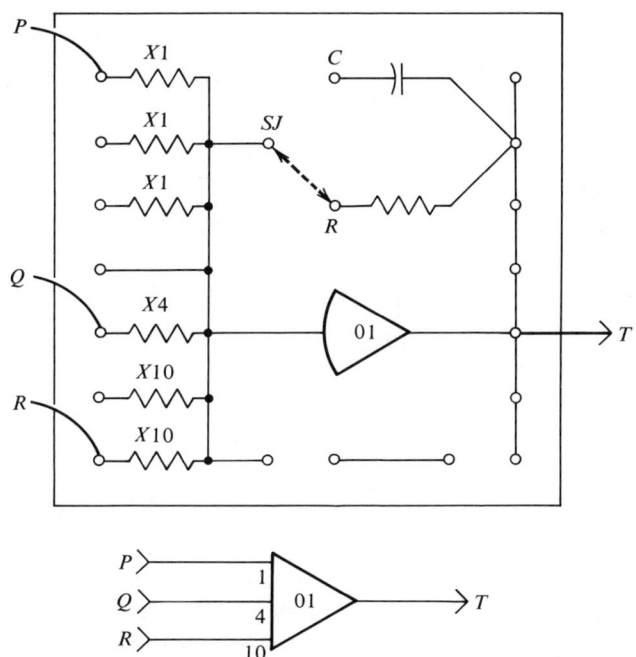

FIG. I-6
Panel Connections and Block Diagram Representation for a Summer.

I-B-4 Integration

A portion of the patch panel associated with a summer-integrator is shown in Fig. I-7. The shorting plug has been moved to connect the left

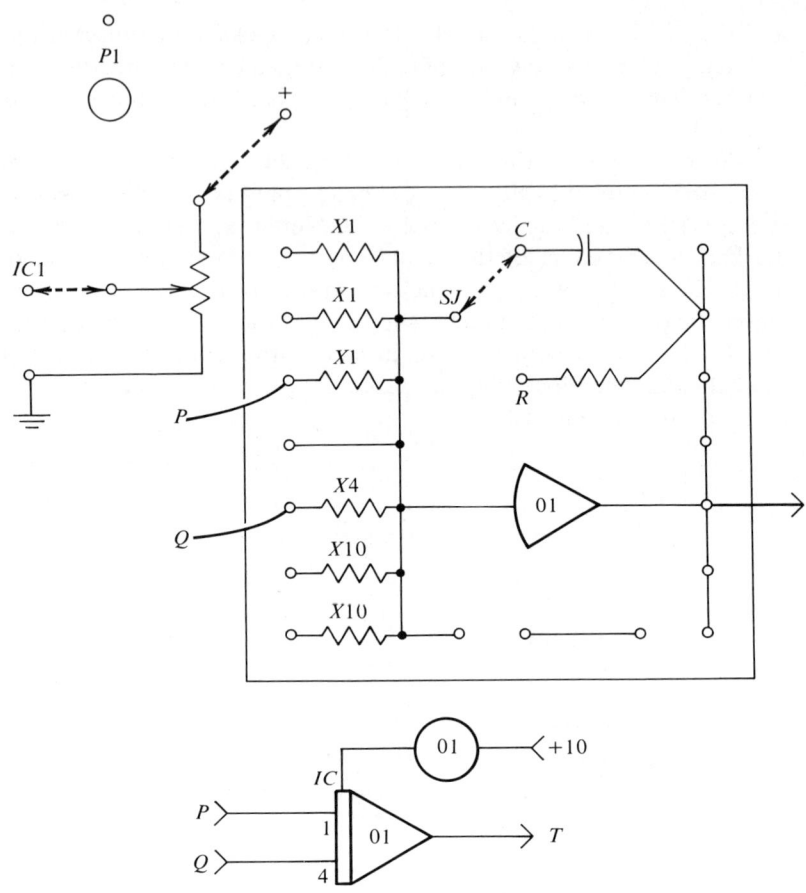

FIG. I-7

Panel Connections and Block Diagram Representation for an Integrator-Summer

terminal *C* of the feedback capacitor and the summing junction *SJ*. Again the similarity between the appearance of the patch panel and the schematic diagram of the integrator should be very evident. If an *IC* voltage is needed on this integrator, potentiometer *P1* should be used as shown in the upper portion of Fig. I-7. The block diagram representation of this INTEGRATOR-SUMMER is shown in the lower portion of the Fig. I-7.

I-B-5 Multiplier

The Burr-Brown Model 600 computer has two multipliers as standard equipment. These multipliers permit the simulation of nonlinear problems

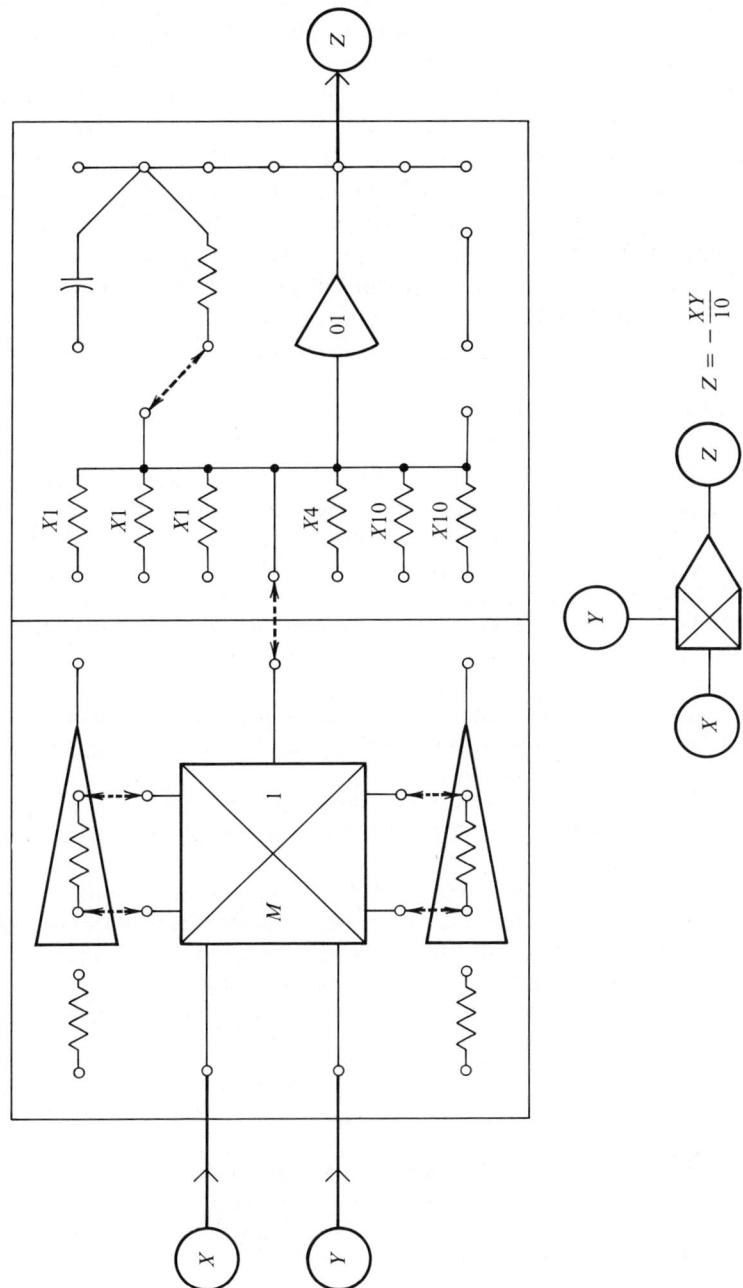

FIG. 1-8 Panel Connections and Block Diagram Representation for a Multiplier.

which involve the products, quotients, and square roots of variables. The two inverters associated with a multiplier plus another amplifier operated as an inverter are required to implement multiplication. The connections for a multiplier are shown in Fig. I-8. The construction of the multiplier is such that the output voltage is the product of the input voltages divided by ten. Thus the product of a voltage of 5 volts and another of 7 volts is not 35 volts, but rather is 3.5 volts. If the same voltage is supplied to both input terminals on the multiplier the output voltage is 0.1 times the square of the input voltage. For example, if 6 volts is fed into both inputs the output is 3.6 volts. Division and square root can also be performed. See the Burr-Brown manuals for details.

I-B-6 General Operation

1. The first step in setting up a simulation on this analog computer is to patch the summer-integrators as summers or integrators according to the assignments made on your block diagram of the analog model which you are setting up. All operational amplifiers must have a feedback element connected to prevent overloads when the computer is turned on.
2. Turn on the computer by pressing the button marked POWER.
3. Press the button marked PATCH to place the computer in the patch mode.
4. Connect the computer elements according to your block diagram.
5. Adjust each potentiometer to the desired ratio according to the procedure given in Section I-B-2.
6. Press the $\times$ 10 range switch on the voltmeter and press the appropriate AMPLIFIER OUTPUT MONITOR button to observe the result of the simulation.
7. Press the button marked COMPUTE to place the computer in operation, and observe the solution on the voltmeter. Check other appropriate voltages to determine if the model is performing satisfactorily.
8. Make any changes in scaling that may be required.
9. Connect the recording equipment and record the desired solutions.

I-B-7 References

Burr-Brown Model 600 Educational Analog Simulator Operator's Handbook, Burr-Brown Research Corporation, Tuscon, Arizona, 1966.

Burr-Brown Model 600 Educational Analog Simulator Laboratory Manual, Burr-Brown Research Corporation, Tuscon, Arizona, 1966.

APPENDIX I

C. ELECTRONIC ASSOCIATES TR-48 ANALOG COMPUTER

I-C-1 General Description

The TR-48 is an all solid-state, precision analog computer. The console is wired to accommodate up to 58 operational amplifiers, 115 potentiometers, 24 integrators, and a large number of nonlinear components. The panel is divided into 12 areas, and each area has five positions for installing computing equipment. The first and third positions accept dual operational amplifier units. The second position accommodates multipliers, diode function generators, and other such units. The fourth position is wired for dual integrator networks or nonlinear units except diode function generators. The fifth position is wired for potentiometer units. The potentiometers together with control knobs are mounted on a panel to the right of the patch panel. The panel to the left of the patch panel has all of the control switches, voltmeters, and

REP-OP display unit. The operating modes for this computer are: POT SET, RESET, HOLD, OPERATE, and REPETITIVE OPERATION. The desired mode is selected by pressing one of the MODE buttons along the lower edge of the control panel. The integrator units may be obtained either with relay mode control, or with electronic mode control for greater precision at higher speeds. An array of three columns of buttons permits the selection of any amplifier output, any coefficient potentiometer, or input trunk for monitoring on the digital voltmeter, or on the panel meter. The digital voltmeter has automatic range and polarity selection. The zero center panel meter can also be connected to the selector circuit, used to manually balance the amplifiers if needed, or to monitor the power supply voltages. The voltmeter has five ranges selected by a rotary switch. The time duration of the solution when in the REP-OP mode is selected by a rotary switch located in the center of the panel. A vernier for the solution time is located in the center of the range switch knob. Below this is located the control for the motor which engages and disengages the patch panel. On the lower left side of the control panel is the array of OVERLOAD indicators. Below this is the power switch which turns the computer on and off. All computing components are located behind the panel and connections are made by means of bottle plugs and patch cords. The input terminals for the REP-OP display unit are terminated at convenient locations on the patch panel. Other recording and display equipment may also be terminated on the patch panel. Mode pushbuttons are illuminated when depressed to show clearly the condition of the computer. When a button is depressed to make an alternate selection, the prior connection is broken, the new one made and the new indicator light turned on.

I-C-2 Multiplication by a Constant

A sketch of a Coefficient Setting Potentiometer Group is shown in Fig. I-9. There are five potentiometers in a group. Four of these are permanently grounded on the lower end and the fifth may be grounded if desired by a single bottle plug. In EAI terminology a double banana shorting plug is a single bottle plug. The right half of the panel for this group contains five jacks for the $+10$ volt reference supply. This area of the panel is colored red. The middle portion of the right side is colored black and has two grounded jacks. The lower right side contains five jacks for the -10 volt reference supply. This portion of the panel is colored yellow. The potentiometers are set by the following procedure.

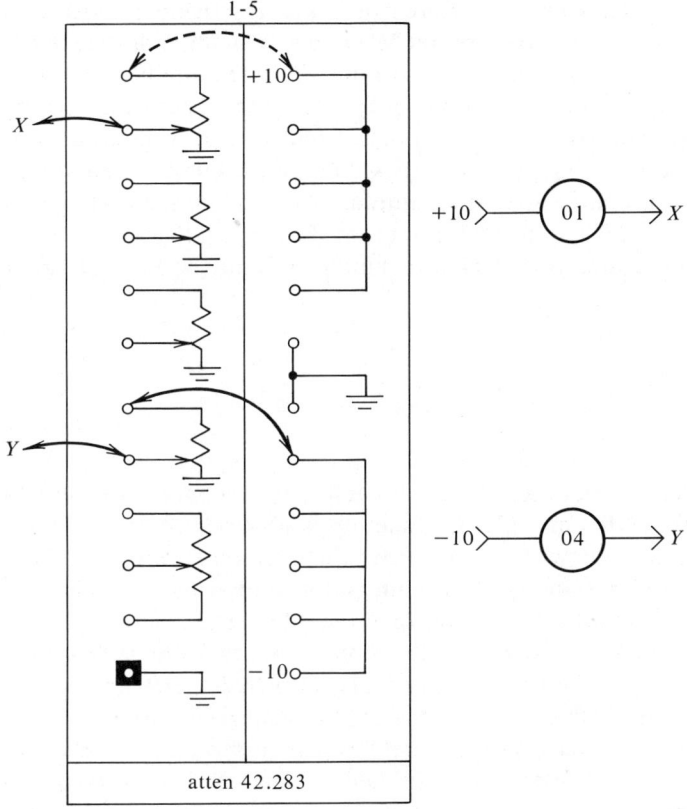

FIG. I-9
Panel Connections for Coefficient Setting Potentiometer Group 42.283.

1. Press POT SET.
2. Select the potentiometer by number with the push button selector.
3. Adjust the potentiometer until the desired ratio is indicated on the digital voltmeter.

If the computer does not have a digital voltmeter, the potentiometers can be set with reference to a master potentiometer in the same manner as on the TR-20 computer.

I-C-3 *Inversion and Summation*

The terminal arrangement for the dual amplifier 6.614 is the same as that for the amplifiers used on the EAI TR-20 analog computer. The quad amplifier modules have a different terminal arrangement with only two unity gain inputs and two output terminals. When the double bottle plug is in place to make an inverter with the QUAD amplifiers, there remain only one input terminal and one output terminal. These amplifiers are intended primiarly for use with nonlinear equipment where one input and one output are adequate. The QUAD amplifiers may be mounted in the lower row in place of five dual amplifiers to expand from 48 operational amplifiers to 58 operational amplifiers. See Fig. I-10 for a sketch of the panel connections of the DUAL amplifiers and the QUAD amplifiers.

I-C-4 Integration

Fig. I-11 shows a sketch of the patch panel connections for a DUAL INTEGRATOR unit (12.1322) such as is used for electronic mode control. A bottle plug with six plugs and three circuits is used to connect the *B*, *SJ*, and *O* terminals of the integrator unit with the corresponding terminals of an adjacent operational amplifier. Single circuit bottle plugs are used to patch the signals to the mode switches. Four are required: one each connecting the pairs of terminals marked *IC*, *OP*, and 0.1β. If the gain of an individual integrator is to be increased by a factor of ten, a single bottle plug is removed from the pair of terminals marked 0.1β on that integrator. The terminal marked *SJ'* makes the summing junction available for special circuits when the other *SJ* terminal is in use. The negative of the desired *IC* voltage is supplied to the single terminal marked *IC*. This connection can be made by a single circuit bottle plug if the proper potentiometer is assigned this function.

I-C-5 Nonlinear Modules

A very large number of modules for performing various nonlinear functions are available for the TR-48. The major kinds of units are as follows: Dual Limiters, Quarter Square Multipliers, Fixed Diode Function Generators, Variable Diode Function Generators, Log Diode Function Generators, Sine-Cosine Generators, Comparators, and Function Switches. See the EAI TR-48 OPERATOR'S MANUAL for details on the use of these units.

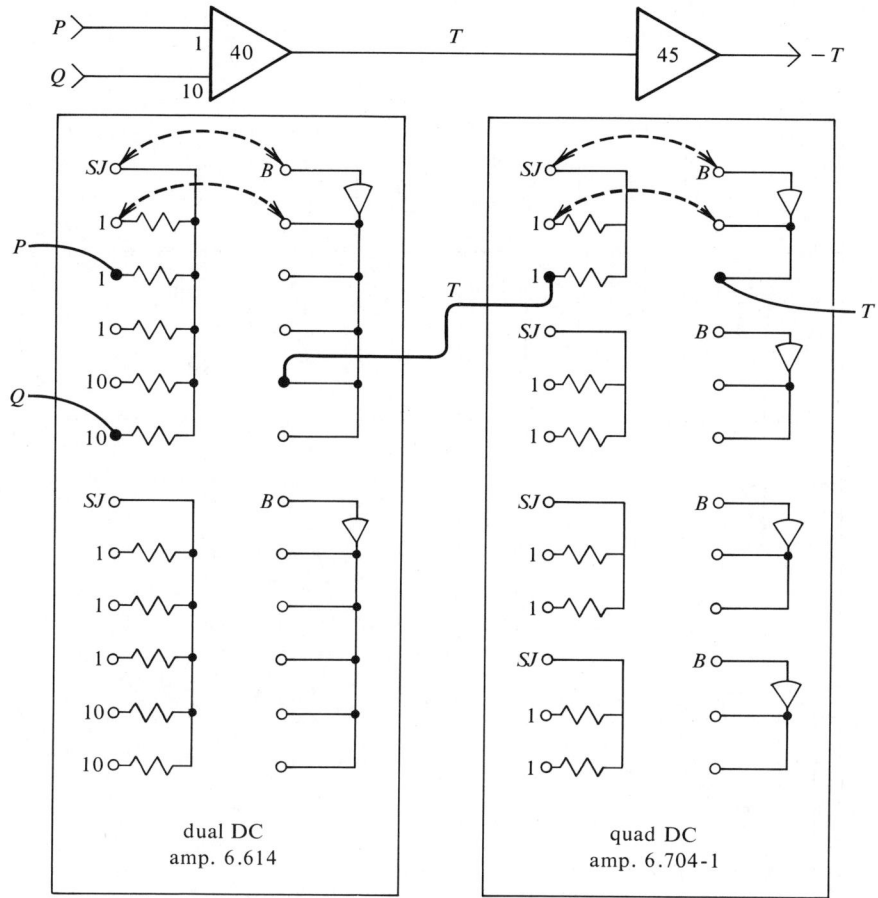

FIG. I-10

Panel Connections for Dual DC Amplifier (6.614) and Quad DC Amplifier (6.704-1).

I-C-6 General Operation

1. Make certain that appropriate bottle plugs are in place to connect all operational amplifiers as either a summer, an inverter, or as an integrator. All amplifiers must have a feedback element connected to prevent overloads. It is also necessary to see that all single bottle plugs required for control of the integrators are in place.
2. Turn on the computer by pressing the POWER switch.
3. Place the computer in the POT SET mode.

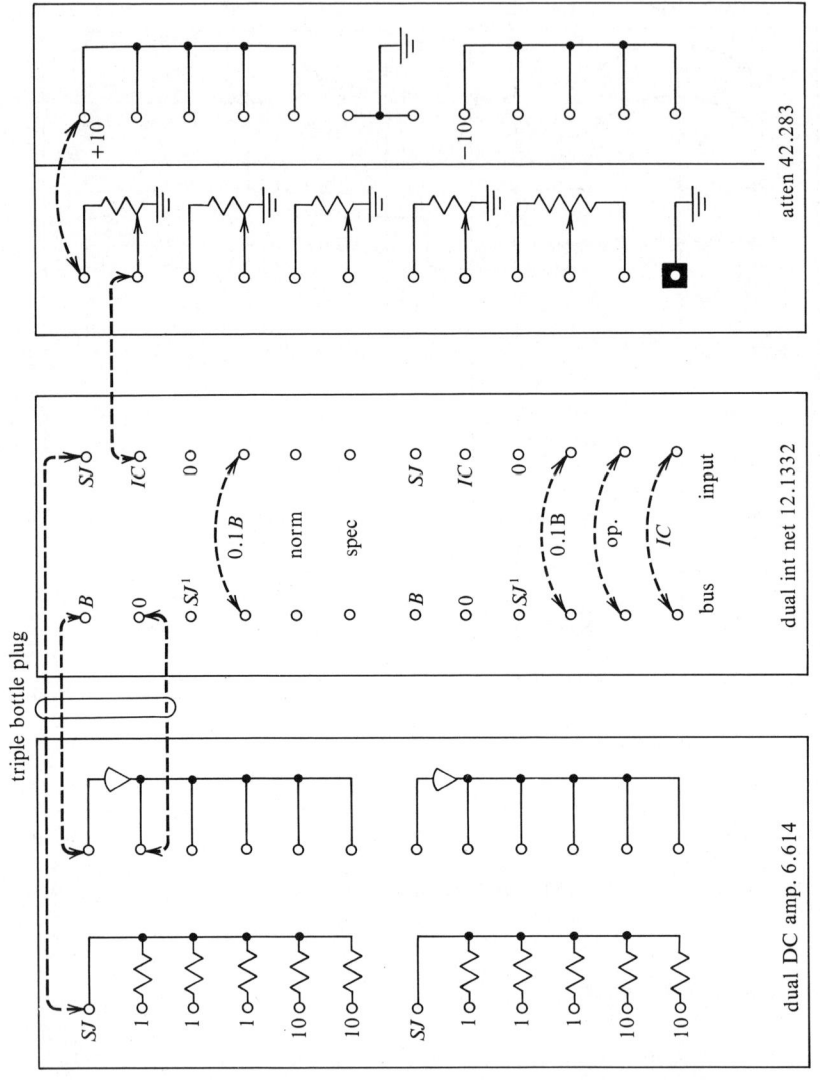

FIG. I-11 Panel Connections for Dual Integrator.

4. Patch the computing elements as defined by your block diagram. Careful assignment of computing elements will maximize the number of connections that can be made by the bottle plugs and hence reduce the clutter of leads on the patch panel. It is helpful to patch all interconnections by functional groups and then to make the interconnections between groups.
5. Adjust all potentiometers by the POT SET procedure described above.
6. Select appropriate voltages for monitoring and check the system response when the computer is placed in the COMPUTE mode. The REP-OP mode is particularly helpful for checkout of the operation of analog models because the entire solution can be viewed at once, and the effect of changes in parameters is readily apparent.
7. After the model has been determined to function properly, record the variables of interest for the range of parameters required.

APPENDIX II

DERIVATION OF ANALOG COMPUTER GAINS

II-A Inversion

        The detailed connections of an operational amplifier as an inverter are shown in Fig. II-1 below. Voltages and currents are identified, and their reference directions are shown. The voltage e_1 is positive if the terminal marked $+$ is indeed positive with respect to the terminal marked $-$. The current i_a is positive if indeed current flows through R_a from left to right. Likewise, the voltage e_o is negative if the terminal marked $+$ is indeed at a negative potential with respect to the terminal marked $-$. Kirchhoff's current law states that

> The sum of the currents flowing into a junction is equal to the sum of the currents flowing out of that junction.

DERIVATION OF ANALOG COMPUTER GAINS

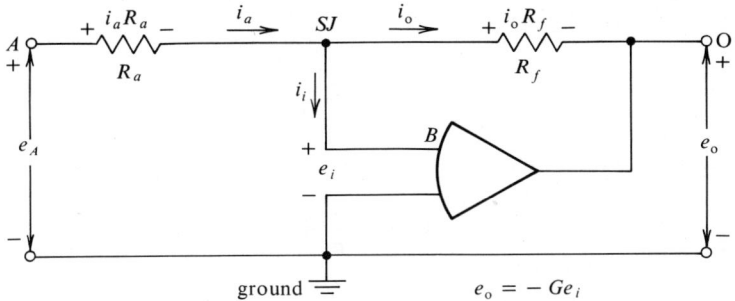

FIG. II-1
Schematic Diagram of Analog Computer Inverter Circuit.

The application of Kirchhoff's current law to the summing junction, SJ yields Eq. (II-1).

$$i_a = i_i + i_o \tag{II-1a}$$

Kirchhoff's voltage law states:

> The sum of the voltage rises in a given direction around a loop is equal to the sum of the voltage drops around that loop in the same direction.

The application of this law to the left hand loop in the clockwise direction, A-SJ-G-A, yields

$$e_A = i_a R_a + e_i \tag{II-1b}$$

The voltage e_A is a voltage rise in the clockwise direction because the reference direction for e_A shows terminal A at a positive potential with respect to terminal G. Similarly $i_a R_a$ is a drop in potential because terminal SJ is at a lower potential than terminal A. Application of the voltage law to the right hand loop, SJ-O-G-SJ, yields

$$e_i = i_o R_f + e_o \tag{II-1c}$$

The nature of the operational amplifier provides two more relations:

$$e_i = -\frac{e_o}{G} \tag{II-1d}$$

$$i_i = \frac{e_i}{R_i} \tag{II-1e}$$

Solve Eq. (II-1b) for i_a:

$$i_a = \frac{e_A - e_i}{R_a} \tag{II-1f}$$

Solve Eq. (II-1c) for i_0:

$$i_o = \frac{e_i - e_o}{R_f} \tag{II-1g}$$

Substitute Eqs. (II-1e), (II-1f), (II-1g) into Eq. (II-1a).

$$\frac{e_A - e_i}{R_a} = \frac{e_i}{R_i} + \frac{e_i - e_o}{R_f} \tag{II-1h}$$

Collect the terms in e_i on the right and substitute Eq. (II-1d).

$$\frac{e_A}{R_a} = -\frac{e_o}{G}\left[\frac{1}{R_a} + \frac{1}{R_i} + \frac{1}{R_f}\right] - \frac{e_o}{R_f} \tag{II-1i}$$

$$e_o = \frac{-e_A\left(\dfrac{R_f}{R_a}\right)}{1 + \dfrac{1}{G}\left(\dfrac{R_f}{R_a} + \dfrac{R_f}{R_i} + 1\right)} \tag{II-1j}$$

Since the value of G is very large, the second term in the denominator becomes very small when the values of R_a, R_f, R_i and G are substituted. For example, typical values of these parameters are as follows:

$$R_f = R_a = 10^6 \text{ ohms}$$
$$R_i = 50 \times 10^6 \text{ ohms}$$
$$G = 100{,}000$$

The denominator then becomes:

$$\text{Denom} = 1 + 10^{-5}(1 + 0.02 + 1)$$
$$= 1.0000102 \tag{II-1k}$$

Thus the inverter configuration of Fig. II-1 has the following gain relation:

$$e_o = -e_A\left(\frac{R_f}{R_a}\right) \tag{II-1l}$$

When $R_f = R_a$ the output voltage is the negative of the input voltage.

II-B Summation

The detailed connections of an operational amplifier for operation as a summer are shown in Fig. II-2. Voltage and currents are identified and reference directions are shown. By application of Kirchhoff's laws in a manner similar to that of the previous section the following equations result:

Kirchhoff's current law at the summing junction, SJ:

$$i_a + i_b + i_c = i_i + i_o \qquad \text{(II-2a)}$$

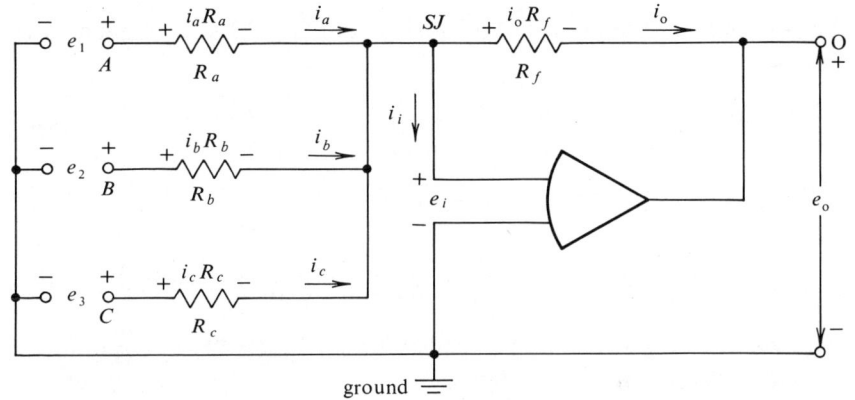

FIG. II-2
Schematic Diagram of Analog Computer Summer Circuit.

Kirchhoff's voltage law:

$$\text{Loop } A\text{-}SJ\text{-}G\text{-}A; \quad e_A = i_a R_a + e_i \qquad \text{(II-2b)}$$

$$\text{Loop } B\text{-}SJ\text{-}G\text{-}B; \quad e_B = i_b R_b + e_i \qquad \text{(II-2c)}$$

$$\text{Loop } C\text{-}SJ\text{-}G\text{-}C; \quad e_C = i_c R_c + e_i \qquad \text{(II-2d)}$$

$$\text{Loop } SJ\text{-}O\text{-}G\text{-}SJ; \quad e_i = i_o R_f + e_o \qquad \text{(II-2e)}$$

The properties of the operational amplifier yield:

$$e_i = -\frac{e_o}{G} \qquad \text{(II-2f)}$$

$$i_i = \frac{e_i}{R_i} \qquad \text{(II-2g)}$$

Solution of Eqs. (II-2b), (II-2c), (II-2d), and (II-2e) for i_a, i_b, i_c, and i_o yields

$$i_a = \frac{e_A - e_i}{R_a}$$

$$i_b = \frac{e_B - e_i}{R_b}$$

$$i_c = \frac{e_C - e_i}{R_c}$$

$$i_o = \frac{e_i - e_o}{R_f}$$

(II-2h)

Substitution of Eqs. (II-2g) and (II-2h) into Eq. (II-2a) eliminates the current variables.

$$\frac{e_A - e_i}{R_a} + \frac{e_B - e_i}{R_b} + \frac{e_C - e_i}{R_c} = \frac{e_i}{R_i} + \frac{e_i - e_o}{R_f} \quad \text{(II-2i)}$$

The terms in e_i are collected on the right:

$$\frac{e_A}{R_a} + \frac{e_B}{R_b} + \frac{e_C}{R_c} = e_i\left[\frac{1}{R_a} + \frac{1}{R_b} + \frac{1}{R_c} + \frac{1}{R_i} + \frac{1}{R_f}\right] - \frac{e_o}{R_f} \quad \text{(II-2j)}$$

The voltage e_i is eliminated by substituting Eq. (II-2f) into Eq. (II-2j). Terms in e_o are also consolidated.

$$\frac{e_A}{R_a} + \frac{e_B}{R_b} + \frac{e_C}{R_c} = -\frac{e_o}{R_f} - \frac{e_o}{G}\left[\frac{1}{R_a} + \frac{1}{R_b} + \frac{1}{R_c} + \frac{1}{R_i} + \frac{1}{R_f}\right] \quad \text{(II-2k)}$$

Solve for e_o:

$$e_o = -\frac{\left(\frac{R_f}{R_a}\right)e_A + \left(\frac{R_f}{R_b}\right)e_B + \left(\frac{R_f}{R_c}\right)e_C}{1 + \frac{1}{G}\left(\frac{R_f}{R_a} + \frac{R_f}{R_b} + \frac{R_f}{R_c} + \frac{R_f}{R_i} + 1\right)} \quad \text{(II-2l)}$$

The right term in the denominator is again very, very small because the amplifier gain G is very large. Hence the output voltage is the weighted sum of the input voltages. Each voltage is multiplied by the ratio of the feedback resistor to the corresponding input resistor.

$$e_o = -\left[\left(\frac{R_f}{R_a}\right)e_A + \left(\frac{R_f}{R_b}\right)e_B + \left(\frac{R_f}{R_c}\right)e_C\right] \quad \text{(II-2m)}$$

II-C Integration

The detailed connection of an operational amplifier as an integrator is shown in Fig. II-3. The application of Kirchhoff's current law to the junction *SJ* yields:

$$i_a = i_i + i_o \tag{II-3a}$$

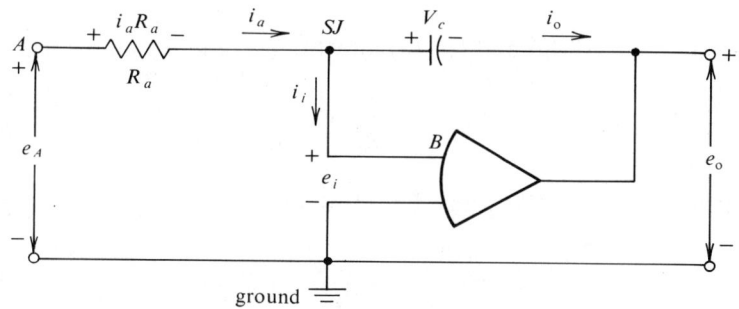

FIG. II-3
Schematic Diagram of Analog Computer Integration Circuit.

The application of Kirchhoff's voltage law to the left loop yields:

$$e_A = i_a R_a + e_i \tag{II-3b}$$

The application of Kirchhoff's voltage law to the righthand loop yields

$$e_i = v_c + e_o \tag{II-3c}$$

The voltage across a capacitor is related by the capacitance to the charge stored in the capacitor.

$$v_c = \frac{q}{C} \tag{II-3d}$$

But the value of q is the $\int i\,dt$ and, therefore

$$v_c = \frac{1}{C}\int i_o\,dt \tag{II-3e}$$

The nature of the operational amplifier again yields

$$e_i = -\frac{e_o}{G} \tag{II-3f}$$

$$i_i = \frac{e_i}{R_i} \tag{II-3g}$$

Solve for i_a in Eq. (II-3b):

$$i_a = \frac{e_A - e_i}{R_a} \tag{II-3h}$$

Substitute Eqs. (II-3g) and (II-3h) into Eq. (II-3a) and solve for i_o:

$$i_o = \frac{e_A - e_i}{R_a} - \frac{e_i}{R_i} \tag{II-3i}$$

Substitution of Eq. (II-3i) into Eq. (II-3e) yields

$$v_c = \frac{1}{C}\int \left[\frac{e_A - e_i}{R_a} - \frac{e_i}{R_i}\right]dt \tag{II-3j}$$

Substitution of Eq. (II-3j) into Eq. (II-3c) yields

$$e_i = \frac{1}{C}\int \left[\frac{e_A - e_i}{R_a} - \frac{e_i}{R_i}\right]dt + e_o \tag{II-3k}$$

Substitution of Eq. (II-3f) into Eq. (II-3k) yields

$$-\frac{e_o}{G} = \frac{1}{C}\int \frac{e_A}{R_a}dt + e_o + \frac{1}{C}\int \left[\frac{e_o}{R_a G} + \frac{e_o}{R_i G}\right]dt \tag{II-3l}$$

Solving for e_0 on the left yields

$$e_o = -\frac{1}{R_a C}\int e_A dt - \frac{1}{G}\left[e_o + \frac{1}{C}\int \left(\frac{e_o}{R_a} + \frac{e_o}{R_i}\right)dt\right] \tag{II-3m}$$

For a sufficiently large value of amplifier gain, G, the second term on the right is negligible compared to the first term and the integrator has the relationship:

$$e_o = -\frac{1}{R_a C}\int e_A dt \tag{II-3n}$$

DERIVATION OF ANALOG COMPUTER GAINS

The capacitor may be initially charged giving an initial condition.

$$e_o = -\frac{1}{R_a C} \int e_A dt + e(0) \qquad \text{(II-3o)}$$

The reciprocal of the RC product is the gain of the integrator where R is measured in ohms and C is measured in farads. It sometimes is more convenient to measure R in megohms and C in microfarads. One megohm is 10^6 ohms and one microfarad is 10^{-6} farad. The powers of 10 cancel out and the result has the proper numerical value. The RC product has units of sec, which is consistent because the integral of voltage with respect to time gives units of volt-sec which yield, when divided by sec, the units of volts.

APPENDIX III   **ELECTRICAL CIRCUITS**

This appendix shows in detail the operation of the electrical circuits used for POT SET and IC.

III-A Pot Set

The potentiometer can be set by a balancing technique that compensates for the reduction in voltage from a potentiometer caused by current flow in the ARM of the potentiometer. This method also makes it unnecessary to have calibrated dials on the potentiometers. The desired ratio is set on the Master Potentiometer, MP. The voltage at the arm of the potentiometer, CP, being set is compared by a millivoltmeter, MV, with the voltage from the Master POT as shown in Fig. III-1. The resistor R_a is the input resistor to which the arm of the potentiometer is connected. A relay grounds the summing junction SJ of the operational amplifiers

ELECTRICAL CIRCUITS   189

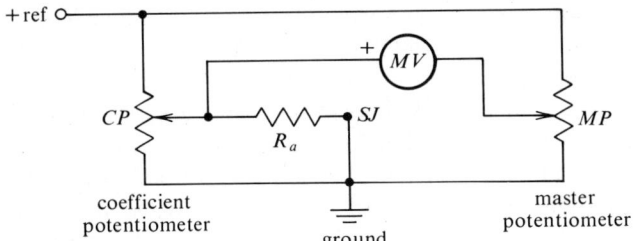

FIG. III-1
Schematic of Pot Set Principle.

in the POT SET mode. This circuit functions very much like the Wheatstone Bridge. When the potentiometer, *CP*, is adjusted so that the reading on the millivoltmeter is zero, the potentiometer *CP* is set for the same ratio as the master potentiometer. Since the resistor R_a is effectively connected the same as when the computer is operating, the loading is compensated properly. If the lower end of the potentiometer *CP* is not grounded, the bridge circuit is not complete and hence will not function properly.

The actual circuit is more complicated. A typical POT SET circuit is shown in Fig. III-2. The Pot Set Relay, *KPS*, switches the terminal *B* from the amplifier input to ground when the POT SET MODE is selected. When SW1 is depressed the contact arms shift from top to bottom. The

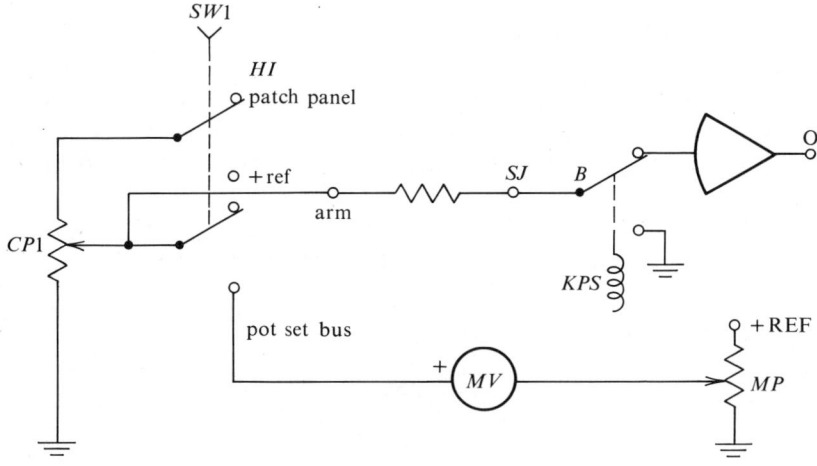

FIG. III-2
Typical Detailed Circuit for Pot Set.

top end of the potentiometer is connected to the +Reference Voltage and the ARM is connected to the POT SET BUS which connects to the left side of the millivoltmeter, *MV*. If the computer is well engineered the needle on the millivoltmeter will move in the same direction, clockwise or counterclockwise, as the knob is moved on the potentiometer, *CP*, which is being adjusted. Thus if the meter shows a downscale deflection, the knob on potentiometer *CP* is turned clockwise to bring the meter to a zero deflection, and hence to set the potentiometer to the desired ratio. The converse is the case for an upscale deflection. When the master potentiometer, *MP*, is being set to match the setting of a coefficient potentiometer, *CF*, the needle on the meter moves in a direction opposite to the rotation of the knob of the master potentiometer.

On computers which have a digital voltmeter, *DVM*, in addition to, or in place of a panel meter, the POT SET is accomplished by connecting the *DVM* in place of the millivoltmeter *MV* and the master potentiometer. This system is more convenient to use because the desired ratio is set only on the coefficient potentiometer, rather than first on *MP* and then on *CP*. These computers frequently have another position on switch SW1 which permits the measurement of the voltage present on the arm of the potentiometer when the upper end is connected to the HI terminal on the patch panel. This feature is convenient for setting a potentiometer whose lower end is not grounded, or for checking to see that the desired voltage is indeed present on the arm.

III-B Initial Condition

Consider the circuit shown in Fig. III-3 below: The resistors *R* have the same value and ignoring for the moment the capacitor *C*, the circuit looks like a unity gain inverter. When the capacitor is considered, the output

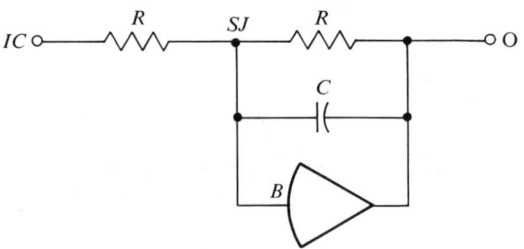

FIG. III-3

Principle of Initial Condition Circuit.

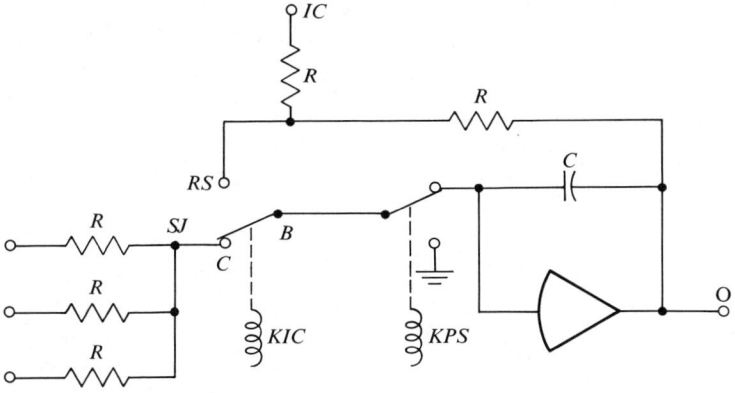

FIG. III-4

Typical Circuit for Establishing Initial Conditions.

voltage will rise after a period of time to the same value as though the capacitor were not there. By choosing a suitable value, R, for the resistor this time can be made as short as desired. Relays or electronic circuits are used to select the mode of operation of an integrator circuit. There are usually three modes: 1. RESET or IC, 2. HOLD, and 3. OPERATE or COMPUTE. One possible circuit is shown in Fig. III-4. When the computer is placed in the Initial Condition, *IC*, mode, the relay *KIC* in each integrator unit switches the arm from the compute position, *C*, to the reset position, *RS*.

When the computer is placed in the HOLD mode, the Pot Set Relay, *KPS*, opens the circuit from the terminal *B* to the input of the operational amplifier. In this condition the input to the integrator is zero and the output voltage HOLDS at the value which it had at the time the HOLD condition was initiated.

APPENDIX IV **STABILITY OF SOLUTIONS FOR ALGEBRAIC EQUATIONS**

Consider the following set of simultaneous algebraic equations.

$$4x + y = 6 \qquad \text{(IV-1a)}$$

$$x + 5y = 11 \qquad \text{(IV-1b)}$$

This system of equations would result in a stable analog computer model if Eq. (IV-1a) is solved for x and Eq. (IV-1b) is solved for y. The solution would be found to be as follows:

$$\begin{aligned} x &= 1 \\ y &= 2 \end{aligned} \qquad \text{(IV-1c)}$$

STABILITY OF SOLUTIONS FOR ALGEBRAIC EQUATIONS

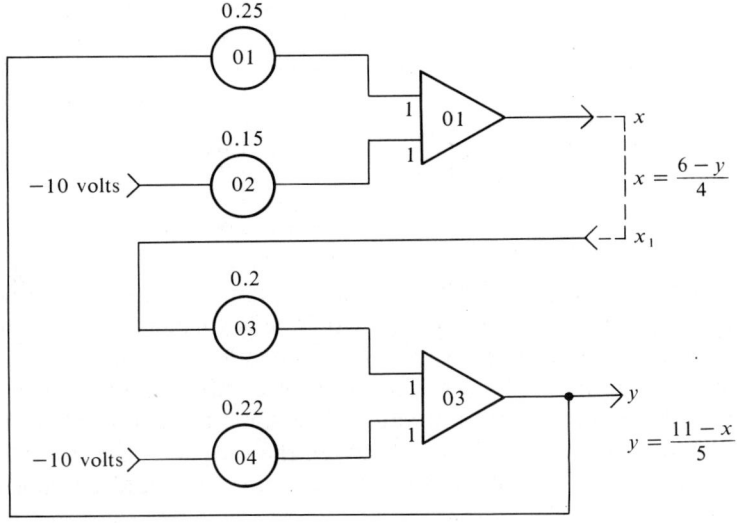

FIG. IV-1
Stable Analog Computer Model for Simultaneous Algebraic Equations.

This fact can be verified by substitution into the original set of equations. If the analog model is amplitude scaled on a one unit per volt basis, the block diagram is as shown in Fig. IV-1. If the circuit is completed between x and x_1, the system will come to equilibrium with $x = 1$ and $y = 2$. Consider now that the connection between x and x_1 is opened and that a variable voltage x_1 is supplied to potentiometer 03. The table below indicates the value of x for various values of x_1. These values can be observed experimentally on the analog computer, or can be computed in the following way:

$$y = \frac{11 - x_1}{5}$$

$$x = \frac{6 - y}{4}$$

$$x = \frac{6 - \left(\frac{11 - x_1}{5}\right)}{4}$$

$$= \frac{6}{4} - \frac{11}{20} + \frac{x_1}{20}$$

$$x = \frac{19}{20} + \frac{x_1}{20} \qquad \text{(IV-1d)}$$

APPENDIX IV

x_1	x
0.8	0.99
0.9	0.995
1.0	1.000
1.1	1.005
1.2	1.10

Note that if x_1 is too small then x is larger than x_1, but still less than the equilibrium value. If x_1 is too large, then x is smaller than x_1, but still larger than the equilibrium value. Thus when x_1 is connected to x, the system tends to move toward a position of equilibrium if x has a value different from the equilibrium value. The same tendency would be observed if the circuit were opened between the output of amplifier 03 and potentiometer 01. The input to potentiometer 01 would be considered as y_1.

Consider now what happens when the equations are reversed before forming the analog model.

$$x + 5y = 11 \qquad \text{(IV-1e)}$$

$$4x + y = 6 \qquad \text{(IV-1f)}$$

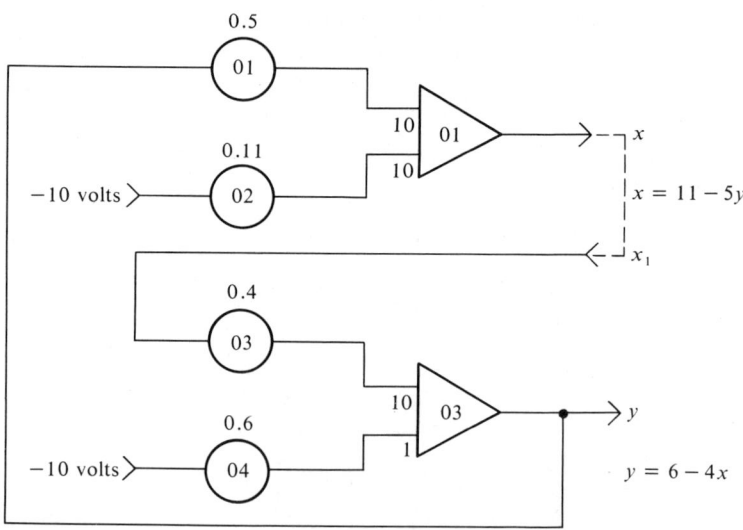

FIG. IV-2

Unstable Analog Computer Model for Simultaneous Algebraic Equations.

STABILITY OF SOLUTIONS FOR ALGEBRAIC EQUATIONS

The analog model is as shown in Fig. IV-2. The assumption is again made that the dotted connection between x and x_1 is opened and a variable voltage x_1 supplied. The results for several values of x_1 are tabulated below based on the relation:

$$x = -19 + 20\, x_1$$

x_1	x
0.9	−1
0.95	0
1.00	+1
1.05	+2
1.10	+3

In this case note that when x_1 is too small, the value of x is even more negative with respect to the equilibrium value than is x_1. When x_1 is too large, the value of x is more positive with respect to the equilibrium value than is x_1. Thus when the connection is made that forces x_1 to be equal to x, any departure from the solution point, $x = 1, y = 2$, causes the values to depart even further from the solution point.

This demonstration of the nature of the instability of the analog model was used because it probably is more meaningful and provides more insight than the argument based on the roots of the characteristic equation formed from the matrix of the coefficients.

INDEX

Acceleration:
  angular, 125
Algebraic equations, 18
  simultaneous, 4, 21, 192
Amplifiers:
  operational, 7, 11
Amplitude scaling, 9, 19
Analog computer, 3
  active, 5
  passive, 4
Analogs:
  of arithmetic operations, 7
  of calculus operations, 33
Angular:
  acceleration, 125
  velocity, 130

Back resistance (*See* Resistance, back)
Balance, 5
Bias:
  forward, 138
  reverse, 138
Blackburn double pendulum, 135
Block diagram, 11, 72

Capacitance, 35
  electrical, 35
  thermal, 92
Capacitor, 35
Cathode ray oscilloscope, 64
Chopper stabilization, 5
Cm, 10
Comparators, 152
Cosine function, 53

Dashpot, 110
Differential equation, 75
Differentiation, 34
Digital Computer, 2
Digital Voltmeter, 190
Diode function generator, 144
  semiconductor device, 138
DVM (*See* Digital voltmeter)
Dynamic system, 71

Electrical charge, 35
Electric current, 35
Electric power, 92

Falling body:
  freely, 84
  with viscous drag, 88
Feedback resistor, 12, 14
First-order system, 70
Forward bias (*See* Bias, forward)
Forward resistance, 138
Freight car, 136
Function:
  cosine, 53
  polynomial, 50
  ramp, 47
  sine, 53
  sinusoidal, 53
Function generator:
  diode, 144
  sinusoidal, 54, 148

Gain:
  integrator, 42
  voltage, 8
Galilei, Galileo, 85
Generator:
  sine-cosine, 148
  sinusoidal, 54
Gravity, 84, 89, 129
Ground, 8

HOLD, 163, 191
Hybrid computer, 1, 6
Hydraulic system:
  two tank, 73
  three tank, 98

IC (*See* Initial condition)
Inertia:
  moment of, 124
Initial condition, 45, 46, 190
Input resistors, 14

198 INDEX

Integration, 40, 162, 169, 176, 185
Integrator:
　gain, 42
Inversion, 11, 160, 168, 175, 180

Kirchhoff's Laws:
　current law, 180, 181, 183, 185
　voltage law, 181, 183, 185

Limiter, 139
Linear equations:
　simultaneous, 21, 40, 192

Modeling:
　mathematical, 3, 72, 73
Models:
　differentiation, 37
　integration, 41
　mathematical, 72, 73
Moment of inertia, 124
Momentum, 85
Multiplication by a constant, 16, 174
Multipliers, 145, 170
　quarter-square, 145
　time-division, 145
　servo, 145

Nonlinear modules, 176
Nonlinear phenomena, 137

Ohm's Law, 8, 12
Operational amplifiers, 7, 11
Oscilloscope (*See* Cathode ray oscilloscope)

Pendulum:
　Blackburn double, 135
　simple, 128
Polynomial function, 50
POT BAL, 17
Potential difference, 8
Potentiometer, 16
　three-terminal, 17
　two-terminal, 17
POT SET, 17, 188
Precision, 2

Quarter-square multiplier, 145

Ramp function, 47
REP-OP mode, 61, 163
RESET, 163, 167, 191
Resistance:
　back, 138
　forward, 138
　thermal, 92

Resistor:
　feedback, 12, 14
　input, 14
Reverse bias (*See* Bias, reverse)

Scale factor, 9
　amplitude, 10
　time, 82
Scaling, 72
　amplitude, 9, 19
　time, 82
Second-order system, 109
Semiconductor device:
　diode, 138
　thermal behavior of, 92
Servo multipliers, 145
Simultaneous algebraic equations, 4, 192
Simultaneous differential equations, 98
Simultaneous linear equations, 21
Sine-cosine generator, 148
Sine function, 53
Sinusoidal function, 53
　generator, 54
SJ (*See* Summing junction)
Spring-mass-dashpot system, 110
Strip chart recorder, 62
Summation, 13, 160, 168, 175, 183
Summing junction, 13
Swinging door system, 120
Superposition, 43
System, 10
　dynamic, 71
　first-order, 70
　hydraulic, 73, 98
　second-order, 109
　spring-mass-dashpot, 110
　swinging door, 120

Terminal velocity, 89
Thermal capacitance, 92
Thermal power, 93
Thermal resistance, 92
Time constant, 81
Time-division multiplier, 145
Time scaling, 82
Transfer characteristic, 139
Trial solution, 72

Velocity:
　angular, 130
Viscous drag, 88
Voltage, 8
Voltage gain, 8

X-Y plotter, 62